Weaving a Virtual Web

Weaving a Virtual Web

Practical Approaches to New Information Technologies

Edited by

Sibylle Gruber
Northern Arizona University

National Council of Teachers of English
1111 W. Kenyon Road, Urbana, Illinois 61801-1096

Staff Editor: Kurt Austin

Interior Design: Doug Burnett

Cover Design: Carlton Bruett

NCTE Stock Number: 56495-3050

Every effort has been made to provide current URLs and e-mail addresses, but because of the rapidly changing nature of the Web, some sites and addresses may no longer be accessible.

Library of Congress Cataloging-in-Publication Data

Weaving a virtual Web: practical approaches to new information
    technologies/edited by Sibylle Gruber.
        p. cm.
    Includes bibliographical references and index.
    ISBN 0-8141-5649-5
    1. English philology—Study and teaching—Technological innovations.
    2. World Wide Web (Information retrieval system)—Study and teaching.
    3. Language arts—Computer-assisted instruction. 4. Information
    technology—Study and teaching. 5. Educational innovations. I. Gruber,
    Sibylle.
    PE66.W43 1999
    808'.042'0285—dc21

                                                                99-049330

Contents

III. Supporting Collaboration and Interaction

(handwritten margin notes: "(use) Good illustration: exercises PowerPoint")

IV. Publishing on the Web

V. Resource Appendix

Foreword

Gail E. Hawisher
University of Illinois at Urbana-Champaign

Cynthia L. Selfe
Michigan Technological University

W*eaving a Virtual Web: Practical Approaches to New Information Technologies* will prove an exceptional volume of essays. While it ostensibly demonstrates how instructors can use the Web effectively in the day-to-day business of teaching, it also grounds itself deeply in the theory and pedagogy that have revolutionized writing and literacy instruction over the past few decades. Taking information technologies into its field of vision, however, this book goes several steps further: it persistently looks to the future and to the important theoretical questions of just what constitutes literacy and the teaching of literacy in the new millennium. Highly practical, as the volume's subtitle implies, the essays within explore the many ways in which the new online space of the Web can abet teaching and learning. But they do so with a sophisticated understanding of the many complexities that attend literacy, always recognizing that the term itself is fraught with difficulties, its power more often than not elusive to those who pursue it.

If there is one underlying theme in the volume, it is that although the many meanings of literacy—with and without technology—continue to evolve, the term never denotes simply a skill or set of skills that can be automatically transferred to online environments or that autonomously ensures prosperity and success in educational or social situations.

As teachers of literacy—and as two English professionals who have been working with computers and composition for almost twenty years—we have not always been so smart about the complicated relationship attending literacy and computers. In *Critical Perspectives on Computers and Composition Instruction* (1989), our first book together, we had the good sense to realize that English professionals, ourselves included, were placing too much faith in computers, but we could not and did not foresee the extent to which electronic environments would change our understanding of teaching and learning; nor were we able to envision the new kinds of literacy environments that would be generated in the next decades.

In our individual chapters for that volume, one of us asked why we were attributing all sorts of power to computers and word processing, but not before she counted some 4,000 student revisions and scrutinized what seemed like hundreds of studies to determine whether students revised and wrote more effectively with computers (Hawisher 1989). In this effort, we were still very much limited by our experience with print literacy and its various forms (e.g., drafts, printouts, papers). The other of us very astutely recognized that computers required yet another layer of literacy learning of students, but failed to recognize that the term *literacy* itself was causing every bit as many problems as the added component of computers (Selfe 1989).

Since those early days, the field of computers and composition has developed an increasingly sophisticated and interdisciplinary understanding of literacy issues. Informed by the related work of literacy scholars (Brian Street 1995; James Paul Gee 1990; Harvey Graff 1987), composition scholars (Elspeth Stuckey 1991; Mike Rose 1989), and computers and composition colleagues (Anne Wysocki and Johndan Johnson-Eilola 1999; Geoffrey Sirc 1999) and Sibylle Gruber, we have continued to gain a more thoughtful—although still developing—understanding of literacy, its practices, and the values associated with it.

We have learned more, for example, about how literacy practices—authoring, designing, reading, analyzing, interpreting—function in culturally and contextually specific ways (Hawisher and Selfe, forthcoming). And we have learned that these effects are always politically charged, never neutral. We've learned that literacy attitudes and practices are determined within and shaped by these particular contexts and that the different ways in which communications are authored, received, or used fundamentally affect the production, reception, and understanding of information; and we have learned that literacy is as often used to help reproduce existing power relationships as to introduce change within cultural systems (Gee 1990; Graff 1987; Street 1995).

But our education about the literacy practices and values associated with electronic contexts (and the social formations that support them) has only begun. It will continue with the essays Sibylle Gruber has thoughtfully assembled for this volume. From these contributions, readers will be reminded that the weaving of virtual webs requires teachers who are ready and able to theorize the Web as narrative (Chapter 1, Gillette), as an important rhetorical space (Chapter 12, Wysocki; Chapter 14, Rehberger; Chapter 18, Smith), as central to technical communication (Chapter 2, Applen; Chapter 17, Egbert and Jessup), as pedagogically appropriate for all levels of schooling (Chapter 6, Boreen;

Chapter 10, Li and Osborne) and, as inherently intertextual or, in Patricia Webb's words, "always already collaborative" (Chapter 4, Golson and Sagel; Chapter 9, Webb; Chapter 13, Burow-Flak).

These essays, as well as others in the volume, clearly indicate that to be literate Web authors/designers/readers—literacy requirements conceived in this decade—teachers and students must draw on multiple theories emerging from many different disciplines (Chapter 5, Sommers). As English studies professionals, this book suggests, we must bring to our authoring those abilities already intrinsic to writing but also those common to artists, graphic designers, and rhetoricians who work in the new media. David Gillette, for example, points to the creative elements of online projects, such as media collages, while at the same time informing his and his students' thinking with narrative theory. In taking various narrative approaches from print, film, television, photography, and painting, Gillette illustrates that "storytelling in all its guises" can serve Web authors and help them create such widely different genres as nonfiction prose and conventional academic research. And he is only one of many in this volume to look to other disciplines for theoretical frameworks.

Other authors turn to visual theory and rhetorical theory for their increasingly sophisticated understanding of meaning and representation. Anne Wysocki, for example, builds on visual theory to help students enlarge their conception of how images work on Web pages in rhetorically effective and not so effective ways. To this end, she has experimented with having students create images and respond to other students' images and arrangement of images, all the while modeling possibilities for them with her own image-making on the Web pages of their syllabus. Through her careful orchestrating of materials, class activities, and response, she was able with her students to create "a place that gave [her and her students] a center for looking—individually and as a class—out at the world and back in at what we were making."

Building on these chapters, then, and from our own experiences in working with students, we can begin to ask a series of even more perceptive—and difficult—questions about the authoring, design, and reading practices associated with Web literacies, as well as the cultural values attendant to these practices:

- How are narratives represented on the WWW? How do Web narratives differ from those represented in print? What narratives are left off the Web? Why? Who has access to the stories and narratives told on the Web? Who lacks such access? Why?

[handwritten margin note: Questions for consideration]

- How do individuals and groups tell their stories in personal and/or organizational Web pages? What are the new literacy strategies/genres involved in constructing personal representations and online identities? Organizational representations and identities? What elements of such narratives/stories are included? What elements are excluded? Why? Who benefits from such choices and how?

- How are public and private narratives handled on the Web? How are they represented? Connected? Hidden? Shaped? To whom are they directed and why?

- How do visual and textual representations share in the task of communicating meaning within Web pages? How does this relationship differ from that found in conventional print texts? In conventional artistic representations?

- What terms/understandings/strategies/rhetorical approaches can teachers and students use to describe the ways in which visual representations make meaning on the Web? In conventional print texts?

- How do authors/designers/readers of Web materials assemble visuals/texts/sounds/video into meaning? Shape these components into effective and satisfying wholes? Gauge their effectiveness? How does communication fail on the Web? When?

- How are teachers and students learning effective strategies for communicating on the Web when they, themselves, often lack Web literacies? And how are students helping teachers to do so? How do teachers and students acquire such literacies? Where and from whom? In what order? With what support?

- How do teachers and students/people of different media generations and ages interpret texts and images on the Web? In what ways are their interpretations similar, different?

- How do peoples from different cultures, ages, races, genders, orientations, and backgrounds create and interpret texts and images on the Web? In what ways are their designs and interpretations similar, different?

- Within educational settings, how are Web literacies being integrated into more conventional literacy instruction? Displacing such instruction? Changing the nature of literacy education?

- How do people interact within Web spaces? How do their Web literacy practices connect them with each other and support collaborative activities? Prevent such connections and collaboration? Complicate them?

■ How are Web literacies being taught, learned, and practiced in the workplace? Who has access to such educational opportunities, communications?

The chapters in this book begin the process of both posing and addressing these critical questions. In this task, they provide the profession with the gift of insight and further challenge. The editor and contributors should be commended for their balanced and tempered treatment of the Web and its possibilities. Their claims are always well considered and tested; the essays themselves are never extravagant or hyperbolic. Taken as a collection, the essays offer teachers and students of composition studies, English studies, literacy, language arts, and many other disciplines a constellation of issues to explore. We are grateful to be a small part of this effort and highly recommend this collection to teachers, researchers, and students looking ahead to the many challenges of an increasingly digital age.

Works Cited

Gee, James Paul. 1990. *Social Linguistics and Literacies: Ideology in Discourses*. Brighton, Great Britain: Falmer Press.

Graff, H. J. 1987. *The Legacy of Literacy: Continuities and Contradictions in Western Culture and Society*. Bloomington: Indiana University Press.

Hawisher, Gail E., and Cynthia L. Selfe. Forthcoming. *Global Literacies and the World Wide Web*. London and New York: Routledge.

———. 1989. *Critical Perspectives on Computers and Composition Instruction*. New York: Teachers College Press.

Hawisher, Gail E., and Patricia A. Sullivan. 1999. "Fleeting Images: Women Visually Writing the Web." *Passions, Pedagogies, and 21st Century Technologies*. Ed. Gail E. Hawisher and Cynthia L. Selfe. Logan: Utah State University Press. 268–91.

Rose, Mike. 1989. *Lives on the Boundary: The Struggles and Achievements of America's Underprepared*. New York: Free Press.

Sirc, Geoffrey. 1999. "What Is Composition . . . ? After Duchamp (Notes Toward a General Teleintertext)." *Passions, Pedagogies, and 21st Century Technologies*. Ed. Gail E. Hawisher and Cynthia L. Selfe. Logan: Utah State University Press. 178–204.

Street, Brian V. 1995. *Social Literacies: Critical Approaches to Literacy in Development, Ethnography, and Education*. London: Longman.

Stuckey, Elspeth. 1991. *The Violence of Literacy*. Portsmouth: Boynton Cook/ Heinemann.

Wysocki, Anne, and Johndan Johnson-Eilola. 1999. "Blinded by the Letter: Why Are We Using Literacy as a Metaphor for Everything Else?" *Passions, Pedagogies, and 21st Century Technologies*. Ed. Gail E. Hawisher and Cynthia L. Selfe. Logan: Utah State University Press. 349–68.

Preface

Whether we listen to the news, read papers, magazine and journal articles, or talk to colleagues, "computerspeak" is part of many stories and conversations. Politicians and proponents of a more efficient workforce are eager to see new information technologies integrated into the workplace. To bridge the gap between corporate America and the educational system, teachers at all levels are encouraged to participate in the "technological revolution" as it relates to their teaching practices. Each issue of the *Chronicle of Higher Education*, for example, includes a section on "Information Technology" where educators can read about incorporating gender sensitivity in online courses (31 October, 1997, A36), about Sloan Foundation grants for online programs which "create a sense of community" (13 November 1998, A23), or about replacing paperbacks with electronic books (30 October 1998, A28). Many teachers interested in providing students with new venues for knowledge acquisition, however, are deterred by the onslaught of information and the many practical, methodological, and pedagogical issues left unanswered. Most books and articles in journals or in edited collections do not provide an in-depth "hands-on" approach to integrating the Web into daily teaching practices. As a result, many teachers remain in a quandary about how to provide students with enough skills to prepare them for future employment while at the same time enhancing their acquisition of academic and literate discourse. Basic questions relate to the creation of Web pages for specific courses and specific course goals, introducing students to various aspects of the Web, finding and linking to relevant sites, and integrating the virtual environment successfully into the face-to-face environment of the classroom.

Weaving a Virtual Web: Practical Approaches to New Information Technologies provides readers with a practical reference guide and a pedagogical introduction to the Web. It is intended for teachers who are trying to integrate the World Wide Web into their classrooms for the first time, and for teachers who have already experimented with the Web and are looking for different approaches to teaching on/with the Web. The contributors to this collection are experienced educators who have been successful in using the new information technology in the classroom. These contributions share a common desire to provide educators with the means to explore the potentials of electronic media without falling victim to the "information overload" and without having to re-invent an already existing Web of information. A Web site created to expand the scope of the book will lead readers to the various Web-based projects created by the contributors and discussed in the collection.

The idea for this book grew out of a conversation with Gail Hawisher, who encouraged me to work on this project and to be visionary. I owe special thanks to her for her trust in me, her wonderful advice, and her continued and unfaltering support. I thank Cynthia Selfe for the positive reinforcement she provided whenever it was needed. I also thank Michael Greer, NCTE's senior editor, for his comments and suggestions. He kept the collection on track and made this project possible. A special thank you goes to Kurt Austin, NCTE staff editor, who made the impossible possible. Many of my colleagues and friends have given me feedback and have offered their support while I was working on this book. I thank them for their constant encouragement. And I also want to extend my gratitude to the contributors of this collection. Without them, the book would not exist.

Introduction: Hypermedia Technologies for the Classroom

Sibylle Gruber
Northern Arizona University

anguage in an electronic forum, according to Gary Heba (1997), "continually invents and reinvents itself through an ongoing negotiation among users, developers, electronic content, and its presentation in a multimedia environment" (22). Stuart Moulthrop and Nancy Kaplan (1994) have described the impact of hypertextual discourse on the construction of text in similar terms. For them, constructive hypertext—hypertext that allows readers and writers to "act"— changes and blurs "distinctions between reception and production" and emphasizes plurality and participation.

constructive hypertext

As a result, readers in a hypertextual environment can follow numerous links that resist fixed and stable categories (220–23). The World Wide Web, then, can create realities which are in constant motion and which are not limited by linearity and monologic discourse often attributed to conventional texts. Accordingly, users of the Web can move beyond current perceptions of textuality toward more dynamic and collaborative forms of writing and reading preferred by many teachers and students. As a consequence, the Web also allows for exploring diverse forms of literacy practices—taking, for example, multimodality into consideration—emphasized in many educational institutions. Hypermedia texts can help teachers provide a means of constructing knowledge by demanding students' active involvement with a constantly changing text.[1] This, as Joyce (1995) has pointed out, can allow users to move through virtual worlds which "language previously only evoked in the imagination" (24). In its ideal form, then, hypertextual discourse—and hypermedia—can enhance innovative teaching practices that promote student participation in the learning process. In other words, the Web can furnish teachers and students with innovative tools for supporting already existing educational goals such as involving students in the learning process, using collaboration as a teaching and learning strat-

multimodality

egy, and creating a space for active learning, exploration, and innovation.

The World Wide Web, according to this viewpoint, does not only contribute to a rapid expansion of information but can also support an accessible and engaging curriculum by foregrounding new ways of approaching knowledge distribution and acquisition. According to Mick Doherty's cover statement in *Kairos: A Journal for Teachers of Writing in Webbed Environments,*

> In hypertextual environments, writers are not only learning to strike forcefully in the traditional sense of presenting the correct words in the proper manner, but are also learning to weave a writing space that is more personal than the standard sheet of paper. We are writing differently; we are reading differently; we are learning differently; we are teaching differently (Mick Doherty, 15 November 1997).

From this perspective, authors and audiences of hypermedia are encouraged—and required—to transform established perceptions of writing and reading practices, and to weave a "virtual web," a writing space that can provide more flexibility than traditional print texts. Authors no longer move through several revision stages from unfinished to finished products, locking them into a rigid pattern of an institutionally approved writing process; instead, texts remain in flux and are "dynamic, open-ended, evolving" (Moulthrop and Kaplan 1994, 221), being revised, changed, and improved on an ongoing basis.

A hypermedia paradigm, then, reconceptualizes the notion of text as a hierarchically organized artifact. Instead, as Victor Vitanza (1996) puts it, "hypertext, to be hypertext, does not have to follow the logic of linear thought but can follow (and some insist *should* follow) associative thought" (186).[2] Consequently, instead of moving through beginnings, middles, and ends without considering alternate modes of presentation, hypertexts and hypermedia allow readers and writers to follow their individual and often very different reading and composing processes more easily (Vitanza 1996; McDaid 1991; Birkerts 1994; Moulthrop and Kaplan 1994; Heba 1997).[3]

Hypertext scholars are certainly not the first or only proponents of texts as dynamic and heteroglossic. Theorists and practitioners from the classical period (see, for example, the Sophists' perspectives on the creation of meaning in texts) to the twentieth century have argued against language and text as stable and fixed entities. Bakhtin (1981), among others, argues that language "is never unitary"; instead, its significance and meaning is determined by specific speech acts (291). Many feminist scholars, poststructuralists, and postmodernists contend that the meaning of words and texts is created not only by the author but is constantly recreated by her readers and the context surrounding the production and consumption of text. From this perspective, Landow and Delaney's (1991)—and other hypertext theorists'—claim that printed texts, unlike hypertexts, are "linear, bounded, and fixed" needs to be modified and revisited. Instead of portraying print texts and hypertexts as binary opposites, we can conceptualize them as a continuum—neither being absolutely linear nor completely nonlinear, and both sharing characteristics necessary for successful communication.

It will become apparent when reading the essays in this collection that hypertexts do not present an entirely new approach to texts and to teaching. Instead, their application in classroom situations enhances many of the already existing educational practices—from teaching writing as a process to increasing audience awareness—by combining newness with familiarity. Teachers, for example, can use the Web to support students' often nonlinear composing processes. Students can be encouraged to conduct research on the Web, select and gather important data, brainstorm and organize their ideas, decide what to include in their drafts, and experiment with new ways of presenting information. These activities can move students from being passive to active learners, encouraging them to explore and evaluate new concepts and new ideas. At the same time, students can learn how to apply their newly acquired skills to already existing frameworks within their fields of inquiry. For example, once they realize that research on the Web can be fun *and* instructive, they might also engage more actively in off-line research.

Teachers can also engage students in collaborative and cooperative learning by exploring the Web as an interactive teaching tool. Collaborative activities, according to Bellan and Best (1992), "by their very nature lend themselves to authentic activity, situated cognition, and socially based learning strategies" (313). Web-enhanced activities can help students hone these skills. The Web—if used in connection with pedagogies that encourage and affirm student interaction—can contribute actively to the creation of connected knowledge. Students can be encouraged to negotiate their roles as members of a group, they can learn how to share responsibilities, they can explore their strengths in specific areas of the collaborative process, and they can be introduced to work with others against current notions of competitive individualism. Teachers, then, can use the Web as a pedagogical tool to ensure that students learn how to build a supportive environment and how to work toward a common goal.

Additionally, the Web can help teachers promote pedagogies that allow students to apply different learning strategies more suitable to their needs. In this environment, students can approach texts from a number of perspectives. For example, they can focus on the linear development of a text; they can also use the links embedded in hypertexts to follow a more associative learning pattern. Furthermore, the combination of text, graphics, and sound can help students understand the intricate connections between different media and their influences on the meaning of texts. Very important, the multiple structures employed by hypertext writers and readers can also bridge cultural differences in approaching texts. Although linearity, a clear structure, and hierarchical organization within a text are considered appropriate by some communities, circularity and a context-based (often nonsequential) organization are preferred by students with different cultural backgrounds. Students who engage in Web-enhanced research activities, for example, can follow a monochronic path (doing one thing at a time—reading the text on one screen) or engage in polychronic activities (doing various things at the same time—reading the text, looking at graphics, following various links for context, moving back to the text). Instead of restricting students' diverse approaches to knowledge acquisition, teachers can use the Web as a tool that encourages students to explore different learning styles.

The Web can also help teachers who want to discourage students' reliance on one text as the main source of information. Hyperlinks within a document undermine the notion of text as isolated artifact. Instead, students can explore the connections between texts, move among different layers of information, gather background information, and investigate texts written on similar topics. Teachers can then encourage students to make the connections they saw exemplified in hyperlinked texts in their own writing and in off-line research.

By foregrounding the new possibilities of hypertexts while also emphasizing their familiarity, teachers can create an engaging curriculum that allows students to move between different layers or webs of texts, visual presentations, and sound. And, because hypermedia texts move beyond words on the screen and incorporate audio and visual elements, teachers can explore the definition and meaning of "text" with their students, establishing new criteria for acceptable communication. Students can no longer be merely concerned with the sequence of words on a page, but they also need to take into consideration new aspects related to aesthetic appeal—background color, clip art, scanned images, sound, font size, and choice of colors all become part of the message an author is trying to convey.

Exploring Web pages and creating online voices can improve students' communication skills while at the same time contributing to a greater awareness of their audiences. Instead of only writing for their teachers and sometimes for their peers, they now have to consider a larger, albeit often undefined, audience. Such an approach moves writing into a larger context, creating a purpose that is absent in many traditional writing assignments. In other words, teachers can enhance and expand already existing teaching methods and can help students understand the writing process, increase audience awareness, and promote independent and critical thinking.

Such new approaches to text and textuality attract many teachers and students to the Web. However, the Web can also create new and often unpredictable challenges. Teachers worry about pedagogical implications, the availability of resources and training, ethical concerns (e.g., misuse of resources),[4] the reliability of online sources, the restrictions imposed by their institution's curriculum, time commitment, and possible longterm effects of integrating the Web into their teaching practices. And although these concerns are shared by many educators who try to work with new technologies, many of these questions have not yet been addressed.

Much excellent scholarship, however, has been done to create a theoretical foundation for educators interested in online communication tools. For example, books and articles on online discourse practices, the effects of online communication and collaborative pedagogies, online power relations and their social, political, and economic implications, feminist and cyborg theories, connectivity theories, and hypertext theories have provided the framework necessary for understanding how new technologies influence us and how we influence new technologies. On the other side of the continuum, many "handbooks" have been published that explain how to access the Web, use search engines, and retrieve information from the Web. However, for the most part, these resources do not address how the Web changes, alters, or continues current theoretical frameworks connected to teaching and research.

What has not been attempted yet, and what *Weaving a Virtual Web* provides, is a volume that builds on already established theories and applies them to practical questions about teaching and pedagogy. In this respect, *Weaving a Virtual Web* signifies a major turning point. It is certainly based on and could not exist without the foundational work of such prominent scholars as Gail Hawisher, Cynthia Selfe, Lisa Gerard, Pamela Takayoshi, Kristine Blair, Richard Selfe, Lester Faigley, James Porter, Johndan Johnson-Eilola, Stuart Moulthrop, Nancy Kaplan, John McDaid, George Landow, and others interested in the theoretical implications of new technologies. The contributors to this volume take the next step by focusing on practical applications of new technologies while at the same time keeping in mind the theoretical implications associated with incorporating new approaches to teaching.

In essence, the contributors to *Weaving a Virtual Web: Practical Approaches to New Information Technologies* consider the Web as an innovative approach for exploring new and established literacies and problematizing current educational, social, and political paradigms. Contributors discuss how the Web has influenced and changed their own teaching practices in the language arts, and they reflect on their past and present experiences with hypertext applications in the classroom. Dealing with different institutional and instructional components, different student populations, and more or less advanced computer technologies, contributors to this volume explore questions like the following:

- What is the pedagogical framework that underlies various uses of the Web?
- What are the planning and preparation stages that teachers have to consider before using the Web?
- How can teachers and students engage in effective research on the Web?
- How can collaboration be encouraged?
- What are the implications for publishing on the Web?
- What practical information and helpful hints will assist teachers and students who want to incorporate the Web into their classrooms?
- What are potential problems for using the Web in an educational setting where traditional texts are favored?

In bringing together representatives from different educational institutions to elaborate on their own practices as teachers, this collection provides insightful narratives and practical examples about how hypermedia can be used in educational settings. The necessity of this volume is highlighted when one listens to and reads about faculty who wish to incorporate new technologies but do not have sufficient support for their endeavors. And although many educators do not consider the help available to them as meeting their needs, more than 40 percent of educational institutions "*require* basic skills for computer or Internet use" (Guernsey, 17 October 1997, A30). The contributors to this collection show how teachers can become competent in using technologies to enhance classroom practices. Throughout the collection, the authors demonstrate how the World Wide Web can become an exciting tool for student learning. They provide writing prompts and writing samples, assignments, instructions, and helpful suggestions for teachers. An extensive corpora of practical information can also be accessed on the Web site which accompanies this book (http://www.ncte.org/books/98/ Gruber 56495.shtml).

    Weaving a Virtual Web, then, provides a great deal more than mere hype for using technology. Instead of falling prey to slogans such as "life without technology isn't an option,"[5] contributors have carefully weighed the impact of technology and the World Wide Web on student learning. The collection is also more than a "handbook" of (re)search techniques on the Web.[6] Although handbooks and research guides provide initial direction on how to access the Web, find various sources, and use correct coding for Web documents, they do not furnish the resources necessary for teachers who need practical, theoretical, methodological, and pedagogical advice on how to include Web-based instruction in their classrooms. The essays in *Weaving a Virtual Web* provide critical perspectives for teachers, educators, and administrators who intend to move beyond traditional instruction and curricula toward incorporating the Web as a tool for enriching current teaching practices.

The Organization of This Volume

A linear, text-based version of essays discussing strategies for integrating the Web—which partly calls into question linear approaches to texts—poses many challenges. The organization in this collection provides a compromise: On the one hand, the papers can be read linearly, moving through a progression similar to the processes involved in writing a paper. In this scenario, the reader examines strategies for planning and goalsetting, researching, collaborating, and publishing. On the other hand, readers are encouraged to move freely from text to text, creating their own links and connections within and among texts. This perspective enables the reader to approach the book less as a traditional volume and more as a hypertext which allows for unpredictable moves while sustaining a cohesive experience.

    To provide a sense of linear progression, this volume is organized into four basic sections: Planning and Structuring Web-Enhanced

Courses; Encouraging Research on and with the Web; Supporting Collaboration and Interaction; and Publishing on the Web.

The first section, Planning and Structuring Web-Enhanced Courses, is comprised of four essays, each of which is concerned with establishing a framework for Web-enhanced instruction. These essays also provide examples of the overall course structure, guiding readers from the beginning stages of Web implementation to possible sample projects. In the first essay in this section, David Gillette explains how to create an English course which focuses on the Web as a media collage where textuality is examined in connection with all elements of the "text" which constitute an "internal narrative logic." Reading "When Media Collide," interested audiences learn how to plan for a course which includes media seminars in which the class analyzes the storytelling "interfaces" of the pivotal media technologies—texts, film, television, still photography, and painting—that interact in a Web-based environment.

In the second essay, "Encountering Hypertext Technology: Student Engineers Analyze and Construct Web Pages," J. D. Applen discusses how to create a course plan which encourages students to read theory about hypertext and the World Wide Web, analyze Web pages, and then construct their own Web pages. Applen shows how careful initial planning enables students to devise a set of criteria that allows them to analyze an effective Web page. Applen also outlines how the specifics of a proposal statement—the objective, problem statement, and audience analysis—prepare students to construct a Web page.

Asking how instructors can cover not only the technical, logistical aspects of the Web but also the theoretical and pedagogical ramifications of using it, Larry Beason's essay shows readers how he structures the different components of a Web project in a course that prepares future teachers for implementing computers in the teaching of writing.

Following Beason's explorations of the theoretical and pedagogical aspects of using the Web is Emily Golson and Eric Sagel's collaborative essay, "The Creation Project." Golson, the instructor of the course, discusses how her pedagogical goals translate into planning and creating a Web project. She examines both the successes and shortcomings of the lesson, and offers suggestions about how to plan future electronic efforts. Sagel, one of the students in the course, discusses how the class reacted to the project and puts forward suggestions and technical advice to students or teachers writing Web documents.

The four articles included in the second section, Encouraging Research on and with the Web, present different approaches to helping students become independent and successful researchers by utilizing the Web as a powerful resource tool. In "Can Anybody Play? Using the World Wide Web to Develop Multidisciplinary Research and Writing Skills," Elizabeth Sommers begins with an explanation of her pedagogical stance and the concept of research that defines the course. Sommers describes the most important skills and knowledge students learn in her course. After providing practical information on how to use the Web for research, she concludes with an overview of what she has learned and what other teachers might expect to gain from incorporating Web-based research and writing in their courses.

Jean Boreen, in her essay "Surfing the Net: Getting Middle School Students Excited about Research and Writing," discusses a university course which provided university students as well as veteran teachers an opportunity to work one-on-one with a group of middle-school students on Web-based projects. Boreen shows how using the Internet as a research tool can influence students' rhetorical choices in their writing and can engage students in an active use of resources, leading them to "take charge of their own education."

Jean LeLoup and Robert Ponterio elaborate further on how the Web can be used as a resource tool. In "Foreign Language Resources on the Web: Cultural and Communicative Wealth on the Wires" they discuss the rationale for using the WWW in the foreign language classroom and provide the pedagogical underpinnings for integrating electronic communications technologies with their wealth of information into the foreign language curriculum. Their sample projects—visiting two "virtual" French museums and presenting a news broadcast in Spanish after students collected information available on the Web—show well-thought-out objectives for language teaching while also incorporating research about a country's culture.

The next essay, "Building a Web for Literacy Instruction," provides a model for English teachers who want to incorporate technology for conducting meaningful and independent research and for writing instruction. In this essay, Sarah Rilling and Enikö Csomay present projects used in a first-year composition course in the United States and a teacher education course in Hungary. They point out that students who were able to use the Web for conducting research "learn not only how to be more independent learners, but they also acquire various learning strategies from their peers."

In the third section, Supporting Collaboration and Interaction, the six contributors elaborate on their experiences with using the Web to encourage teamwork and cooperative learning among students as well as with audiences outside the academic setting. Describing her work with students in college composition courses, Patricia Webb's essay, "Changing Writing/Changing Writers: The World Wide Web and Collaborative Inquiry in the Classroom" provides an example of how the Web can support and encourage collaborative inquiry. As a result of integrating the Web into her class, Webb found that students started to view "writing and thinking as part of a dialogic process in which we are in continual conversation with others." Discussions were richer, students had more of a sense of their audience, and they took more responsibility for the collaborative writing they produced.

Aijun Anna Li and Margery Osborne discuss collaboration on the Web as a major component of student learning in a fifth-grade classroom. In "Using the Web to Create an Interdisciplinary Tool for Teaching," Li and Osborne look at a teacher in a "real" instructional setting to understand the dynamics and social processes of community building and information sharing in the classroom. Li and Osborne show how the fifth-graders collaboratively—with only minimal equipment—use the Internet and other information technologies in everyday instruction.

In her essay entitled "Alewives," Katherine Fischer explores the possibilities of the Web as a "living sea" which allows students to interact not only with each other but with an audience outside the conventional classroom walls. She stresses the immediacy of the Web and the capability of interaction between students and sources—such as war veterans responding to students' queries online—which creates an experience of literature as "living and breathing."

The metaphor of "living" is continued into the next essay of this section, "Writing Images: Using the World Wide Web in a Digital Photography class," where Anne Wysocki argues that the structures of her class and of the class's use of the World Wide Web can be compared to a city. Not only did the Web pages built by students feel like city streets, but they encouraged the interactions that can happen in cities, leading to spirited communication and interactions rarely attained in regular classrooms.

Building communities on the Web also informs Elizabeth Burow-Flak's essay, "From Castles in the Air to Portfolios in Cyberspace: Building Community Ethos in First-Year Rhetoric and Composition." After addressing how to translate new technologies into one's teaching method and pedagogical goals, Burow-Flak documents how students can learn to evaluate new technologies critically, and how Web activities can establish community not only in cyberspace, but also in face-to-face interactions in the classroom. She shows how students in her classroom have grown—through World Wide Web construction—"into a critically savvy community of writers."

The fourth section, Publishing on the Web, contains papers which explain the impact of creating hypermedia environments that allow students to publish their texts. The contributors here discuss how published Web pages influence students' perceptions of their texts and the texts of their peers. In "Living Texts on the Web: A Return to the Rhetorical Arts of Annotation and Commonplace," Dean Rehberger shows how the Web can be used as a tool to help students focus on portfolios, workshops, group projects, collaboration, revision, and process. Rehberger argues that the Internet can be used by instructors to create more effective assignments and responses to student writing. Using the Internet as a writing tool, according to Rehberger, allows instructors to merge older rhetorical arts of linking, cataloguing, annotating, and collecting emphasized by hypertext with contemporary theories of writing and cultural studies, creating what Rehberger terms "living texts," thus expanding Fischer's and Wysocki's use of the term to include not only the environment of the Web but also the texts created on the Web.

The structure of Douglas Eyman's hypertextual class in his essay "Students as Builders of Virtual Worlds: Creating a Classroom Intranet" moves students from creating public personal narratives (acting as individual writers, but writers with a real audience) to working in collaborative teams to produce knowledge bases which can be linked to and explored by other students. The four primary assignments discussed in this essay are an autobiographical description intended for a small, known audience (the class itself); the writing of an individual hypertext essay, organized as linked lexia; the linking of the previous essays to other students' essays, with the creation of "bridge" pages which explore the process of collaborative intertextuality; and the creation of a hypertext journal.

The following article, "Using the Web for High School Student Writers" by Ted Nellen, relates his experiences as a New York City public high school English teacher who recounts some of the activities of his students in his Cyber English class in which each student publishes on the Web. He provides specific writing examples and gives advice and tips to those who wish to electrify their classrooms. This teacher, who calls himself a constructivist, has used many resources on the Internet to excite his students and to draw the best from them. Their Webfolios and international collaborations make Cyber English an important Internet application in education and proof positive of the Internet's effect in the English classroom.

Publishing for authentic audiences is at the forefront of Joy Egbert and Leonard Jessup's essay on "Systems Analysis and Design Projects: Integrating Communities and Skills through the Web." In this project, learners participate in a process to develop Web pages for a client in the community. As Egbert and Jessup point out, these projects provide community members and teammates as authentic audiences with whom learners interact socially and professionally while learning critical skills such as problem solving, decision making, synthesizing, summarizing, and working cooperatively.

Audience awareness in publishing on the Web is also an important aspect of Catherine Smith's essay, "Nobody, Which Means Anybody: Audience on the World Wide Web." Smith sketches a teacher's recognition of including a "public commons" for Web discourse in client Web sites developed by technical/professional writing students. For guidance on accountably teaching "audience" in this stage of Web evolution, Smith proposes a synthesis of rhetorical principle, Hannah Arendt's ethics of public life, and recent theory of human-computer interaction.

The last essay in this section leads us into "MOOspace." In "Donut Shoppes and Tea Rooms: Getting in the MOO(d) for Hypertext," Mick Doherty and Sandye Thompson explore the pragmatics and theoretical value of utilizing "MOO" technology—a shared synchronous writing space—to help students reconceive of the writing process as it is applied in multilinear environments. The major contributors to this essay are students from several electronic writing classes, who discussed the pros and cons of MOOing, and what they learned from the experiences. The authors note that all of the resources cited in this essay are electronic publications, a rhetorical choice of the authors encouraged by the student participants, as a means of further validating the epistemological value of the pixelated word.

The volume concludes with an extensive reference essay by Kevin Leander in which he provides excellent Web-based resources for teachers and students. As a reference, "The Craft of Teaching and the World Wide Web: A Reference Essay for Educators" is designed as a brief guide for educators who are novices on the Web and wish to have a broad sense of a variety of valuable Web resources. Sections contain links, descriptions, and extended reviews, and vary topically from institutional projects to examples of student work, from online journals to digital libraries and professional development resources. As an essay, the piece argues for constructivist, dialogue-based pedagogies with the Web, especially those which have the potential to engage educators and their students with dispersed and diverse communities of practice.

The essays in this volume provide readers with answers to many questions connected to using the Web for instructional purposes. The authors elaborate on how to plan a Web-enhanced course and how to design activities for students. They also show how to encourage research on the Web and how to integrate collaborative strategies in a Web-enhanced classroom. Finally, the contributors address the impact of publishing student work on the Web. And, because the contributors are also teachers at different institutions, their essays center on the importance of hands-on material to provide specific examples for those interested in Web-enhanced instruction. The plethora of sample syllabi, writing exercises, handouts, and tips makes this collection an invaluable resource for educators at all levels.

Notes

1. Landow (1992) argues that Roland Barthes' "ideal textuality" encompasses the features of a computer hypertext as a "text composed of blocks of words (or images) linked electronically by multiple paths, chains, or trails in an open-ended, perpetually unfinished textuality described by the terms *link, node, network, web,* and *path*" (3).

2. Vitanza (1996) here refers to Sven Birkerts's (1994) distinction between print culture and electronic culture. According to Birkerts, print culture is "vertically cumulative" while electronic culture is "laterally associative" (207).

3. Not all critics consider the unstructured nature of hypertexts as positive. Birkerts (1994), for example, sees the "proto-electronic era" as eroding current language practices and moving toward "plainspeak," flattening historical perspectives, and undermining the private self (211–13).

4. For an in-depth exploration of the theoretical foundations of rhetorical ethics for Internet users, see James Porter's *Rhetorical Ethics and Internetworked Writing.*

5. Taken from an advertisement by Datatel in the *Chronicle of Higher Education,* 20 November 1998, page A23. Other keywords in the ad include *technology as a friend, designed to help you succeed, instant access,* and *more productive.*

6. Handbooks on Web research include Rodrigues's (1997) *The Research Paper and the World Wide Web,* Clark's (1997) *Working the Web,* Crump and Carbone's (1996) *English Online: A Student's Guide to the Internet and World Wide Web,* Branscomb's (1998) *Casting Your Net,* Leshin's (1998) *Student Resource Guide to the Internet,* and Anderson, Benjamin, and Paredes-Holt's (1998) *Connections.*

Works Cited

Anderson, Daniel, Brett Benjamin, and Bill Paredes-Holt. 1998. *Connections: A Guide to On-line Writing.* Boston: Allyn and Bacon.

Bellan, J., and T. Best. 1992. "Pixels instead of Pens and Paste." *Visual Communication: Bridging across Culture.* Blacksburg, VA: International Visual Literacy Association.

Birkerts, Sven. 1994. "Into the Electronic Millennium." Reprinted in *CyberReader* (1996), edited by Victor Vitanza, 203–14. Boston: Allyn and Bacon.

Blumenstyk, Goldie. 1997. "A feminist scholar questions how women fare in distance education." *Chronicle of Higher Education,* 31 October: A36.

Branscomb, H. Eric. 1998. *Casting Your Net: A Student's Guide to Research on the Internet.* Boston: Allyn and Bacon.

Clark, Carol. 1997. *Working the Web: A Student's Guide.* New York: Harcourt Brace.

Crump, Eric, and Nick Carbone. 1996. *English Online: A Student's Guide to the Internet and World Wide Web.* New York: Houghton Mifflin.

Datatel. 1998. "Life without technology isn't an option." Advertisement in the *Chronicle of Higher Education,* 20 November: A23.

Doherty, Mick. 1997. "Cover Statement." *Kairos: A Journal for Teachers of Writing in Webbed Environments* [Online]. http://english.ttu.edu/kairos [November 15].

Guernsey, Lisa. 1997. "E-mail is now used in a third of college courses, survey finds." *Chronicle of Higher Education,* 17 October: A30.

Heba, Gary. 1997. "HyperRhetoric: Multimedia, Literacy, and the Future of Composition." *Computers and Composition* 14: 19–44.

Joyce, Michael. 1995. *Of Two Minds: Hypertext Pedagogy and Poetics.* Ann Arbor: University of Michigan Press.

Kiernan, Vincent. 1997. "Linguists hope a new computer program will advance the study of sign language." *Chronicle of Higher Education,* 7 November: A27.

Landow, George P. 1992. *Hypertext: The Convergence of Contemporary Critical Theory and Technology.* Baltimore: Johns Hopkins University Press.

Landow, George P., and Paul Delany. 1991. "Hypertext, Hypermedia and Literary Studies: The State of the Art." *Hypermedia and Literary Studies.* Ed. Paul Delany and George P. Landow. Cambridge, MA: MIT Press.

Leshin, Cynthia B. 1998. *Students Resource Guide to the Internet: Student Success Online.* Upper Saddle River, NJ: Prentice Hall.

McDaid, John. 1991. "Toward an Ecology of Hypermedia." In *Evolving Perspectives on Computers and Composition Studies: Questions for the 1990s,* edited by G. E. Hawisher and C. L. Selfe, 203–23. Urbana, IL: NCTE.

Moulthrop, Stuart, and Nancy Kaplan. 1994. "They Became What They Beheld: The Futility of Resistance in the Space of Electronic Writing." In *Literacy and Computers,* edited by C. L. Selfe and S. Hilligos, 220–37. New York: MLA.

Rodrigues, Dawn. 1997. *The Research Paper and the World Wide Web.* Upper Saddle River, NJ: Prentice Hall.

Vitanza, Victor. 1996. *CyberReader.* Boston: Allyn and Bacon.

I Planning and Structuring Web-Enhanced Courses

1 When Media Collide

David Gillette
University of Central Florida

Treating the Web as a Media Collage

If sculpture is not chiseling and casting and welding, what is it? If painting is not painting on canvas and selling it to buy more paint to put on more canvas, what is it? . . . because all the arts face the same technological pressures, they are going to find, create, new relationships through that technology, through their new digital equivalences. Such equivalences pose the most fundamental, and most obvious, challenges to the structure and purpose of the university arts curriculum, and to the place of literary study in it.

R. Lanham, "Literary Study and the Digital Revolution"

Once a student puts her work up on the Web, includes links to other sites, spots her pages with an animated GIF or two, adds in many personal and public photos, installs a film clip to illustrate her point, and then tacks on a MIDI track of a Bach piano sonata playing in the background, only a small portion of her overall work can actually be considered standard writing and composition. What do you do when you're asked to evaluate her work as an English instructor? Do you ignore everything else and just focus on the text? That certainly doesn't seem fair. But then by what standard do you approach the nontext elements in her work?

My tendency as an instructor is to look at the entire creation and evaluate it as a singular composition, an interactive digital collage assembled from many divergent pieces. I consider everything created for the Web as a collage of elements working together to make a unified statement. Sometimes the statement arises easily from the collage, and sometimes the statement is obscured by a misuse of one or more elements in the collage. A Web site can strike us as a brilliant piece of work because the creator understands the media elements at play within her work and therefore uses the strengths of each element to create a strong, unified argument. Equally, a Web site can be an ugly, confusing mess because media was used poorly in the presentation.

When evaluating student Web work—which I do in the technical writing courses I teach—we need to take into account the entire media collage the student has assembled for us. Did the student have a reason to include each GIF, video clip, music track, audio file, and graphic in her final work? Are there elements in her work that seem to have no reason to be there? Did the student have a plan in mind when he linked one page to another, or does his linking seem random? Is the statement of the work itself clear and concise, no matter which part you look at, or does the point of the piece contradict itself as you interact with the project?

To prepare students for this level of analysis, we first need to show them how to create a successful collage that builds upon the strengths of its individual parts. We need to introduce our students to the individual media elements that exist in a typical Web creation. Finally, we need to tie together the analysis of these media elements with a structure that most of us instinctually understand and use every day. We need to show students how narrative structure, storytelling in all its guises, can serve as the foundation for everything they create on the Web, be it fiction or nonfiction prose, scientific instruction and fact

---

Media Collage Tip #1
How to evaluate nontextual student work.

- *Treat student Web work as a media collage.* Examine how well the entire structure hangs together. The argument or point of the collage should be clear from the outset.

- *Ask students to explain every aspect of their Web collage.* Require cohesion and thoughtful purpose in their answers. Any answers not well founded or which fail to support the goals of the collage indicate the element in question is a weak part of the whole and must be reconsidered.

- *Keep track of how often you get lost.* If you are lost too often, something is wrong and the collage is still not complete. Getting lost in a Web collage is not your fault, it is the fault of weak design and indicates there is still work to be done.

- *Require everything to work properly.* Is there something you can't read, see, or use in the Web collage? If so, the collage is still not complete.

gathering, game-like interaction, or publishing the results of standard academic research.

Using Narrative as Focus When Looking at the Web

> *Narrative poetics outlines the competence required of readers and tellers of narrative. Like language (langue), narrative can be understood as a system underlying individual texts: narrative poetics is to a given narrative what grammar is to a given utterance, so a reader's knowledge of how narrative operates as a system partly determines the sense he or she makes of a text. Such competence is not limited to so-called literary texts or even to fictional ones. It is, moreover, culturally learned, reinforced by narratives of all sorts: novels, short stories . . . but also newspapers, advertisements, histories, myths, letters, anecdotes, jokes, popular entertainments, and public ceremonies.*
>
> S. Cohan and L. M. Shires, "The Structures of Narrative: Story"

In my hypertext/hypermedia courses I talk about the Web as a new way to intermix established communication technologies into a creation that, as an evolving collage, has its own style of argumentation. However, the unifying structure beneath everything presented in this collage is the energy of narrative construction and internal narrative logic. No matter how any collage comes together, the desire to tell a story to someone else remains the center of everything that takes place. The narrative can be fictional or factual, it can be linear or may be independent of time, but the underlying structure of a successful, engaging media collage retains its focus by how it interlinks its narrative elements.

My courses depart from and return to two central lessons designed to help students produce interesting, cohesive work on the Web. First, I teach students about the structure and logic of the various narrative approaches represented by print, film, television, and painting/still photography. Second, I show students how those narrative approaches can interact with each other to create an individual, self-contained collage on the Web. During the span of one semester, I introduce students to the most prominent media technologies resident in an average Web collage. We look at and discuss film, television, printed and bound text, still photography, and other means of oral and visual storytelling.

By studying these narrative technologies individually, we find that as each one arrives on the computer screen it no longer functions as it did in its original form. Yet each media element remains a definable part of a larger, more complex whole. A Web collage is powered by the combined strengths of its individual elements that create an overall impression with an identity separate from its parts. If you remove any individual element, the collage changes, substantially altering the ultimate meaning. Additionally, if you understand and use the strength of each media element to its fullest potential, the collage itself will become stronger. When a Web collage finally comes together, it actually evolves into a new medium on its own.

Bringing the Media Collage to the Classroom

The first thing I explain to my students is that my hypertext courses are not courses in how to write HTML, nor are they courses about hypertext as some kind of literary genre. I tell students we are going to study how narrative is structured by a variety of media elements, all of which play a vital role in creating a cohesive Web collage. While my courses are not strictly about developing writing skills, I do tell my students they will be required to produce a fair amount of dense, thoughtfully prepared text in response to questions about their work. Additionally I inform students that I expect their final Web projects to contain a substantial amount of text. Text is one of the most powerful and adaptive technologies ever invented, and it therefore remains a vital part of all my courses.

Because most of what I teach is offered under the Technical Writing rubric, I explain that even though we are focusing on the narrative aspects of collage, the course is not a fiction writing work-shop. While what students produce does require creative effort, their projects should mostly be nonfictional or technically informative in nature. Additionally, while at least half of our time in class revolves around discussion of our readings, the other half is devoted to hands-on development of student Web projects. I therefore warn students that they will be continually shifting gears throughout the semester, from careful reading and analysis to detailed, time-consuming production.

To introduce students to the individual elements of the Web, I lead them through two- to three-week seminars during which we analyze what I refer to as the storytelling interface of each media. When I use the term *interface* in this context, I refer to the representation of space and time in each media, and how that representation is received by readers, viewers, or users. Even though the Web collage is composed of many media elements and continues to add more nearly every day, I currently limit my discussions to the most frequently used narrative interfaces borrowed from printed text, film, television, and still photography/painting.

I initiate and conclude the discussion of each media element with some deceptively simple core questions that become increasingly complex and elusive each time we apply them to our work in class.

As we explore each medium with more detail, we return to our core questions repeatedly, discovering different answers each time. Eventually our answers form the basis for the students' final projects, which range from highly personal interpretations of a single-class discussion to abstract theoretical presentations dealing with large course-length themes.

Structuring One Semester of Media Seminars

The first part of the semester (usually three to four weeks) is devoted to the study of the linear, structured-logic narrative interface of traditional text using the codex form of presentation (a printed and bound book with individual sheets of paper contained between a cover of some kind with a defined front and back). In the past I have used a number of traditional literary works for this print-based seminar, focusing on

---

Media Collage Tip #2
How to focus on narrative in nontextual media forms.

Asking the following questions may help you and your students define and examine the narrative "interfaces" of media such as film, television, still photography, and the printed word.

- How does this media function as a storytelling device?

- How is this media different than the other ones we have studied thus far?

- What is the most powerful narrative aspect of this media technology?

- What is the weakest narrative aspect of this media technology?

- How does this media relate to or interact with its intended audience?

- How does this media deal with narrative representations of time?

authors who also discuss various ways in which we write about, talk about, and live within our conception of time. Lately I have found some literary science fiction and metafiction works that are ideal for this purpose, such as *City of Glass* by Paul Auster, *Slaughterhouse-Five* by Kurt Vonnegut, and *If on a Winter's Night a Traveler* by Italo Calvino.

We then move on to a seminar examining the stream-of-consciousness, immersion narrative interface of film narrative. For source material, we usually examine simple, popular films such as *Jaws*, *Night of the Living Dead*, or *The Birds* along with a more complex use of film narrative such as *8 1/2*, *Citizen Kane*, *Wings of Desire*, or *Ran*. Along with close viewing of the source films, we read analyses of the films by their directors and by critics focused on the technical aspects of the films' construction.

Two weeks of the course are devoted to the personal, multichannel narrative interface of the television commercial. I ask students to review current commercials and to storyboard their own commercials designed to sell the Web as a new and improved method of storytelling.

In the final media seminar, we spend two weeks examining the static, instantaneous narrative interface of still photography and painting using work from Postimpressionist movements (most of which can be found on the Web at various museum sites), recent printed and online collections of photojournalism, and recent critical writings about twentieth-century art, Cubism, collage theory, and performance art.

At the conclusion of each media seminar, I require students to design their own Web collages which they accompany with oral and printed or hypertextual presentations explaining the connection between their collage and the media under consideration in that seminar.

The final third of the course turns into a workshop in which students work together and independently to create a Web collage representing their responses to that semester's seminars. During this final workshop phase we occasionally stop to reconsider past discussions in light of ongoing student work, and also debate the changing definitions of terms such as *publishing, storytelling, narrative,* and *collage.*

Text as Narrative Technology

I always begin my courses by analyzing a medium familiar to everyone. Therefore I begin by looking at how printed text presents narrative to its reader. We examine text as a technology, and how that technology, combined with the interface design of the codex, helps to create a

Media Collage Tip #3
How to arrange a semester of media seminars.

- *Choose source texts, films, photos, and television productions with a similar theme.* This is not necessary, but it does help focus class discussion if students can see how different media deal with the same topic. This also makes it easier to establish comparisons between the narrative interfaces used by each medium.

- *Be flexible with the class schedule.* The range of foreknowledge and comfort with different media formats varies from class to class. A class composed of English majors can move through a "Text and Codex as Narrative Interface" seminar much more quickly than can a class composed of computer science students who may not be as familiar with the history and development of the book and printed literature. Seminars on the narrative interfaces of still photography and painting can take longer than expected depending upon the level of art history students have been exposed to before taking this seminar.

- *Reserve time for in-class work on the Web.* Students need to have time, in class, with the instructor present, to work on their projects, ask technical questions about HTML, surf the Web, and show their work to each other. Students have to do a great deal of outside work for this course, so providing a good number of in-class workshops helps lighten the load. In-class workshops can also lead to impromptu lectures that may solve many problems quickly, by addressing concerns that would never be raised in a standard lecture/response/discussion format.

- *Discourage the use of too many media formats in a final Web collage.* Students will want to experiment with each of the narrative interfaces you introduce them to in class. Experimentation is fine, but students also need to learn the basic artistic and writing dictum that "less is more." Help students understand the value of editing their work (both textually and visually) for precision and clarity.

specific narrative interface for the reader, and thereby defines the limits for what is usually considered a useful or understandable printed narrative. As a theoretical basis for this seminar I refer to Walter Ong's *Orality and Literacy* or Eric Havelock's *The Muse Learns to Write*. Both of these books examine how the ability to read and write text is an outgrowth from a specific set of thinking and physical technologies which directly influence how we view time, and thereby also influence how we construct narrative.

For source material I often use Kurt Vonnegut's *Slaughterhouse-Five* which, while claiming to be a fractured narrative, is actually a straightforward narrative construction designed to be read in order, from front to back. The narrative is constrained by the interface of the printed book. Vonnegut's novel uses a narrative format driven forward by the slow, careful accumulation of plot and character detail. While nearly any conventional novel could pose as a model for how codex and text technology define and restrict narrative structure, *Slaughterhouse-Five* contains a number of useful discussions about how we see time and how our time perception alters the way we create and relate stories.

As an example of how time perception defines narrative, Vonnegut introduces an alien culture, The Tralfamadorians, a race of creatures who see time all at once, and therefore do not share the human conception of beginning, middle, and end. For Tralfamadorians, everything happens simultaneously. A novel reads like a collection of telegrams, a cluster of tiny but perfectly conceived bursts of information scattered throughout the span of time contained by the novel.

The beauty of a Tralfamadorian narrative is defined by the overall impression given to the reader viewing thousands of information bursts simultaneously. In other words, a Tralfamadorian novel is really an elaborate narrative collage, a cluster of perfectly selected tidbits that resonate together, responding to each other's strengths and weaknesses, creating a singular, overall impression. My students have found that the Tralfamadorian novel easily becomes a shorthand reference for what we do when we create a narrative structure for the Web. Ultimately, in a Web collage we're trying to allow all the tidbits of information on a Web page to resonate together to create a singular, cohesive impression. In many ways, the Web is a Tralfamadorian novel.

To connect this analysis of print's narrative and its relationship to the Web, I ask students to try a few of the following exercises:

- Imagine the codex format was never invented. How else could you collect or display a textual narrative? Develop a prototype of your design and explain how the interface of your design alters the narrative structure of the work contained inside it (or outside it, or around it, or beside it). Adapt your prototype to a Web site that does nearly the same thing.

- Take a narrative specifically designed for the codex interface (any section from an eighteenth- or nineteenth-century novel would do) and adapt the story to a Web creation that attempts to mimic the original codex format as closely as possible. Consider everything about the original, including type of cover, any graphics or designs on the pages or cover, information on the front and back pages. You should consider even the quality of the paper, the type of ink, and the binding method.

- Create a Web narrative that cannot be presented in the codex format. In other words, create something that can only exist on the Web. Remember, printed text is quite flexible and can present nearly any type of information. Your narrative has to be structured in such a way that moving it to codex format would destroy it completely.

Film as Narrative Technology

When we turn to film as a narrative technology, we begin with an analysis of simple screenplays to examine how print explains something that will ultimately be completely nontextual. I often use current screenplays to ensure that most of the class has already seen the film in a theater. We then view one or two films which we pause, rewind, and fast-forward to closely examine and discuss how camera movement, camera position, editing, lighting, and the use of music combine to create a stream-of-consciousness narrative.

I explain to my students how when we view a film in a theater, it comes at us all at once, allowing us no control over the story once it begins to unfold. Therefore, a film uses an emotionally intense, plot-driven narrative structure to help create a sense of experience in the mind of its audience. Film narrative focuses on the compression of time and does not provide the audience with space for reflection or reconsideration of what is being presented. Being placed into a film narrative is similar to being cast down and rooted into the bed of a fast-moving stream—the story flows toward you in one continuous rush of emotional and logical connections, the force of the narrative is completely beyond your control. All you can do is watch and be tossed back and forth as the story rushes around and past you.

To connect this analysis of film's narrative interface and its relationship to the Web, I ask students to try a few of the following exercises:

- Take a popular Web site and turn it into a one-minute film. You need to present nearly everything available on the main pages of the site in your short film. Be prepared to explain how your film narrative interface mimics, or radically departs from, the interface of the original Web site.

- Take a section from a popular film and turn it into a small Web site. You need to present nearly everything contained in your film selection on the pages of your Web site. Be prepared to explain how your Web site interface mimics, or radically departs from, the narrative interface of your chosen film.

The Classroom as Instructional Collage

I use a lecture/response/workshop structure that repeats, in nearly every detail, from one media seminar to the next. I begin with lectures, followed by detailed questions the students must respond to on a class Internet discussion group before the next class meeting. Their responses are graded on a pass/fail basis. We bring the Internet discussion into class by presenting the text of the discussion on the instructor's machine, projected for the entire class to see. Then I give another lecture, create another response session, and then we devote a few classes to in-class workshops, taking time out every so often to review work in development.

Workshops are followed by one or two classes that allow students to present their work. At the end of every media seminar I expand upon questions I posed after my lectures and post the entire list of questions on the class discussion list. I give students a week to choose one of the questions and respond to it, in detail, with an e-mail response to me which I then grade and return.

Students seem to work quite well with this structure, but for both the instructor and student it can be demanding to maintain. I spend nearly twice my standard course preparation time just keeping up with this schedule. Also, students can easily become too deeply involved with their projects and lose perspective. After all, this is just a class. Immersion in their work is good, but if not treated carefully it can lead to students taking everything more seriously than is necessary or useful. A sense of humor and play, for both student and instructor, is essential for this type of course to succeed.

Continuing the Collaboration

If any of my work interests you and you wish to find out more about what I and my colleagues are teaching in our hypertext and hypermedia courses at the University of Central Florida, feel free to contact me at dgillett@pegasus.cc.ucf.edu, or visit my department's Web site at http://pegasus.cc.ucf.edu/~english to view some of our student's work.

Appendix #1

Hardware and Software Suggestions
Computer Hardware Suggestions for Class Workstations

- Pentium or Power PC Chip
- 1 GIG hard drive
- 16 MEG RAM
- 17" color monitor
- Sound card with external speakers
- Individual Internet connection (28,800 modem or faster, or T1 connection)
- CD-ROM drive

Additional Hardware Suggestions for Classroom

- Dependable, rapid Internet connection for every machine
- Fifteen or more individual workstations
- Videotape player with dedicated monitor (or hooked up to the computer overhead display)
- Bright projection system connected to the instructor's machine. You should be able to view the screen with all or most of the lights turned on.
- CD/tape player
- Standard overhead projector
- A number of work tables to allow groups of four to eight students to sit together and spread out printed versions of their work for presentation, review, and editing
- Access to a number of portable storage systems such as Zip or Jazz drives, allowing students to bring into class, and take home, files larger than 20 to 30 MEG
- High quality color flat-bed scanner

Software Suggestions for Class Workstations

- At least one HTML text editor, such as BBEdit, Hot Dog Pro, HTML Pro, Web Weaver, etc.
- At least one WYSIWYG HTML editor, such as Netscape Gold, FrontPage, Claris Home Page, PageMill
- A number of good clip art packages with photos and illustrations in GIF or JPEG format. Should also include viewers.
- MS Word or WordPerfect
- Photoshop or Painter
- Powerpoint or Persuasion
- Director
- Both Netscape Navigator and Microsoft Internet Explorer

Constructing Web Pages : Questions to consider

2 Encountering Hypertext Technology: Student Engineers Analyze and Construct Web Pages

J. D. Applen
University of Central Florida

Engineering 2A, 2B, and 2C constitute a sequence of linked writing courses that satisfy the core composition requirements at the University of California at Santa Barbara. In this sequence, first-year engineering students practice writing the kinds of documents that will situate them in the discourse of the engineering community. A fundamental characteristic of these courses is the synthesis of design techniques in technical writing with the corresponding design strategies in engineering. In Engineering 2A, the students work on quarter-long projects where they research an emerging technology and present a technical survey report. In 2B, the engineers produce or redesign products for the physically disabled—products such as portable fold-away writing surfaces that could be attached to a wheelchair. In both classes they practice the traditional skills of library sleuthing and proposal writing that incorporate the relevant visual materials such as graphs, schematics, tables, and scanned-in photographs.

Engineering 2C is a logical extension of the first two courses in that it is built on the research and design skills mentioned above, but it involves the analysis and construction of Web pages. I wanted the students to better understand the theoretical scope of electronic media, as it has potentials that the traditional writing spaces mentioned above do not. Web pages are bright, bold, and interactive, and these elements combined with the speed with which one can move around in hyperspace make them an attractive means of communication.

There is also a practical benefit to using the Web because increasing numbers of technical and engineering organizations are using the WWW for the purposes of information transmission and acquisition. For example, the multimedia elements of the WWW facilitate the ongoing redocumentation of end-user engineering manuals (Sullivan 1997) and software (Rajlich 1997). They also promote the expeditious and cost-effective exchange of technological information between engineers working in distant venues and separate companies such as those that make up the North Sea Drilling Group (Evans 1996). Additionally, corporations such as Bellcore have implemented "virtual project offices" so that project managers and engineers can better coordinate their activities (Questore 1996).

While the WWW possesses many attributes that traditional print technologies cannot offer, it also has some limitations—extended texts are easier to read in hard copy form, much of the information found on the Web does not meet the standards of texts in print (anyone can author a Web site), there is no organized database that one can consult when researching a particular topic, and at this time there is still much more substantive information that can be found in a university library than on the WWW.

Because of these strengths and weaknesses of the WWW, I wanted my students to be able to devise a rhetorical rubric that compared the power of electronic literacy with the more traditional literacy and research skills that the students had developed in the first two courses. This would allow them to become discerning and efficient consumers of the expanding volume of data available on the Internet and enable them to become effective Web page engineers so they could produce Web sites for organizations that they would work for in the future. While this course was designed to meet the needs of a group of first-year engineers, the pedagogy that I will be describing can be transferred to any introductory college-level course, especially a composition course based on the analysis of electronic information. In this chapter I will discuss the following areas of theory and pedagogy:

- How the information on the Web differs from other kinds of information
- How students can devise a set of criteria that allows them to see the advantages and disadvantages of the Web
- How the specifics of a proposal statement—the objective, problem statement, and audience analysis—can prepare students to construct a Web page
- How the generation of a preproduction links schematic can allow students to better conceptualize their projects
- How to implement group work in Web page projects

In the first week of the course the students examined the arguments in Michael Heim's "Infomania" (1993), an article that draws attention to the deluge of data that emerges from new information technologies. From their journals it was clear that the students understood Heim's overall thesis that we "lose our capacity for significance" when we are overwhelmed with information (10). To help frame Heim's ideas in the context of their own lives, I asked the students to think about the most intriguing or interesting beliefs and thoughts that they had attributed significance to, and where they had discovered them. Were they ideas they had been told in quiet conversation with a parent, friend, or mentor; were they understandings they had figured out on their own by putting together bits of information that initially seemed discordant or tangential; or did their ideas come prepackaged from the ambient media, popular culture, or technology?

I like to start with Heim because he challenges those who would like us to believe that the advent of the "Information Superhighway" really enhances our ability to think. To counter the idea that more information is better, I employ a reader-response exercise that compels the students to make meaning out of a traditional written text. In class, I asked the students to "enact" Carolyn Forché's poem "The Visitor" (1981, 15), a poem that has both a narrative structure that students can follow and an enigmatic quality that challenges them to read carefully before they make their interpretation. After several students read the poem aloud, they formed groups and produced a short film script. The students posed as collaborative directors who must convey to cinematographers, set directors, writers, and actors just how they wanted their film to look. They had to come up with their presentations collaboratively, then explain their conceptions before their classmates. This exercise asked students to bring their own experiences into their collective interpretations, work with others, and articulate a complex cinematic vision from the relatively spare text of fewer than eighty words.

In the next few classes we performed exercises with the purpose of generating a set of criteria that constituted effective homepages. I stressed the importance of a sound homepage as they are the marquees of the WWW; they need to be informative and alluring to compete against the many other homepages that viewers could so easily move on to. Between class meetings, the engineers searched for a homepage that was designed in a way that held their interest and then brought a copy of it to class so they could describe to others why they thought it was effectively designed. As is often the case in rhetorical analysis, most students chose pages that were interesting because the content was important to them. I think students should be examining pages that they would take a personal interest in, but when they do this, they often fail to separate the value of the content from how the content of the page was enhanced by the persuasive devices that it employs to grab and hold the viewer's attention.

To enhance the students' understanding of audience awareness, I put the students into groups and asked them to produce some quick sketches of homepages that we would design for professional sports teams. I chose this exercise because many of the students had not viewed homepages that were devoted to this subject, yet this was an area that almost everyone would know enough about to be able to produce such a page. Some of the items they selected to include in their pages included team logos, aerial views of the home stadiums, a key player in action, or the team photo; most of the groups chose combinations of these items. We discussed the potential audiences for the different emphases. For example, a fan who wanted to view a homepage for no other reason than to see her team celebrated might want to see some action photos, whereas someone looking to buy some tickets for an upcoming game might better be served by a homepage that had a picture of the seating pattern in the stadium followed by a link that listed the team's home schedule. In the technical survey reports that the engineers produced in the first quarter, they were asked to choose cover pages that required a visual element and a title that designated the document's subject and at the same time suggested something that would engage the reader. The homepage of a Web site was the corollary to the technical survey report's cover page, but a homepage could also offer an opening menu that suggested inner links to the page, much as a brief table of contents might suggest the content in printed texts.

In Engineering 2B we had discussed the concepts of *ethos* and *logos* as they related to students' design proposals. However, up until this point in 2C, I did not foreground the exercises outlined above with a discussion of any rhetorical concepts because I wanted the engineers to become practiced in the very difficult work of trying to identify their own criteria that explained why a Web document succeeded in attracting them and holding their interests. The next step was to provide a more prescriptive rubric, and I did this by handing out a copy of Sarah Yeo's "Designing Web Pages That Bring Them Back" (1995, 14), a three-page article that describes what one has to be concerned with regarding (1) the layout of the homepage, (2) ease of printing, (3) links, (4) typography, (5) page length, (6) line length, (7) graphics, and (8) backgrounds. Except for "ease of printing," I assigned each separate group of engineers one of these criteria and asked them to embellish Yeo's ideas by using them to more precisely examine the Web pages that they had already studied and written about in their journals. By the end of this class session, the engineers had a fair idea of some of the things that they would have to keep in mind when they analyzed or constructed their own Web pages. In the written assignment that followed, they generated rhetorical analyses of Web pages of their own choosing by illustrating how the elements that Yeo enumerated contributed to the rhetorical success (or failure) of the page. Below is the heart of the assignment description.

Choose a Web page and evaluate it in terms of what makes it an effective body of information. You might look at Yeo's essay and ask yourself, "Would I return to this Web page? If so, why would I?" If you do not want to bring yourself into it, then define the audience of the page. You may describe the content of the Web site, but what we are most interested in is how the content is expressed. Use Yeo's criteria and the criteria of any of the other theorists in our reader. You do not have to describe everything in terms of Yeo's analysis, just what stands out. If you have any additional criteria that you or your classmates have come up with, make sure that you use them too.

Goals:
1. As analysts, we will examine the devices a Webmaster uses to make a Web site effective.
2. As writers, we will produce a well-developed essay that analyzes and explicates a Web site's rhetorical elements.

Method:
1. What does the Webmaster achieve? What does she make the audience feel?
2. Using the following questions, devise a theory that explains how the Web designer accomplishes this task:
    *   How does she present the content of her Web page?
    *   If she were to change some of the stylistic strategies or techniques that she employs, yet retain the same essential content, in what ways would the site's effectiveness change?
3. In your essay, focus on the relationship between the site's effect and the audience. Back up each of your statements with an example from the Web page, and explain how the example illustrates your theory.

Figure 2.1. Web Page Analysis Assignment

The strength of this assignment was that it required the engineers to examine how each stylistic feature contributed to the overall look of a Web site. The best papers produced cogent descriptions of how these features enhanced the content.

After gaining a sense for the theoretical dynamics of WWW pages, the engineers began planning their own Web pages, working collaboratively in groups of three. By this time in the quarter, I knew the interests of the students well enough to place them in small groups. Before going into construction, they wrote proposals that described the content of their Web pages as a function of the needs of their targeted audiences. The proposals began with an objective statement that was to be only one or two sentences long. (For example, "Our objective is to construct a Web page that will help all first-year engineering students with their coursework. We will lay out all of the required first-year classes, and then offer advice on how they should study for these classes.") I see the objective statement as similar to the classic thesis statement in that it allows the students to better focus their production efforts. I also have the students write out what I call a "problem statement" that allows them to understand the purpose for their pages. To give them a sense of the scope of a problem statement, we discuss the following set of questions adapted from *Technical Communication* (Lay 1995, 163):

- What is the problem?
- When and where does the problem take place?
- Why does the problem happen?
- Who is affected by the problem?
- Why is the problem significant—what are the short-term and long-term costs?

For the UCSB Dormitory page, the group proposing this project demonstrated that there was no university document written for incoming students that told them what it was really like to live in a dorm. The documents that were offered by the campus dormitory officials described the costs and rules, and offered the traditional gloss that made dormitory life seem idyllic, yet they did not offer any substantive suggestions such as "Don't room with a friend from high school" and "Forget studying in the dorm. Study in the library," suggestions written by people who learned about how to make the best uses of dormitories after they had been living in them for the better part of a year. Writing a problem statement is a good way to make sure that the students find subjects for their pages that will have real value as information on the WWW. It also empowers them because they find that they do possess an expertise in something that they can share with their peers and others.

Both the objective and problem statement prepare them to move on to the next step, writing a description of their imagined audience and what they need to do to produce an effective Web page for this audience. To prompt them, I offered a list of questions adapted again from *Technical Communication* (Lay 1995, 72):

- Identify your audience. Is it simple and homogeneous? Multiple and heterogeneous?
- What are the needs of the audience that will be reading your page? Is there something that you want to convince your audience of? How will you do this?
- Do you need to supply any background information, explanations of terms, or other information to your audience?
- What does your audience know that you can already build on?
- What is your audience's educational background?
- What are their personal interests?

Additionally, I asked the groups to specify in their proposals just how they were going to divide the work within each group. Even though there were many times when the students would sit as a unit before the computer constructing their Web page, such an activity would not be very efficient for the entire construction process. The students divided the labor into such tasks as composing the written text of the page, surfing the Internet to find suitable images to download or other pages to link to, or putting the actual texts of the pages together using HTML. I also asked the students to turn in a Gantt chart or timetable with their project proposals that would later be followed up by an informal progress report that they would e-mail to me, all standard practices in the field of engineering (Vest, Long, Thomas, and Palmquist 1995, 15).

George Landow's "The Rhetoric of Hypermedia: Some Rules for Authors" (1991) nicely describes how a thoughtfully defined links system can aid in producing an internally coherent text that keeps readers from getting lost in space, yet at the same time allows readers the freedom to move around in a hypermedia environment. Landow provides nineteen "rules" for an effective links system, such as employing devices that get the reader to explore, utilizing stylistic devices that make navigation an enjoyable experience, and including organizing overviews for the reader (86, 89). Although Landow demonstrates these features using an Intermedia hypertext presentation of Charles Dickens's *Great Expectations,* I feel that our discussion of his rules enabled my engineers to better understand the need to envision a blueprint of a links system for a Web page before designing one, a suggestion consonant with their other introductory engineering coursework that stressed careful design and planning strategies before going into production.

   After our group conferences, we met in class and produced such blueprints. The engineers produced sketches of their links systems, then drew them on the board and explained the organizational logic behind them. Below is a links schematic of the "How to Survive Dormitory Life" Web page:

blueprint of links [handwritten marginalia]

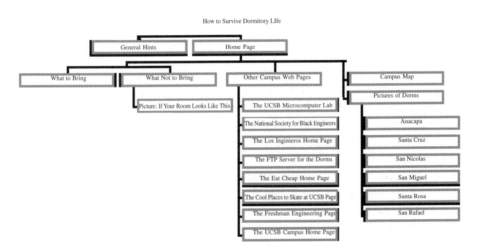

A links schematic provides the architecture of the page in one space, which is contrary to the way one can view the actual Web page on the Internet with all of its attendant links. Starting from the homepage, we can see how the first tier of links leads us into the Web site's actual content. However, a links schematic can be somewhat deceiving in that all of the sublinks seem to possess the same quantity of information. In fact, there was much more information in the "What to Bring," "What Not to Bring," and "General Hints" links, as they all contained about two screens worth of written text and some graphics. The production of the links schematic is similar to an exercise we went through in the first courses where the engineers produced outlines of their technical survey reports and design proposals. As with a traditional outline, the schematics provide an organizing structure where students can "see" what they have to do, but the schematics also allow the students to imagine how they might be able to connect their middle and lower tier links to other homepages. For instance, in addition to getting to the "Cool Place to Skate" homepage through the "Other Campus Web Pages" link, it was easy to see that they would also be able to make a connection to it from the "What to Bring Page" if they wanted to suggest that students bring their skateboards. Conversely, after producing a schematic that included a homepage devoted to the skateboarding sites on campus, it might be suggested that incoming students bring their skateboards.

To construct their pages, the students used the Hypertext Mark-up Language (HTML) code that can be viewed by Netscape and other Internet browsers. While a number of students purchased an inhouse publication on HTML, others found HTML documents on the Web that they simply printed out. I discovered that having access to a hard copy version of the HTML codes is important, but I naively assumed that these manuals would allow the students to see a marker, read a description of what it could add to a page, and then place the marker on their page. However, this is somewhat akin to going to a foreign country with a popular phrase dictionary and believing that one will be able to converse with the locals. To understand what the myriad of HTML markers can actually do, one has to see them in context. Perhaps the best strategy is to give the students a sufficient amount of time to find other sites on the WWW that they would like to emulate in terms of formatting and style, and then have them study how the HTML tags "behind" the sites produce the look in which they are interested. On Netscape 4.0 one can do this by going to the "page source" function found on the "view" menu.

The students had very little trouble learning how to use the basics of HTML during the time we spent in the computer lab, but being engineering majors, many of them possessed considerable technical aptitude and facility with computers. However, I can see how learning HTML could be a daunting task for many students and instructors. Since I first taught this course, some very powerful WYSIWYG (What You See Is What You Get) editors have come into widespread use. For example, Netscape 4.6's Composer allows one to produce Web pages without using HTML code; this software allows students to concentrate on the actual style and content of their pages and avoid some of the frustration that can attend learning HTML. However, HTML purists would argue that these editors do not allow us to produce very sophisticated Web pages and that we need to know HTML code in order to debug our Web sites if we encounter difficulties after we have ported them to the WWW.

When I teach the course again, I will place greater emphasis on the complex rhetorical quality of the WWW that writers such as Richard Lanham (1994) and Jay David Bolter (1991) articulate; I want the students to better understand the Web as something other than just a new way to acquire and distribute information. As John Slatin has pointed out, the hypertext links system allows us to see the "relatedness" between ideas and bodies of information, but it is at its "weakest when it comes spelling out what these relationships entail" (1990, 880). Margarita Ramirez, one of the engineers who took the course, offers us an interesting insight in her paper when she writes, "Whenever I think of the Net and its hypertext, the movie *Pulp Fiction* comes to mind. Like hypertext, the movie was not created with a beginning, middle, and a conclusion. Rather, it was shown in sections." When I hear this, I feel that my work as a writing instructor has just begun. Why, I would like to know, does the Web have the effect on us that it does?

Works Cited

Bolter, Jay David. 1991. "Topographic Writing." In *Hypermedia & Literary Studies,* edited by P. Delany and G. P. Landow. Cambridge: MIT Press.

Evans, D. 1996. "Application of World Wide Web Technology in a Learning Organization." In *Proceedings—Petroleum Computer Conference 1996,* 235–43. Richardson, TX: Society of Petroleum Engineers (SPE).

Forché, Carolyn. 1981. *The Country between Us.* New York: Harper & Row.

Heim, Michael. 1993. "Infomania." In *The Metaphysics of Virtual Reality,* 3–11. New York: Oxford UP.

Landow, George P. 1991. "The Rhetoric of Hypermedia: Some Rules for Authors." In *Hypermedia & Literary Studies,* edited by P. Delany and G. P. Landow. Cambridge: MIT Press.

Lanham, Richard. 1994. *The Electronic Word: Democracy, Technology, and the Arts.* Chicago: U of Chicago P.

Lay, M., B. Wahlstrom, S. Doheny-Farina, A. Duin, S. Little, C. Rude, C. Selfe, and J. Selzer. 1995. *Technical Communication.* Chicago: Irwin.

Questore, J. 1996. "Project Management and the World Wide Web." In *IEEE International Engineering Management Conference 1996,* 491–93. Piscataway, NJ: Institute of Electrical and Electronics Engineers.

Rajlich, V. 1997. "Incremental Redocumentation with Hypertext." In *Proceedings of the First Euromicro Conference on Software Maintenance and Reengineering,* 68–72. Los Alamitos, CA: Institute of Electrical and Electronics Engineers Computer Society Press.

Slatin, John M. 1990. "Reading Hypertext: Order and Coherence in a New Medium." *College English* 52(8): 870–83.

Sullivan, S. 1997. "Solving the Burden of Power Plant Documentation." *Power Engineering* 101(5): 26–30.

Vest, D., M. Long, L. Thomas, and M. E. Palmquist. 1995. "Relating Communication Training to Workplace Requirements: The Perspective of New Engineers." *IEEE Transactions on Professional Communication* 38(1): 11–17.

Yeo, Sarah. 1995. "Designing Web Pages That Keep Them Coming Back." *Intercom* (March): 13–15.

3 Preparing Future Teachers of English to Use the Web: Balancing the Technical with the Pedagogical

Larry Beason
University of South Alabama

Here's an all-too-familiar story. Not long ago, a writing teacher told me how hard he and his department had worked to obtain funding for a computer-equipped writing classroom. These teachers were so caught up in making the appeal that they neglected to prepare for what would happen once they actually got what they wanted. They received a roomful of handsome computers but did not fully understand how to incorporate them *meaningfully* into the teaching of writing. The result, as my colleague told me, was that he found himself making gratuitous assignments using the computer simply to justify the computer-equipped classroom to students and administration. Furthermore, to accommodate the twenty-four computers, the classroom became cramped, and the computer desks were permanently arranged in ways that made group work difficult. The teacher's use of computers actually interfered with learning—not because of technology per se but because of the lack of planning and training.

In light of such problems, the department of English at my school elected to offer Computers & Composition, a course intended to enable future teachers to understand how computers could be used to teach writing. When this course was first offered in the late 1980s, it focused on word processing. With the dramatic growth of e-mail, the World Wide Web, and the Internet in general, the emphasis has changed. When last teaching Computers & Composition, I decided to focus on the Web. This change was based on the input of students, but I also considered the amazing growth of the Web in education, commerce, government, and people's personal lives. Whether they want their students to compose WWW pages or simply understand how to do research by using the WWW, teachers of writing should help students use this form of literacy.

One problem I faced was how to achieve a balance between helping prospective teachers with the technical aspects of the Web and helping them consider the pedagogical implications. In particular, teachers need to go beyond the "gee whiz" reaction to high-tech innovations for the classroom and decide how—or perhaps *if*—the technology should be used to improve students' writing and thinking skills.

By describing how my students used the Web in Computers & Composition, I wish to offer one way to achieve this balance between practicality and pedagogical theory. My approach centers around one assignment that integrated other aspects of the course. While intended for a course specifically devoted to CAI (computer-aided instruction), the basic approach could be used in more general courses designed to prepare English teachers.

My approach helped the prospective teachers better understand the nature and value of the WWW, but I also confess to having to adjust my curriculum based on what I myself learned about using the WWW in the classroom. In fact, the course itself often seemed much like a Web page—evolving, experimental, and occasionally in need of a reload.

The WWW Assignments

Simply put, the core assignment was building a Web page, but my students received a support system by means of other activities. The purpose of these activities as a whole was to help students acquire technical skills and—just as important—to encourage them to develop their own approach and rationale for using the WWW in their future classrooms. The Web can serve a multitude of pedagogical purposes for English teachers. Indeed, one problem with the Web is there are so many possibilities with it that, as David Gillette (1999) points out, a teacher's task can be hampered if he or she does not find a focus and purpose for CAI.

In this essay, I do not wish to present all the various reasons why an English teacher might use the WWW. As discussed in this volume alone, the Web allows the teacher to access student work from various points in the writing process (Nellen 1999), can promote learner autonomy (Rilling & Csomay 1999), and can create a critically savvy community of student writers (Burow-Flak 1999). And those are just a few of many reasons for having students read and write Web pages. Here, though, I wish to deal with factors that go beyond any one reason or goal and, instead, concentrate on how to help future teachers design their own Web goals and implement them in their classrooms. Specifically, I wanted the future teachers in Computers & Composition to appreciate three pedagogical issues:

1. the need for teachers to use the Web in meaningful ways by matching Web activities to sound goals that they develop;

2. the ways in which Web pages reflect a unique form of communication that cannot be taught in the same way that a traditional classroom paper might be taught;

3. the need for students and teachers who use the Web to take into account collaboration and multiple perspectives of the Web—such as small group, whole group, professional community, and general public perspectives.

Based on students' teaching interests, I formed four groups of three to four students apiece, and each group was responsible for putting together three linked pages on the WWW. Students received a handout similar to the one shown below (the due dates are based on an eleven-week quarter).

Students fulfilled this task in various ways. Some groups built pages for teachers of a particular subject, including lesson plans, bibliographies, and information on related professional organizations, conferences, and journals. Some included pages just for students in a writing course, providing important definitions and strategies for writing along with links to writing-related sites on the WWW. One group built pages publicizing the school's MFA program.

To build a Web page, students had to understand the nature of the Web and how to use it, so this hands-on, collaborative project became the central mechanism for helping students acquire the needed technical skills, as well as helping them examine the more theoretical aspects in light of actual use. They were not completely set loose without assistance, though. What follows is a description, largely chronological, of how various components of the project worked together to help these future teachers understand both the technical and pedagogical aspects of the Web.

Building a Page

Goals: To enable you to understand the benefits and shortcomings of using the WWW (especially in your future classroom), to give you technical skills for using the WWW, and to allow you to share your teaching ideas with others on the WWW.

Task: You and your partners will construct a home page with at least two other pages linked to it. These pages should somehow relate to the teaching or learning of composition, rhetoric, literature, creative writing, linguistics, technical writing, or speech. Consider the types of information that would be useful to a particular audience or hierarchy of audiences. We will place your pages on the WWW for at least three months.

Also, write a two-page reflection on this experience, noting the work you yourself did for the group, the strengths and weaknesses of publishing on the WWW, and any other thoughts or feelings you have about the project. You will hand in this paper at the end of the project and discuss it with the class.

Evaluation: Your pages should be "contentful"—have substance and be worth reading. They should also "look good"—be user-friendly, professional in appearance, readable, and visually appealing. You and your partners will receive the same grade unless you make a compelling case for doing differently.

Due Dates:
>   Decide on a focus or purpose .... Week 2 Day 5
>   Submit URL & titles of relevant pages .... Week 3 Day 5
>   Submit a draft or outline to class .... Week 6 Day 1
>   Submit disk copy of pages w/tags .... Week 9 Day 1

Figure 3.1. Assignment: Building a Homepage

Component 1: Lecture and Discussion of Basics

Before discussing the page-building task, I devoted two class periods to covering basic information that would allow students to understand technical and practical matters:

- the history of the Web and browsers such as Mosaic and Netscape;
- the computer and software requirements for using the Web, building pages, and turning a computer into a Web server;

- the Web's often-arcane terminology (which proved of great interest to the linguistics students);
- the hypertextual, nonlinear format of linked pages;
- the role of tags in building pages;
- an overview of sophisticated features that can be built into a page (chatrooms, downloading, e-mail, sounds, etc.); and
- the least you need to know to surf the Web using Netscape.

At the end of one class meeting, the fifteen students managed to huddle in the department chair's moderately spacious office as I gave a quick demonstration of using the Web.

Another helpful resource for the basics was a how-to manual for using the WWW. A required text for the course was Paul Hoffman's (1995) mass-market guidebook, *Netscape and the World Wide Web for Dummies* (I was worried that the title might offend, but the students enjoyed this humorous text despite its unabashed "dumbing down" of the subject). The text is so clearly written that the readings rarely needed additional clarification from me.

Component 2: Hands-On Exploration

The major goals of this second element were to help students learn to use the WWW, to develop some initial thoughts on how to evaluate pages, and to start considering some uses of the WWW in their future classrooms. In this exploratory stage, my emphasis was on the process of hands-on exploration and discovery, but to facilitate this process some of the tasks had concrete goals for students to work toward. Indeed, the students seemed to appreciate both the open-endedness of some exploratory tasks and the security of knowing that they had tangible products to strive for on other tasks.

During one class period when we met in the computer lab, I paired students so that those with some proficiency with computers (if not the WWW) could tutor those students with limited experience. At this point, students had not received the page-building handout but knew the gist of what was coming. In pairs, students began working on three tasks intended to help them learn to use the Web and to stimulate prewriting for their own pages. These three tasks are as follows: (1) examining various pages listed on a handout I provided, (2) surfing the Web as they wished, and (3) beginning work on a task requiring them to find particular types of pages. This third task ("Find the Pages") is shown below.

Find the Pages

Goal: To help you explore the Web and find some relatively useful information.

Task: Write down the URLs and the page titles for the types of pages requested below. Be able to give a 60-second overview of each page.

1. Three pages that deal with (1) education in your area of specialization or (2) actual practice in your area of specialization (e.g., technical writing)

2. Two pages of interest to a scholar or researcher in your area of specialization

3. One page that offers downloads (e.g., shareware) of any sort

4. One totally useless, silly page

5. One page on a hobby or special interest of yours

Figure 3.2. Assignment: Finding Web Pages

When completing these tasks, students were also asked to take notes on the apparent goals and audience for the pages they visited. Once students completed these exploratory tasks, we met as a whole group to discuss them as well as the assorted goals and audiences of the pages the students visited. In addition to discussing the technical issues that arose (e.g., error messages and steps for downloading compressed files), this follow-up meeting allowed us to consider a basic question: *Who* reads all this material on the Web—and *why*? That is, we examined the rhetorical situations involved in writing and reading Web pages:

- the nonlinear and unpredictable ways in which people read pages or even a single page;
- the multiple levels of readers of a page and their goals;
- the apparent purposes (or often the apparent *lack* of purpose) a given page-builder seems to have; and
- the factors that help and hamper readability of a page (e.g., the amount of scrolling involved, and the use of sounds, images, and background textures).

This discussion naturally led us to consider criteria for evaluating a Web page and the different reasons why students and teachers might benefit from using the Web. In fact, each of my students a few days later shared an idea for using the Web in their future classrooms. This was in large part a warm-up for later in the course when they more formally submitted and shared lesson plans for using the WWW and other CAI (see Appendix A).

Component 3: Discussion of Readings

To participate in dialogues that extend beyond our classroom, the students read and discussed various articles. Throughout the term, they read numerous scholarly articles representing theoretical, empirical, and pedagogical perspectives on using the WWW, hypertext, and the Internet in the classroom (e.g., Cohen 1994; Shirk 1991). Because the general public's assumptions (and misconceptions) of the Web will affect teachers, I also asked my students to bring and discuss articles from the popular press that dealt with the Internet (especially articles in which the Web and education were mentioned). In addition to providing insight on the possibilities of the WWW in teaching, these readings served as a reminder that teachers should largely base their approaches to using the Web on the diverse perspectives found in research, theory, and the popular press. Any approach to teaching, CAI or otherwise, should be similarly grounded, but it seems especially important to consider multiple perspectives with the Web. Being such a new yet influential medium, the Web is still an unknown element in many regards, and it is incumbent on teachers to stay knowledgeable of this technology and its impact.

Component 4: Collaborative Planning

An obvious goal of this component was to encourage the exploration and prewriting that benefit nearly all writers. But another goal was again to foster an appreciation of the various perspectives people have about the Web and designing a page, hence my emphasis on small-group planning. Because of the complexity and multifaceted nature of the Web, planning is especially important, for it permits the page designer to consider and evaluate the many options that arise.

In fact, I initially allotted too little time for planning sessions and had to adjust my schedule so that students would uncover mistakes and problems before committing themselves to a particular approach. Occasionally, some class time was allotted for small- and whole-group discussion of the page-building task, but the groups were responsible for devising their own procedures and arranging time to work together. My hope was that students would tailor my general procedures to meet their individual needs and schedules. In retrospect, I should have done a bit more to facilitate small-group meetings. Despite the maturity and responsibility of these graduate students, they sometimes reported frustration at finding time to work together and developing a way in which each member was contributing equitably. My belief is that students at all levels should learn not to rely on the teacher for solving their problems with small-group tasks and communication. Nonetheless, these graduate students were close to being overloaded with the technical and theoretical concepts of the course. Their final products (especially their Web pages) as well as the process of exploring and using CAI would have been even better if perhaps one or two more class periods or small-group meetings were allotted for planning. I am hesitant, particularly with graduate students, to specify each step of group work, but I learned that these students (possibly because of their high expectations for themselves) needed more direct assistance from me. In fact, I had to adjust due dates considerably by allowing more time for them to produce their Web pages (the task handout given earlier takes into account the adjusted schedule).

Another unexpected development, though, was for the better. One assignment I gave was called "E-mail Commentary and Response" (see Appendix B). With this task, students improved their e-mail skills, brainstormed regularly with their groups about material covered in class, and saw one way in which e-mail could be used in their future classrooms. I did not expect this e-mail task to directly relate to their Web assignments. But once the students and I realized that they needed more time to discuss the logistical, technical, and theoretical aspects of creating their pages, our e-mail discussions gravitated toward these matters, thereby providing timely assistance and dialogue.

Component 5: Feedback on Drafts

Feedback was indeed critical in building these pages. Because it is difficult to predict how people will actually find, read, and use a Web page, the students needed diverse readers to examine their page; this was one reason for having students work in groups to build Web pages. Even working within a small group, it is easy for students to talk themselves into assuming too much about how Web readers might navigate through a given page or set of pages. Halfway into the quarter, we thus reached the next major step: The groups shared with the class a draft of their Web pages. This time, my reluctance to over-specify procedures paid off. I asked students to share a draft in hard-copy form, and each group brought something different based on where they were in the process. The group with the most Web expertise shared a printout of pages they had already put on the Web, although their pages were still very much under construction. Another fairly advanced group brought a printout of the source code complete with the appropriate tags, allowing other groups to see and discuss Web pages "behind the scenes." The third group brought a visual diagram on a large sheet of paper indicating how they planned to link pages together and what each page would accomplish. And the fourth group brought in a detailed outline of what each page would include. My original thinking was that groups would share something more along the lines of a traditional draft, but all groups put their thoughts and plans into a written form that best suited their needs.

This peer-response session evolved into a discussion of how we would encourage our future students to share drafts if they were creating WWW pages. The consensus was that a teacher should present peer-response options such as the ones seen in our session, but that it would be a better learning experience if students were encouraged to consider the format for peer response that best suited their needs. This discussion itself reminded us of a thread we had seen throughout our course: Teaching students to write on the Web is a form of literacy much different from traditional "hard copy" discourse, and our pedagogy must adjust to fit this new form. For instance, the drafting stage alone can involve steps not seen in writing regular papers, such as the formatting of tags or testing out a draft copy overnight on possibly hundreds of users who could respond immediately via e-mail. Because of such complexity and assorted options, teachers may have a difficult time in giving the class one set of steps intended to lead to a product. Overgeneralizing "the" writing process has always been a danger in writing classrooms, but it became apparent that this is a bigger problem when having students write on the Web.

My students received useful feedback from one another, but the most common concern was that the page authors were indeed not taking into account the varied ways in which readers might approach a page. Most often, a sufficient revision strategy was to provide contextual information reminding readers of the intended purpose of the pages, what the group's entire set of pages consisted of, and how to navigate to the group's other pages. Because the intended audience of the groups' pages consisted of students as well as teachers, my students still felt they were doing too much second-guessing of how readers would use their pages. Thus, I would now recommend that students also receive feedback from someone outside the class, preferably a member of the target audience for their Web pages.

Component 6: Follow-up Activities

My goal for this final stage was to allow students to reflect on the often chaotic nature of page design and exit the course with some overall conclusions, approaches, and questions for using the WWW in English classrooms.

When the pages were due toward the end of the quarter, I put them onto a Web server (my office computer) and tried them out myself. Although students had by this point also trial-loaded them, most pages still had a few technical problems, and at this point I tried to work them out myself so that the class could view the pages in a timely fashion. The class met once more in the lab to view all the groups' pages and take notes. At the subsequent meeting, the students offered final feedback to other groups, shared their two-page reflections (see my assignment handout given earlier), and offered guidelines for helping students read and write on the Web. Some of these guidelines are as follows:

- In creating a page, the author should clearly alert users to his or her goal and intended audience, and the author should base nearly all authoring decisions (e.g., page format, colors, length, complexity) on this goal/audience determination.

- Often, the fancy "bells and whistles" are counterproductive because they hamper readability, increase download time, and overcrowd a page.

- A page should have—more often than not—its own substance rather than merely being a page of links to other pages.

- Writing teachers and students alike must realize that teaching Web literacy cannot be based simply by wholesale adoption of the assumptions, genres, and approaches used to teach traditional writing.

- The strength of the WWW is also its weakness—anybody can put virtually anything on the WWW so that potentially millions of people can read this material. Students thus should be given solid instruction on evaluating the quality of the content—not just the format—of Web pages.

Even after this wrap-up discussion, I felt my students were overwhelmed by all the possibilities as well as new problems of this emerging form of literacy. Thus, I added a final activity: an oral debate on the pros and cons of using the Web (and CAI in general) in the writing or English classroom. Arbitrarily, I formed a pro and con group and gave them half a class meeting to plan their arguments. In the spirit of negotiation rather than confrontation, however, I formed a third group composed of two people charged with synthesizing the various arguments and making recommendations to the other two groups. While the pro and con groups planned their arguments, the synthesizing group discussed the nature of negotiation and synthesis (a useful starting point was Catherine Lamb's 1991 article on what it means to go beyond argumentation in feminist composition). In part, I included this "synthesis" group to model the behavior that I would hope the class would use in the future when the students become full-time professionals working with their peers.

With these follow-up activities, the students were better able to go beyond their one rewarding but challenging experience with authoring on the Web and consider the future role of the Web in education and their own classrooms. As one student pointed out, the Web may be frustrating because it changes so quickly, but that alone is worthwhile because it reminds teachers that they themselves must be lifelong students to keep pace with education in a technological era.

Summary and Suggestions

In this final section, I wish to bring these different components of the course together and reflect on the strengths and problems of using the WWW in a teacher-preparation course.

Putting It All Together

Figure 3.3 shows an outline of how a teacher-preparation course might incorporate the Web, though keep in mind that other CAI issues and strategies would be covered as well.

Things to Look Out for

In using the WWW in ways such as the above, the teacher of a teacher-preparation course faces several challenges. Preparing teachers to deal with conceptual issues as well as day-to-day teaching is a difficulty in itself; incorporating new technology such as the Web can, despite its value, present an additional level of complexity. Hence, I wish to summarize some pitfalls and suggestions for using the Web in a teacher-training course.

1. *Anticipate "mercenaries" and "fix me's"*: Some students will understandably want to know more about the Web simply to make them more marketable or more Web-literate. The teacher should make it clear that those factors are secondary to helping future teachers evaluate CAI pedagogy.

Overview of the Page-Building Task & Related Activities

Topic & Task	Goal	Timing
Component 1: *Lecture & Discussion of Basics*		*Week 1 or 2*
• History of Web	Improve awareness of what the Web is.	
• Technical requirements for reading & writing Web pages	Provide practical info on using the Web.	
• Nonlinear nature of Web pages & other aspects unique to Web literacy	Stimulate thought on nature of the Web & its effects on writing instruction.	
• How to surf the Web (with demo)	Model the process of using the Web.	
Component 2: *Hands-on Exploration*		*Week 1 or 2*
• Examination of teacher-selected sites	Improve practical skills using a specified, goal-directed task.	
• Open-ended Web surfing	Improve practical skills using an open-ended process-oriented task.	
• "Find the Pages" Task	Improve practical skills & prepare for follow-up class discussion.	
• Follow-up discussion of technical issues, goals and readers of pages, & criteria for evaluating WWW pages	Address practical problems & develop approaches to writing, reading & critiquing Web pages.	
Component 3: *Discussion of Readings*		*Throughout*
• Scholarly & professional articles	Examine recent issues, promote theory-building, & examine empirical assessments of CAI.	
• Popular press articles	Consider the impact of society-wide events & thinking on CAI.	
Component 4: *Collaborative Planning*		*Throughout but esp. in first half*
• 4 in-class planning sessions	Share ideas with teacher assistance.	
• 3 out-of-class planning sessions	Share ideas more independently.	
• Whole group comparison & discussion of plans	Provide feedback from outside the group.	

continued on next page

Figure 3.3. Page Building and Related Activities

• Group meeting with teacher	Offer individualized instruction on group pages.	
• Ongoing e-mail discussions	Allow opportunities for receiving help & exploring ideas on building & using the WWW.	
Component 5: *Feedback on Drafts*		*Middle of the term*
• Feedback within each small group	Promote revision & exploration.	
• Feedback from other groups & teacher	Promote revision & exploration.	
• Feedback from someone outside the class (preferably a member of the target audience)	Promote revision & exploration.	
Component 6: *Follow-up Activities*		*Last week*
• Class discussion of each group's revised pages & students' individual two-page reflections on the project	Offer critiques of pages & opportunity for self-evaluation.	
• Submission of CAI packet including lesson plans using the WWW	Share teaching ideas & receive suggestions.	
• Class debate & synthesis	Develop rationale for using the WWW in English classrooms.	

Figure 3.3. Continued

2. *Get students beyond the "gee whiz" reaction*: Hardly anybody seems immune from being so impressed (or intimidated) by the high-tech presentation that he or she is distracted from critically evaluating the content of WWW pages. Before designing their own Web pages, students should develop ways to read and evaluate existing pages.

3. *Be prepared for unknowns*: The Internet is constantly undergoing new developments; thus, any use of the Web in the classroom will in many ways be a first for a teacher no matter how many times he or she has used the Web previously. In addition, it is hard to anticipate how much experience a class will have with the Web. Because of these and other unknowns, the teacher would be wise to be both flexible and clear about what is expected. The teacher might do so by (1) being ready to change the syllabus and assignments and (2) offering as much

clarity as possible on assignments by providing tentative due dates and suggesting basic procedures for a Web project.

4. *Facilitate group work:* Because of the complexities of the Web, group work is useful in allowing students to teach one another. However, these same complexities often mean there are many more decisions that students have to make about writing Web pages than when writing traditional hard copy. Thus, the teacher should take extra steps to help students with group work, such as allowing substantial class time, formally and informally meeting with groups on their progress, and obtaining individual feedback (e.g., through e-mail) on the state of the group's work.

5. *Obtain multiple feedback*: Possibly because students are accustomed to the linear nature of hard text, their hypertext pages will likely not reflect the myriad ways in which people might locate, read, and use their pages. The teacher should allow many opportunities for having people outside the group provide feedback—especially during the planning stages to forestall problems.

6. *Synthesize*: A teacher-preparation course using the WWW will cover so many technical and methodological issues that the big picture might be lost. More than most courses, this sort of course needs to conclude with various attempts to back away from logistical or day-to-day issues and return to the larger issues of why the WWW is or is not useful as CAI, the ramifications of this emerging technology for society, and the extent to which Web pages constitute new genres of literacy.

7. *Model the goal-setting process*: To remind students that setting clear, sound goals is preliminary to using the Web in their future classrooms, the teacher should provide models of goal-setting in CAI methods—such as in the teacher's own assignments and in sample lesson plans developed by other teachers.

Connecting Teachers' Methods with Goals

The last tip above is central to my essay. The course was particularly conducive to reminding these prospective teachers of the need to evaluate their teaching methods according to clear, reasonable goals they have developed. Most teacher-preparation courses, of course, emphasize this tenet of education, but too often it still does not seem to sink in. Simply coming up with a goal and somehow connecting it to a method are not enough. The goal must be realistic, theoretically sound, and meaningful to students. And the methods must not—as is often the case—be gratuitously connected with the goal, nor must the relationship be rationalized. Methods should be powerfully connected to the stated goal, connected in such a way that the teacher can determine that the students have reached the goal because of the methods.

The page-building assignment and the related tasks in the course seemed to make the prospective teachers realize the full extent of the goal-driven nature of methods. Certainly, our class and small-group discussions indicated such was the case, and I believe my students' close attention to goal-setting was the result of two factors.

Read

First, our early explorations of the Web highlighted the fact that many existing pages suffer from having little if any central purpose. A given page might be at once self-expressive ("Here are my likes and dislikes" or "pictures of my pets" sections), informative (a section of useful links), and persuasive (strident assaults on Microsoft or Macintosh products). We discussed how a related problem occurs when classroom activities lack a clear purpose. Thus, these future teachers were constantly reminded in surfing the WWW that fancy gimmicks are useless unless the page designer or teacher, whichever the case may be, bases these around goals that suit a given audience.

N.B.

Second, the Web assignments required significant collaboration, not only in designing pages but in evaluating them for revision purposes. In many classroom assignments, group work appears imposed on students rather than being a logical extension of the task at hand. Because of the newness and complexity of the WWW, my students had to rely on one another on many levels, such as sharing technical information, contributing to the content of the pages, and exploring the format and design options available with the Web. The richness of this collaboration naturally meant that small-group discussions were lively, on task, and thought provoking.

In short, exploring the WWW reminded students of the problems that occur in any situation when people cannot discern a goal. And my students' substantive collaboration on designing pages managed to promote—in an organic way—solving problems by returning again to the importance of having worthwhile goals. In these two ways, the Web assignment reinforced the notion that methods for the teaching of writing must be clearly based around sound teaching objectives. This all-important concept too often becomes lost in the logistics and demands of day-to-day teaching of any sort, but particularly when the methods involve the high-tech glitz and complexity of computer-aided instruction. CAI and the Web bring along "fun and games" implications that could just as easily be distracting as motivating in terms of course objectives.

Thus, in addition to helping teachers use technology, teacher-preparation courses such as the one described here should themselves center first and foremost around the goal of helping teachers evaluate CAI in light of their own course objectives. The Web has much to offer students in K–college, but it also can be a particularly useful medium for preparing teachers to fully appreciate the importance of matching methods to goals.

Works Cited

Burow-Flak, E. 1999. "From Castles in the Air to Portfolios in Cyberspace: Building Community Ethos in First-year Rhetoric and Composition." In *Weaving a Virtual Web: Practical Approaches to New Information Technologies*, edited by Sibylle Gruber. Urbana, IL: National Council of Teachers of English.

Cohen, L. 1994. "Augmenting Instruction in Business Communication Courses with the Internet." *The Bulletin* 57(4): 31–35.

Gillette, David. 1999. "When Media Collide." In *Weaving a Virtual Web: Practical Approaches to New Information Technologies*, edited by Sibylle Gruber. Urbana, IL: National Council of Teachers of English.

Hoffman, P. E. 1995. *Netscape and the World Wide Web for Dummies*. Foster City, CA: IDG Books.

Lamb, C. 1991. "Beyond Argument in Feminist Composition." *College Composition and Communication* 42: 11–24.

Nellen, Ted. 1999. "Using the Web for High School Student Writers." In *Weaving a Virtual Web: Practical Approaches to New Information Technologies*, edited by Sibylle Gruber. Urbana, IL: National Council of Teachers of English.

Rilling, S., and E. Csomay. 1999. "Building a Web for Literacy Instruction." In *Weaving a Virtual Web: Practical Approaches to New Information Technologies*, edited by Sibylle Gruber. Urbana, IL: National Council of Teachers of English.

Shirk, H. N. 1991. "Hypertext and Composition Studies." In *Evolving Perspectives on Computers and Composition Studies: Questions for the 1990s*, edited by Gail E. Hawisher and Cynthia L. Selfe, 177–202. Urbana, IL: National Council of Teachers of English.

Wresch, William, ed. 1991. *The English Classroom in the Computer Age: Thirty Lesson Plans*. Urbana, IL: National Council of Teachers of English.

Appendix A

CAI Packet

Goal:

The purpose of this assignment is to integrate CAI into your future classroom by building on what we have studied in this course.

Task:

Put together a packet containing at least eight lessons or activities that involve *various* forms of CAI. These eight lessons can be loosely based on other teachers' ideas (e.g., something you've read), but the majority of your lessons should reflect your own design, approach, and procedures.

Your lessons can all be geared toward the same types of students and classes, or you can vary the intended audience. Be clear, though, about who the intended audience is.

Try to include various forms of CAI, such as word processing, e-mail, software, etc. You do not have to cover every single type of CAI, but use the WWW as a primary or secondary resource in at least two lessons.

Format:

Follow the format presented in William Wresch's *The English Classroom in the Computer Age.* If possible, you might also include actual instructional aids (e.g., handouts or examples). Think about what sorts of aids you would actually use with a given activity.

Submit a hard copy of your lessons, but do not permanently bind the lessons together. A manila folder should be fine unless you enclose disks or other small items.

In addition, submit a disk copy of your packet. I will put a copy of everyone's packet onto your disk so that in your future teaching you can draw on your peers' ideas.

Evaluation:

I will primarily assess your packet based (not necessarily in this order) on the following:

- the clarity of your explanations of the lessons,
- the extent to which each lesson meets specific goals,
- mechanical correctness of your writing,
- the extent to which you follow the above directions, and
- the overall pedagogical soundness of the lessons (e.g., the likelihood they will be effective and their practicality).

Appendix B

E-mail Commentary and Response

Goals:

The purposes of this assignment are (1) to allow you to give and receive feedback regarding course content and (2) to suggest ways in which you might use e-mail in your own classrooms.

Procedures:

By **Tuesday** of each week, e-mail a **commentary** to me and to your group members. A "commentary" is a reaction to something in English 556 (specifically, during the previous week).

By **Thursday** of each week, e-mail **responses** to the commentaries from your group members. **Be sure to address all mail to me and your group members.** Your group members can't respond to mail they don't receive, and I can't give credit for mail I don't receive.

- *Commentary:* Each new entry must be about 150 words long and should discuss any or all of the following: (1) something we read for the class, (2) a class or group discussion, (3) something I said in a lecture or presentation. **Remember to address every commentary to me and all of your group members and to send your mail by each Tuesday.**

- *Responses:* Respond to the commentary of each person in your group. Each response must be about fifty words long. **Remember to address every response to me and all of your group members and to send your mail by Thursday.**

Grading:

For each entry, you'll receive a checkmark if the entry meets the above requirements and is sent by the stated due date. You'll receive a minus for each entry or response that is incomplete, off-topic, or late. The final grade will be based on this scale:

Up to 1 minus	4.0
2 minuses	3.0
3 minuses	2.0
4 minuses	1.0
5 or more minuses	0.0

E-mail messages will not be graded based on mechanical correctness.

In the space below, list the usernames for me, yourself, and your group members. Separate them by commas (no spaces) as shown in the example.

example: LBeason,engl5560101,engl5560102,engl5560103

4 The Creation Project

Emily Golson
University of Northern Colorado

Eric Sagel
University of Northern Colorado

Overview

This essay traces the growth of a class project from the instructor's pedagogical goals and objectives through the students' conception and development of the project to the constructed site (http://asweb.unco. edu/depts/english/~creation/themes.html). The latter part of the discussion includes a section on technical information as well as sections on problems and suggestions. The piece features two voices: the first, the voice of the instructor, and the second, the voice of the student. Although the voices never change, there are moments when the instructor reveals what she learned and the student discusses pedagogical insights, thus providing a practical demonstration of both paper and project collaboration and lending insight into the various compromises and negotiations that characterized our work. As we would like the Internet to become a place for reflective as well as transactional writing, we hope that others will design projects to help students become more aware of the way in which their thoughts may be woven with the thoughts of others in the texture of discourse.

From the Instructor: Pedagogy and Project Design

The Creation Project evolved from an interest in exploring both the pedagogical and creative potential of the Internet. As one of the teachers and researchers supporting the integration of technology and writing in our university, I had already participated in several technology initiatives and projects, such as designing a computer writing lab, introducing word processing into general education writing classes, and sponsoring the creation of various student-created *HyperCard* projects in intermediate and advanced writing courses (Golson 1995). As the student demand for more experience in this area increased, the next logical step seemed to be publishing on the Web. Thus, when our Macintosh writing lab became hooked to the campus backbone, I immediately began to design a collaborative Internet Project.

From the outset, I wanted the Project to address three goals:

1. To introduce intermediate and advanced writers to differences in writing for a print and Internet audience;

2. To encourage the creation of a student-centered Internet project that would promote writing for a purpose yet reflect student skills, interests, and needs;

3. To study the various attitudes and behaviors that accompany the writers' growth and development when moving from writing in a print to writing in an electronic hypertext environment.

In considering these goals, I needed to address two anticipated problems: faculty reaction to using technology in traditional print-oriented writing courses and student acceptance of nontraditional approaches to writing. I teach in a department which emphasizes creative writing and multiple approaches to reading English literature. For the project to gain acceptance, I knew it would have to remain within the framework of department expectations while addressing student needs. As I had been revising the department's advanced essay course for the past three years, shifting from a colleague's emphasis on proper usage and preconceived form to what Elizabeth Sommers describes elsewhere in this collection as a process approach based on a combination of cognitivist, social constructivist, and expressivist theories (Faigley 1986), it appeared that the best place to continue experimenting with different approaches to writing was English 303. As I traditionally required that one of the students' five writing projects be submitted to a target publication or some other public forum, it seemed natural to suggest that an Internet project could fulfill this requirement.

In addition to working within the framework of course specifications, I wanted the project to address student needs. As the only required course for writing minors, English 303 draws junior- and senior-level students from all majors. These students have highly analytical and creative minds, as evidenced by higher grade points and class standings than most students in the university. Many of our writing minors hope to make a living by writing; consequently, they expect their required writing courses to provide the practice and growth that will move them closer to this goal. In the past, as students began to value the experience of writing in diverse electronic environments, increasing numbers of students had opted to work on *HyperCard* assignments in lieu of traditional imitation assignments. Although most were pleased with the results, final course evaluations indicated that the students liked the notion of optional participation in projects which involved technology. Thus, my project grew from the following imperatives: first and foremost, the project must be directed toward writing; second, very little class time could be devoted to learning software or Net applications; and third, participation should be optional. In keeping with the second and third imperatives, I decided to concentrate on writing and call for volunteers to code the project.

Objectives

With the above reservations in mind, I created a lesson plan for a collaborative Internet project that would fulfill the following objectives:

> Objective 1: Students will demonstrate the ability to perform an Internet search.
>
> Objective 2: Students will demonstrate an ability to evaluate materials found on the Internet.
>
> Objective 3: Students will differentiate between writing for print and writing for electronic audiences.
>
> Objective 4: Students will demonstrate the collaborative skills expected of those who work in a linked electronic environment.
>
> Objective 5: Students will demonstrate an awareness of the creativity involved in writing for an electronic audience.
>
> Objective 6: Students will write for an electronic audience.

Lesson Plan

The lesson plan for the project was as follows:

Day 1: Introduce Students to the Internet

> a. Give students a handout with instructions on an Internet search.
>
> b. Walk students through the handout.
>
> c. Circulate another handout with URLs directing students toward sites constructed by other composition or creative writing classes.
>
> d. Allow students to explore their own writing interests by visiting Net sites of their choice.
>
> e. Show students how to move from one environment to another by requesting they take notes in a word document.
>
> Homework: Write reactions to the possibility of publishing on the Internet.

Pedagogical Aims and Concerns

The first day was designed to address the difference between writing for electronic and print audiences (Goals 1 and 2). I wanted students to realize that Web documents often contain graphic as well as prose elements and that Web prose often presents fragmented thoughts or pieces of information that are connected to other fragments through a series of linked Web pages. In addition, I wanted students to interact with the electronic environment by learning how to perform an Internet Search (Objective 1) and how to move back and forth from Word documents to Internet connections (Objective 2).

Day 2: Evaluate the Internet as Writing Source

    a. Read and discuss reactions to the Internet.

    b. Outline differences between writing for electronic and writing for print audiences.

    Homework: Brainstorm possible suggestions for an Internet project.

Pedagogical Aims and Concerns

The second day was designed to further our comparative study of writing for print and electronic audiences (Objectives 2 and 3) by exploring the notions of chaos, freedom, and choice. I expected some students to enjoy the freedom of nonlinear development and others to be appalled by the writers' apparent "lack of control" over the readers' movement through Webbed pieces. As I encourage students to articulate changes in attitudes or reactions, I also expected some students to address the ways in which those who work in electronic environments must negotiate differences of opinion (Objective 4). I hoped that the discussion would facilitate my understanding of the limitations of introducing Web projects to advanced writers with novice computer skills (Goal 3).

Day 3: Collaboration

    a. Introduce a topic.

    b. Read "beginnings" of pieces on the topic.

    c. Articulate the ways in which hypertext facilitates associative thinking.

    d. Review the difference between reading and writing in an electronic hypertext environment and reading and writing in a print environment.

    Homework: Write drafts for Net projects.

Pedagogical Aims and Concerns

As I wanted this to be a student-centered as opposed to a teacher-centered project, I decided that I would not dictate the shape the project would take (Goal 2). Furthermore, although I expected disagreement, I vowed to allow students to settle their own differences, thereby encouraging the development of collaborative skills (Objective 4). Day 3 was designed to solicit possible suggestions for the project and promote creative thinking and prepare students for collaboration.

Day 4: Begin Project Design

> a. Read drafts aloud.
>
> b. Discuss potential links.
>
> c. Begin to shape the project.
>
> Homework: Revise drafts.

Pedagogical Aims and Concerns

At this point, I hoped for a transferal of creativity from writing print documents to creating linked Web documents (Objective 5). As I knew the students would not easily relinquish control over their writing, I hoped the collaborative creativity would emerge in the conception of a metadocument.

Day 5: Work on Visual Aspects of Project

> a. Illustrate the ways in which writing for the Internet requires visual as well as verbal skill.
>
> b. Seek suggestions from students who appear to be technophobic.
>
> c. Finish shaping the project.
>
> d. Introduce new print assignment.
>
> Homework: Begin drafts for print assignment.

Pedagogical Aims and Concerns

I saw this assignment as furthering collaborative skills (Objective 4), enhancing creativity (Objective 5), and laying the foundation for the eventual demonstration of the ability to create an electronic Web document (Objective 6).

Day 6: Finish Project and Evaluate

> a. Show Prototype.
>
> b. Open discussion evaluating project.

Pedagogical Aims and Concerns

The discussion of the project as well as day three's written assessment of the difference between writing for print and writing for electronic audiences were intended to encourage self-reflection and fulfill the goal of studying the various attitudes and behaviors that accompany the writer's growth and development when moving from writing for print to writing for an electronic hypertext environment.

The Growth of the Project: Focal Points for a Discussion of Hypertext

The introduction to the Internet went well. Students explored composition Web sites containing student essays and decided their writing was equal to the writing of peers in other universities. Two students, Lynette and Matthew, became convinced of the value of publishing on the Internet when they discovered creative writing sites that invited writers to add to the text. Others were surprised by George Landow's scholarly site as well as by commercial sites offering selections from well-known authors, such as William Blake (<Up> word 1996). Still others were fascinated with Project Gutenberg, a vast library of electronically stored books, mostly classics, that can be downloaded for free and viewed offline. The following day's reactions to the possibility of creating a class Internet project focused on the following issues:

1. Copyright
   How do we protect what we have written? Will connecting to other pieces "devalue our creative efforts"?

2. Freedom, Anarchy, Coherence, and Fragmentation
   What happens when my ideas become a part of other writers' ideas? How can I orient the reader to my piece? How do I maintain continuity and coherence? How do I respond to the possible fragmentation of my ideas? How can I make my reader finish my piece before going on to the next? What about closure? What about openings?

3. Audience Awareness
   How does interaction really work? Will the audience be able to respond?

4. The Use of the Visual
   How will the use of graphics—backgrounds, pictures, etc., change the way I write? Will there be less imagery in my writing? Will I feel unfulfilled if I do not use graphics to complement my text? Some of the graphics seem like cartoons. How do I create and/or find graphics that will "match" my writing? Even though they exist on the same page, are graphics

just another link to my writing? Can I just borrow from anybody's paintings, drawings, etc.?

5. Technology
   How do you create a Web page? How much time will it take away from writing?

The Emerging Project

The answers to the above questions emerged throughout the events of the next few days as the project began to take shape. When Chad addressed the issue of coherence by suggesting that the class write linked creation myths, Eric, a self-acknowledged computer hack, announced that he would do all the coding. When Laurie volunteered to edit the pieces, Glenna, an amateur photographer, volunteered to take photographs of the writers. When Dorina, an illustrator, suggested we use illustrations to complement the writing, Clint volunteered to research copyright issues. Finally, when Tonya suggested we include a page for reader comments, Denny mentioned that we should find a way to market our work.

Before writing, we discussed the introductions to several published creation myths. During the next meeting, students read their myths aloud. As expected, students wrote diverse pieces, ranging from the creation of the world to the creation of rest. Baffled by the diversity, the class searched for commonalities, for the thread that would shape the metamyth. The first three myths, written by males, resounded with echoes of destruction. This generated two speculations: (1) all myths contain destruction, and (2) males tend to be more destructive than females. As we read on, different themes emerged: love, hate, change. Still, the shape of the piece evaded the students. Realizing that their readers would have similar difficulties shaping meaning, the students began listing themes on the blackboard. As the list grew, the commonalities emerged. Finally, the class had settled on a chronological and thematic ordering of mythical experience that would be represented by two images on the homepage: a clock and a thematic square. For the next few weeks, as we returned to writing traditional print essays, various members of the class provided occasional updates on the project. Toward the end of the term, when the prototype was complete, Denny interviewed his classmates and wrote a press release for the local paper. Due to institutional problems, we could not launch our piece until the following term. In February of 1996, however, the Web was launched, the local paper picked up the story, and the project was featured on local TV.

Technical Information: From the Student

As a student in English 303, I was eager to participate in the project for three reasons: I wanted to see my own essays on the Web, I wanted to learn Hypertext Mark-up Language (HTML), and I wanted to learn about the concept of hypertext itself. I volunteered to do the coding for the class and taught myself HTML. The following represents the technical aspects needed to complete the project.

The Web is one of the easiest parts of the Internet to participate in. Yet, the Web, like most computer-based systems, relies on a particular set of jargon and terms. Students and teachers new to the Web can become confused by the plethora of terms and acronyms that the Web delights in. The first step to a successful project is to demystify the Web for both the teacher and the students. The following are the terms that provide the basis for understanding, using, and developing a Web: *server, domain name, URL, HTTP, HTML, ASCII, GIF, JPEG, image map, hypertext, link,* and *browser.*

In order to launch your project on the Internet, you must have a *server.* The server is the computer permanently connected to the Web that your project will be stored on. The server is registered with the agencies that maintain the Web and, for a small fee, is given a *domain name* that serves as the base address of the computer on the Web. The domain name of the computer that the Creation Project was stored on is asweb.univnorthco.edu. Domain names are usually broken into three parts. The first part is usually *www, web, www2,* or is left blank. This identifies the domain as a Web-based server. The second portion is the unique name of the server, such as *univnorthco, netscape,* or *CNN* (www.cnn.com, which is the Web site for the Cable News Network). The final element of the domain is the type of organization that supports the server. Schools and universities use the *.edu* prefix, which stands for "education." Others include *.com* for "commercial" and *.gov* for "government."

When a person using a Web browser such as Netscape or Microsoft's Internet Explorer tries to find a particular page on the Web, the browser uses the page's *Uniform Resource Locator (URL)* to determine what computer to connect with to be able to get the information stored on that computer and display it in the browser window. The URL for the Creation Project is http://asweb.unco.edu/depts/english/~creation/themes.html. The term *http://* tells the browser that the document it is looking for is a Web document. Next comes the domain name *asweb.unco.edu.* The */depts/english/~creation* tells the browser to look for a folder named *~creation* within a folder named *english,* which is within a folder named *depts*. Finally, */themes.html* tells the browser to look for an HTML file named *themes* within the folder *~creation*. The browser then asks the server for that file, and if everything is working right, the server sends the file to the browser. The browser then reads and displays the information contained in the HTML file on the computer that the browser is on. *HTML* is the computer language that Web pages are written in. It is a text-based language that tells the browser how to display the text and art that are on the Web page. The file itself is a standard *ASCII* file, which is the most common format to store text on a computer. This file contains all of the directions needed to correctly display your text and art on the browser. In general, the text portions of a Web page are stored directly in the HTML file while the art files, *.gif* and *.jpeg* files, are stored separately and are simply referred to in the HTML file to be called and displayed by the browser when needed.

The power of a Web page is its ability to display information that is linked to other information through *hypertext*. A link in a Web page is a selection of text or an image that has been coded in such a way to tell the browser to go out and get additional information, images, or Web pages. The reader activates the link by clicking with a mouse on the highlighted text or image.

The first step in the Creation Project was getting the students' essays into a single format. With twelve different essays, I knew that each person would be working on different machines, IBM or MAC, and different programs, Microsoft Word or WordPerfect, and that this variety of formats could cause me problems as I put the Web page together; therefore, I asked everyone to submit their essays to me on an IBM-formatted disc in a basic ASCII text format. This gave me greater flexibility in working with their essays. Most current Macintosh computers can read both IBM and Mac discs. By having the students save their essays on IBM disks, I was able to access the essays on nearly any computer in the university's computer labs, and by saving the essays to a *.txt* format, I was able to open the essays with any word-processing program. At the same time that the students gave me their essays, I had them give me art and graphics they wanted to go with their essay. With the essays, the art and photographs, and class discussion on the project format, I was ready to start putting the page together.

If you have a server, creating your own Web pages and publishing them on the Web is simply a matter of "writing" the html documents and loading the html files and all of the art files to the server. Writing your html documents can be done in many different ways. The following programs, available on the Internet or in stores, will help you:

Microsoft Word, WordPerfect, Microsoft Front Page, and HoTMedaL. Most new versions of word-processing programs now include html templates or plug-ins that will lead you through the process of Web publishing. Also, the major online services—AOL, Prodigy, and CompuServe—provide both the server and software to help streamline the process of publishing on the Web. However, if these choices are not available, all you need to publish is a word-processing program, a server, a Web browser to check your work in progress, and a smattering of html coding knowledge.

What I Learned: From the Student

Working on the Creation Project was a challenge and, to be honest, a lot of fun. I had only the briefest introduction to the Internet and the World Wide Web before I was considered the class expert. What I did know was that the process was simple, and I had only a little to learn to be able to do what the class wanted. So, when I volunteered to do a Web page for the class, I was excited on several levels. I looked forward not only to the prospect of having my own writing on the Web, but also I liked the idea that I would be writing Web pages for the whole class. I was extremely pleased that a teacher would propose a project that addressed my strengths and, as I learned later, the strengths of my classmates as well.

Before we began the project, we agreed to make writing central to the entire process. Slowly, however, we discovered that our notion of writing was based on a print rather than an electronic culture. Our decision not to include internal links, linking at a micro level, for example, came out of a concern for the integrity of each myth. Gradually, however, we began to look at writing in a different way. As we began to understand that we were writing not in a closed system but rather in an open system of both space and time, we realized that pieces of our myths could be connected to other myths, and that the writing and the electronics were both central to our project; nevertheless, we could not bring ourselves to break up our narratives. The space that we created is very organized. There is only one entrance to the site, and while movement within the project is open, the project, as of yet, does not have multiple links to other sites. To compensate for our inability to open up our narratives, we began to see our writing as temporary. We knew that at any time we could edit, change, or expand on what we had written, and we even talked about the possibility of our project being linked to students' essays in other classes and even other universities. I now know that our decisions were a compromise prompted by the openness of the Internet. In reaction to the chaotic nature of the Web, we created a space that defies that chaos yet still suggests the associative possibilities of Web authoring.

When I go to the Web site now, I feel that the presentation and organization of the project could be better. The site's main page is slightly confusing and does not explain the project's purpose or how to navigate the project very well. Other than the clock face on the main page, which I am happy with, the artwork is simple and in some cases may be distracting. Once in the site, there is a feeling of being trapped because the links do not lead anywhere but to the project itself. All of these issues aside, however, I look back at the project with a certain amount of pride. Given a limited amount of time and a limited amount of exposure to the Web, our class produced an interesting variation of the various essays that were randomly posted on the Web by classes in other universities. The myths are varied, and the connections we made to each other's myths were revealing. If you go to all the "theme" pages, for example, there is only one theme that contains all the myths: the deconstruction page. This reflects a universal discovery that for something to be created, something must be destroyed.

Through our discussion of linking the essays, we came to a conclusion about myths and creation. However, I think it goes beyond just the idea of finding keywords or shared ideas that led us to this observation. We were working in a new working space, a writing space that modeled the associations and connections that we were making. In trying to fit our essays into that writing space, we allowed ourselves to make connections and associations that I do not think we would have otherwise made. The idea that all creation contains destruction, while obvious once stated, was a surprise to our class. This observation came about when we juxtaposed our need to create groups of associations between the essays and our desire to create a metaphor of time out of the linear yet looping arrangement of the essays. As you navigate the clock from midnight back to midnight again, a world is created and destroyed, over and over again.

Problems

On the surface, the students fulfilled every goal and met every objective while working on the Internet project. In that sense, the project was a success. Formal end-of-semester evaluations consistently praised the Internet as offering immediate avenues for students to share their work

and the Creation Project as being one of the most innovative assignments in the university. But throughout our work, we encountered
several philosophical, legal, and technical problems which threatened
to undermine the conception and realization of the piece.

First, there were philosophical and pedagogical problems. Although the students were accustomed to a workshop approach to
writing, they had never participated in a collaborative writing project.
They saw their writing as unique, as coming from within, as having no
relation to their peers' writing. And they liked it that way. Even though
they admitted that writers borrow freely from other writers, and that
writing inevitably contains other voices, they saw joint efforts as
devaluing individual work. This attitude emerged several times throughout the project. One variation occurred when a student resisted the
possibility of creating links to interior portions of their myths. As the
student said, "I want readers to finish reading my piece before they go
on to one that differs radically in style and content."

The difficulty with collaboration extended to difficulties with
understanding the nature of hypertext. Although the students were
fascinated with their introduction to the Internet, they did not grasp the
ways in which hypertext's chaotic fragmentation changes the relationship between readers and writers. As the students saw it, form controls
meaning and writers control form. Rather than expand the potential
meaning of their myths via numerous exits and entrances to the site—
and thereby giving readers more freedom and control over their
respective meaning-making processes—the students in English 303
chose to present a unified, coherent metamyth with limited connection
to thoughts or ideas in other parts of the Internet. Although I would
have liked more links to the outside, I constantly fought the impulse to
impose my authority by interjecting teacher-centered suggestions. I did
not want to take the project from the students even if it meant projecting
only a partial understanding of hypertext to the rest of the Internet
world. Thus, as we continually struggled to negotiate differences
within and between ourselves by seeking compromises to impulses and
suggestions, we ended by creating a project that reflected only a partial
acceptance of the ways in which ideas and realities intersect and interact
in a hypertext writing environment. As the students reflected upon
their experience, a few expressed disappointment mingled with pride.
Our evaluation of the project is more than a bittersweet reflection on the
realities of compromise, however; it is a testament to what can be
learned when weaving a virtual web.

Next, there was the issue of copyright. The students suggested using published illustrations to complement their writing. The library's official position on copyright was that we could not duplicate an entire piece. One librarian cautioned that she would interpret a published illustration as an entire piece. Further inquiry on computer and writing listservs yielded conflicting advice. Thus, to be safe, we had to settle for clip art instead of the beautiful illustrations chosen by the students. This significantly affected the look of our web and made some students uncomfortable, as Eric so elegantly voiced in the previous section.

Finally, there were technical and protocol problems. When we asked for server space to launch our web, we were told that our work would have to be approved by a university committee. Upon presenting our work to this committee, we were told that we could not launch our project until several committees had approved of the newly drafted, official university Web page standards and protocols. When we asked how long this would take, we were told that someone would get back to us. In the meantime, however, a systems analyst from another division offered to launch our project on his division's server.

Suggestions for Teachers

The Creation Project formed a good introduction to the Internet for writers trained in and committed to print publication. In the future, however, I plan to incorporate the following suggestions into my work:

- Devote more time to exploring and explaining hypertext, encouraging students to go beyond merely using the Web as a place to publish student work by providing a stronger framework for students to discover the possibilities for reading and writing in hypertext.
- Allow more time to work on the project.
- Research copyright issues to enable students to take advantage of the visual nature of the Internet.
- Provide more focus on the notion of a metamyth, thus strengthening the possibilities for an expansive, collaborative piece with multiple interior links to interior portions of classmates' writings as well as other Internet Web sites.

Suggestions for Students

- Explore the Web to see what is out there and what is possible.
- Try to imagine ways that your writing could be published on the Internet.

- Be open to the idea that your work will be connected to others.
- Allow those connections to generate associations that go beyond your work and the collaboration.
- Don't let the technology of the Internet keep you from making creative associations.
- If your institution has Web space for students, create your own homepage.
- If you belong to an Internet service provider, explore their online writing opportunities.

Works Cited

Blake, William. 1996. *The First Book of Urizen.* <Up> word Communications. http://www.upword.com/blake/ur.html

Crump, Eric, and Nick Carbone. 1997. *English Online: A Student's Guide to the Internet and World Wide Web.* Boston: Houghton Mifflin.

Faigley, Lester. 1986. "Competing Theories of Process: A Critique and a Proposal." *College English* 48: 527–42.

Golson, Emily. "Student Hypertexts: The Perils and Promises of Paths Not Taken." *Computers and Composition* 12: 295–308.

Landow, G. 1996. Web sites created and managed by George P. Landow. http://landow.stg.brown.edu

National Center for Supercomputing Applications. 1999. "A Beginner's Guide to HTML." http://www.ncsa.uiuc.edu/General/Internet/WWW/HTMLPrimer.html

Project Gutenberg. 1996. http://www.gutenberg.net

Sagel, Eric, and Emily Golson, et al. 1995. *The Creation Project.* http://asweb.unco.edu/depts/english/~creation/themes.html

II Encouraging Research on and with the Web

5 Can Anybody Play? Using the World Wide Web to Develop Multidisciplinary Research and Writing Skills

Elizabeth Sommers
San Francisco State University

Introduction

As the teacher for Electronic Research and Writing, a multidisciplinary undergraduate research and writing class at San Francisco State University (SFSU) that integrates computer-mediated instruction (CMI) and learning, I want students to grasp what they need to know about academic discourse, the content and methodologies of the disciplines, and to tackle any computer-related projects within that framework. I know the way to do this is to construct carefully scaffolded assignment sequences (Applebee and Langer 1983) that require increasing analytical depth of students while making room for personal voice as well, assignments that teach students how to use technology in the context of learning about language, thought, belief systems. While giving students great leeway about the form and content of the projects they construct, I am reluctant to let them totally self-select topics, knowing most of them tend to avoid their weaknesses, turning to narration, avoiding what Vygotsky (1962) calls the zone of proximal development, that place where students and teacher or more experienced peers can meet, the zone in which learning takes place. This essay provides an overview of the Web-based curriculum I construct to meet these challenges: why I use the Web, examples of course activities and methods, and a distillation of the most valuable pedagogical and technological lessons.

Our Definition of Research

In Electronic Research and Writing, "research" is gradually defined as the complex relationships between scholarly technique and scholarly purposes, between gathering information and synthesizing such information into disciplinary or multidisciplinary knowledge. Students begin to distinguish ways and means of knowing and ways and means of making meaning in their own and other disciplines. They often grow interested in peering into the form of the forms of thought (Whitehead 1933), discovering the assumptions beneath our everyday concepts. Maverick types of communication begin to seem compelling while taboo topics take on fresh meaning. Centered in humanistic stances, students learn to look beyond information to meaning, detecting and selecting layers of meaning, ways of knowing, means of expression, finding both symbol and sign, doing so in greater depth and with greater interest and subtlety than I have observed in typical writing courses.

Why I Use the Web to Teach Research and Writing

While the Web is not the only technology used in Electronic Research and Writing, it is one of our most valuable resources. The Web gives us a new forum, a new playing field on which to think simultaneously and creatively about form and content, the ways to present and select information, the means to meld seeming incongruous patches of knowledge, an interactive forum in which we can respond to the ideas spun by other participants. Some of these ways are new, others familiar, but all of them provide unexpectedly provocative results.

First, encouraged to collaborate with one another as well as to experiment with various ways of presenting their knowledge—by discussing readings asynchronously, learning both scientific terminology and literacy terms, developing homepages, studying their own disciplines through the lens of another—students learn to see knowledge as a social construct which is not restricted to individual disciplines. Many begin to understand that knowledge changes with time, information, form of thought, academic discipline, synthetic and analytical expertise. Second, academic genres become more real, more important, crucial to understanding. Students learn that true genre knowledge involves much more than formal conventions and dull disciplinary templates (Coe 1987). Experiencing the making of meaning in asynchronous conferences, written texts, and oral classroom discussion on a regular basis, they tend to discover that knowledge is contextualized, communicable, and community-owned, dynamic and shifting.

Third, many students begin to approach research as a dynamic exploration rather than a static recitation of facts as they grapple with new forms to express their own interpretations. In part this is due to the pedagogical foundation of the class: the humanistic center, the course questions, the readings, the curriculum, the goals (Lawrence and Sommers 1996). But in part this is also due to the subtle yet insistent ways that the Web—a new form and forum offering new opportunities to interpret and shape content—seems to urge us to reexamine our ways of thinking and knowing, our ways of sharing and creating ideas. As we study form and its significance, the new forms make us self-conscious about older forms. Students can and do ask the right questions about the purposes of research, its audience, and the relationship of form to content. Students also can and do ask what is "good" research? Should it provide information, patch together new knowledge, acknowledge wisdom or even strive toward a wisdom of its own?

In short, fresh enough and novel enough to provide multitiered possibilities, the Web becomes an environment for students learning to understand ideas, scholarship in the disciplines, themselves, and one another. Multidimensional, fluid, transitory, and playful, the Web also provides a playing field on which participants can and do experiment with ideas, knowledge and wisdom, the boundaries between genres, and disciplines; and the participants' roles—writers and readers, viewers and listeners—blur in the process. Other writing invitations in traditional forms, no matter how carefully scaffolded, rarely seem to have the same intense effect on those students who too often bring narrow ideas about research and proceed with the stunted writing processes that have never served them well. Using the Web, they seem to become eager to look beyond the conventional, below the surface, moving through the commonplace to find the means to weave together the most original thoughts, feelings, and beliefs to be gleaned from their own, one another's, and professionals' work. Below I explain specific ways that teachers can create a course such as this.

As at so many universities, many students at SFSU want to move beyond the conventional definitions and limitations of their disciplines and explore the nature of human knowledge itself. They are interested in Kuhnian (1962) paradigm shifts, the history of scientific and humanistic thought, the social and cultural implications of technological innovations. While these students often possess less expertise at critical thinking, reading, and writing than I might wish, most arrive with a great and insatiable curiosity about the nature of knowledge constructed by human beings as well as a healthy skepticism about the classification systems and taxonomies used to illuminate (or obscure) such knowledge. By and large these are students who are fully aware of the artificial constraints of the academy but who are intent on learning what they can within its boundaries. The Web provides a fine vehicle for exploring the form writing takes in various disciplines, a way to exemplify academic genres by contrasting them to Web-based scholarship, and a way to find knowledge about topics.

In Electronic Research and Writing, I endeavor to teach undergraduates not only how to use computer resources but also how to comprehend ways in which computers, in particular the World Wide Web mediate knowledge, helping them at the same time to explore and experiment with various academic disciplines. We study and construct both academic and computer-mediated discourse, questioning ways of knowing throughout the course. We do so in many ways, the Web helping us to explore both scholarly method and content with great thoroughness and thoughtfulness.

The Web proves vital in a number of other ways as well. It is not only an invaluable research tool but also a new medium in which students participate in a wide variety of ways by creating their own projects (for example, developing Web sites). Participants also contribute to Usenet groups, a powerful way, as Day points out, to develop a sense of both audience and purpose (cited in Monahan 1994). They also use e-mail, join Web-based communities such as the Well, feminist organizations, genealogical societies. The Web is valuable as an essential new way to reap information (Hunter 1995; Reeves 1996; Riel and Harasim 1994), adding to rather than replacing the ideas students receive from books, from talk, from individual thought. It is valuable as well as a contrast to other genres, in particular traditional academic genres. Finally, the Web is essential because increasingly it is a primary medium through which our students learn and communicate (Green 1995), and it is one of the media, perhaps the primary medium, in which our students will communicate in the future. Many already do, whether they are students of art, literature, or computer science.

Participants begin to think and write about the nature of academic discourse, the various genres they have been taught to read and write, the realm of permissible thought and feeling allowed by given disciplines, the computer's role in changing or maintaining this control. Many students begin to question whether all human knowledge or feeling should be allowed expression and communication within the academy and society. The often glaring differences between emerging Web discourse and traditional academic scholarship are useful to examine and accentuate the importance of various aspects of scholarly communication: form, content, etiquette.

How We Use the Web to Facilitate Our Quest

At first the group of twenty-five students works face-to-face for about half of each weekly three-hour session, talking about and critiquing texts, comparing ideas, comparing genres, linking computer-mediated discourse and research to the traditional ways in which students have learned to read and write texts (see Appendix A, Course Materials). These face-to-face meetings are very important. As one participant explained to me, the meetings' depth and intensity give students the knowledge that they are the thinkers, the experts, the scholars who integrate method and meaning, a sense that their humanistic beliefs and values, rather than the technology, are central. I offer technophobic students one hundred dollars if they can make smoke waft out of the computers, and I make mistakes myself, real mistakes, hoping these real gaffes show that while nobody is infallible, human beings' quests rather than the computer's capabilities are of central importance. Later class meetings are often held in a fully equipped campus classroom with twenty-five state-of-the-art computers with full Internet connectivity. Although the computers are set in rows (rather than in the pods I prefer), the computer classroom provides us with an overhead projector, an LCD, a scanner, and a laser printer. Students can and do work outside of class in many other campus facilities and on their own personal computers.

Gradually the Web plays an ever more important role in our work. Students participate in an asynchronous conference environment created at SFSU, Conference on the Web (COW), create hypertexts, Web sites, and collaborative projects that express complex, evolving, and formerly fragmented knowledge, the technology providing us with a means to understand and sometimes transcend time boundaries, disciplinary ways of knowing, and conventional genres.

What Students Learn in Electronic Research and Writing

- Accessing Library Resources: Students thoroughly explore the massive holdings of both traditional and electronic libraries (CAUSE 1996) and learn to use technological tools such as CARL UnCover, ERIC, Silver Platter, Lexis/Nexis.

- Honing Library Methods: Students learn how to gain remote access to various scholarly search tools and databases, in both paper and digital forms, relying both on library research tools and a site designed for students and faculty at SFSU, the Humanities Educational Leadership Program (H.E.L.P.) (Sommers 1996).

- Using Popular Search Engines: Students discover that many popular search engines, while providing access to powerful and lengthy databases, often include more popular citations, shaky knowledge bases, and meandering Usenet group commentary than scholarly information (Campbell and Campbell 1995).

- Evaluating Scholarly Sources: Students determine how to assess the value of sources (Harnack and Kleppinger 1997), appraising their authority and accuracy in part on the scholarly reputation of the publisher, the use of other sources in presenting an argument, the author's reputation in the field, and the strength of corroborating studies.

  In class, for example, we explore the differences between a highly effective and less effective Web site by comparing sites, generally agreeing that a clear sense of audience and purpose are fundamental, that display of ideas should be clear and relatively simple (Gibbs and Cheng 1995), that links to other scholarly sources are essential, and that content should include original synthesis based in part on scholarly research.

- Writing for Academic Audiences: Writing for one another as well as for the teacher by working in collaborative peer groups, with careful education in how to respond to one another's work, students ascertain what their peers—their fellow academics—expect and want (Sommers 1995; Sommers and Lawrence 1992).

- Writing on the Web: Experimenting with designing Web pages, students begin to master principles of effective page layout and uses of graphics. They become aware of the differences between writing on the Web and academic writing, perceiving that shorter discourse, bulleted or hot-linked lists, and parsimonious use of flashing gadgets are most effective (Dougherty 1997; Nielsen 1997). Such work allows students to synthesize interests, to use discursive, visual, and aural means, and to receive immediate audience feedback. Projects include Web sites devoted to an exploration of the similarities and differences between horror films and fashion, an exploration of consciousness itself, and a living site devoted to students' native Web art.

- Writing in Traditional Academic Genres and Other Electronic Genres: A surprising number of students decide to write some of their work in traditional academic discourse, perhaps intrigued by their new grasp of academic disciplines, the contrast to Web-based scholarship serving to clarify conventional form and content for them. Most also move from traditional forms—the research-based essay, for example—to begin writing and exploring in new forms, experimenting with new challenges and possibilities. An archaeology student interested in Greek ruins learns to use Hypercard to create an educational hypercard stack that includes graphic illustration of the site, Knossos, and interactive possibilities and traditional academic discourse explaining and analyzing the artifacts and ruins that fascinate her. Still others—a journalism major, for example—use a hybrid of traditional tools, in one case a video camera and impromptu interviews about students' educational experiences on the Internet, to explore the above questions.

- Citing Traditional and Web-based Scholarship: Using both online and print sources, students learn to cite e-mail messages, Usenet groups, Web sites, books, electronic and paper journals, and peers' online comments.

- Reading and Writing Hypertext: This work provides a microcosm of the Web research students later do. By discussing how they navigate through links in a self-selected manner, by sharing how they experiment with reading and writing in various colors and fonts, by analyzing the effects when they encounter and create images and sound, students learn fundamental skills that serve them well as Web designers and writers (Bolter 1991; Bolter, Joyce, and Smith 1990; Joyce 1995; Landow 1992).

How I Teach Students

- Asynchronous Conference: The Conference on the Web (COW) provides us with ways in which to discuss readings and course questions at any time of day or night. Since the COW also allows and encourages students to write HTML if they wish, they can begin to learn how to code, how to link, and how to import graphics and sound.

- Reading and Experimenting with Various Genres: Diverse course reading allows exploration of a wide variety of content, from scientific information to fiction and allows analysis of academic genre (see Appendix A). The readings focus deliberately on technology and its implications for late-twentieth-century society, allowing students both to consider and critique the technologies they use (Rouzie 1995).

- Encouraging Collaborative Projects and Group Response: Collaborative projects allow participants to negotiate about important concerns, to learn both content and process from one another, to develop a sense of a classroom community, and to share and respond to one another's writing. To be effective, students need careful education in developing collaboration skills and learning to respond to peers' writing (Lawrence and Sommers 1996).

Asynchronous/
Synchronous
Communication

- Providing Mentors: One or more experienced peers, students who have already taken the course, are always welcome to join us to help the newer students. These more experienced peers are helpful in a number of ways, providing a core of interested and knowledgeable students who can help students not only to master the course's intellectual content but also to learn how to use technological tools such as software and search engines; how to refine database searches; how to write hypertext markup language (HTML), and how to place a Web site on the server.

- Cultivating Technological Expertise: Since the technologies we use for the course are neither uniform nor transparent, I am not able to get on with the work of research and writing without some consideration of them. I recommend that teachers expect to have students with a wide variety of skill levels in their classrooms; that you rely on more advanced peers to assist whenever possible; that you learn to accept the fact that students will often know more than you do about various technological nuances and uses (mine often do); and that you let students know that relative inexperience with technology will not hurt them. Inexperience can be valuable, in fact: as students learn to read, write, and think in new forms, they become more conscious of formal conventions and the reasons for them.

Potential Problems in Web-Based Teaching

Self-sponsored Web sites, asynchronous conference transcripts, hypertextual writings, and other novel language forms made possible by technology can be problematic for a traditional teacher who prefers to remain the primary authority in the classroom, expects a homogeneous group of students, or fails to provide careful scaffolding for students to learn about both language and technology. In Electronic Research and Writing I experience very few of these problems, in part because I rejected a teacher's current traditional authoritarian role long ago, in part because expert peers can help when I cannot, and in part because I keep the focus not on the technology but on research and writing. Yet I do struggle with thorny issues of a different sort: class always seems too short; many students need to rely on out-of-class asynchronous communication but have trouble with access (Krause 1994); students continue projects into the summer or graduate school without reaching closure. While I try to provide students with as much access and continued support as I can, both as classroom teacher and advocate, I have not yet learned how to continue helping former students when each semester I have three or four more classes full of students who need the same care and concern. Though often rewarded with few institutional incentives (Rouzie 1995), the amount of time and effort that Web-based teaching involves can be staggering.

Another sort of problem is typical in many student-centered writing courses that challenge traditional notions of authority and ways of knowing and learning: some self-selected students exclude themselves from the group, keeping a safe distance between us and them. While these students cannot be grouped according to any particular racial, ethnic, or gender classifications, the most tenacious rebels do have a number of traits in common. They seem to see school as an obligation, the teacher as an authoritarian figure to be defied or tricked, their peers as rivals or fellow inmates, the course content as academic cafeteria spinach. Even though few of the students in Electronic Research and Writing fit this pattern, those who do cause problems due to absences, lack of preparation, unwillingness to commit themselves to projects, and shallow relationships with the rest of the group. I recommend that when such students form a majority, teachers work together to scaffold classroom activities, assignments, and deadlines even more rigorously, insisting that each student complete each stage of the work before being allowed to continue. Such means should help teachers of students who intend not to learn but to pass yet another course. But such students seem to be in the minority when teachers take the steps described above.

Conclusion

Can one curriculum, one community, and multiple technologies accomplish everything we want, no matter how carefully we plan? Even though perfect classes are impossible to create and even though Web-based teaching is not easy, certain curricular decisions seem crucial. Above all, think of your teaching goals long before you begin to use the Web. Does the Web have any value to you as a language educator? If not, don't use it. Try not to succumb to pressure to use the expensive new scanner, the color printer, software programs you didn't select and don't see as useful. Unless your own teacherly goals are served by the technology, it is irrelevant, even harmful.

All of us need help (Silva and Breuleux 1994), from more experienced teachers, technical staff, students, books, conference presentations. Before you venture into a Web-based teaching environment, I advise you to observe as many classes as you can, talk to as many teachers and students as possible, study lesson plans and the philosophy behind them, and learn to use some of the Web's capabilities. Don't think you need to know everything before you begin, though, since the Web and a particular school's technological resources change so quickly. Start when you feel close to capable and plan to continue to rely on a support system. Realize that sharing your learning process with students is important too, maybe just as important as sharing your expertise. I also recommend that you collaborate with your colleagues, using some of the ideas central to collaborative learning to rescue isolated teachers: form writer's groups, participate in e-mail discussion groups, observe one another's classes, mentor newer teachers, write together, talk through the difficulties as well as the breakthroughs in your classrooms, arrange working groups, share findings with your peers. Students often make stellar classroom researchers too, especially once they realize that you value their input as collaborators and fellow scholars.

Realizing that much of the academy still demands academic discourse in linear form, think carefully about the implications of encouraging students to experiment with a new literacy if they have not mastered the dominant code. Realize, too, that while students might both read and write hypertext documents in their careers, few such texts will be explorations of consciousness, the nature of knowledge and wisdom, or a critique of ways of knowing in the sciences and humanities. Rather, these documents will demand that students build and walk along pathways toward information and knowledge they need as engineers, computer scientists, nurses. If your goals are primarily professional, the ways the Web is used in Electronic Research and Writing might be more abstract than you want. But as long as you know your objectives, you can adjust the methods suggested above to serve your needs.

Students participate in courses such as Electronic Research and Writing because they want to learn about humanistic and scientific ideas and their relationship to new technologies, forming a thriving community of genuinely inquisitive and searching scholars. While time will tell us whether fascination with new technologies is the main reason such a learning environment develops, I think most students want to possess not only knowledge but also the ways of knowing that writing teachers offer to teach them: critical thinking and reading, written analysis and synthesis, thoughtful self-scrutiny, and the value of group collaboration. Though many students have been injured by poor or indifferent schooling, these very students often seem among the most eager to learn when they realize they have a real opportunity to do so. In various ways, through different means, the participants in

Electronic Research and Writing arrive at unique conclusions about the nature of knowledge and information, the limitations of any given way of knowing and the infinite possibilities that open up when many symbol systems, many ways of knowing are embraced.

Works Cited

Applebee, Arthur, and Judith Langer. 1983. "Instructional Scaffolding: Reading and Writing as Natural Language Activities." *Language Arts* 50: 168–75.

Bolter, Jay David. 1991. *Writing Space: The Computer, Hypertext, and the History of Writing.* Hillsdale, NJ: Erlbaum.

Bolter, Jay David, Michael Joyce, and John Smith. 1990. *Storyspace.* Watertown, MA: Eastgate.

Campbell, Dave, and Mary Campbell. 1995. *The Student's Guide to Doing Research on the Internet.* Reading, MA: Addison-Wesley.

CAUSE. 1996. *Realizing the Potential of Information Resources: Information, Technology, and Services.* Proceedings of the 1995 CAUSE Annual Conference. Boulder, CO: CAUSE.

Coe, Richard. 1987. "An Apology for Form; or Who Took the Form out of Process?" *College English* 49(1): 13–27.

Daedalus Integrated Writing Environment (DIWE). 1995. The Daedalus Group, Inc. Austin, TX.

DeLillo, Don. 1986. *White Noise.* New York: Penguin.

Dougherty, Dale. 1997. "Don't Forget to Write." *Web Review* (26 Oct.). http://webreview.com/97/10/10/imho/index.html.

Gibbs, William, and He-Ping Cheng. 1995. "Formative Evaluation and World-Wide-Web Hypermedia." In *Eyes on the Future: Converging Images, Ideas, and Instruction: Selected Readings from the Annual Conference of the International Visual Literacy Association.* Chicago, IL: International Visual Literacy Association.

Green, Kenneth C. 1995. *The Sixth National Survey of Desktop Computing in Higher Education.* Encino, CA: Campus Computing.

Harnack, Andrew, and Eugene Kleppinger. 1997. *Online! A Reference Guide to Using Internet Sources.* New York: St. Martin's Press.

Holtzman, Steven. 1994. *Digital Mantras: The Languages of Abstract and Virtual Worlds.* Cambridge, MA: MIT Press.

Hunter, Leslie G. 1995. "Decade of Change." *History Microcomputer Review* 11(2): 50–52.

Joyce, Michael. 1995. *Of Two Minds.* Ann Arbor: University of Michigan Press.

Krause, Steve. 1994. *Gopher Is No Longer Just a Rodent: Using Gopher and World Wide Web in Composition Studies.* ERIC Document Reproduction Service, No. ED 377 490.

Kuhn, Thomas. 1962. *The Structure of Scientific Revolutions.* Chicago: University of Chicago Press.

Landow, George. 1992. *Hypertext: The Convergence of Contemporary Critical Theory and Technology.* Baltimore: Johns Hopkins University Press.

Langer, Susanne. 1942. *Philosophy in a New Key.* Cambridge, MA: Harvard University Press.

Lawrence, Sandra, and Elizabeth Sommers. 1996. "From the Park Bench to the (Writing) Workshop Table: Encouraging Collaboration among Inexperienced Writers." *Teaching English in the Two-Year College* 23(2): 101–11.

Monahan, Brian D. 1994. *The Internet in English Language Arts.* ERIC Document Reproduction Service, No. ED 378 577.

Nielsen, Jakob. 1997. "How Users Read on the Web." *Alertbox* (27 Oct.). http://www.useit.com/alertbox/9710a.html.

Reeves, Thomas C. 1996. "Technology in Teacher Education: From Electronic Tutor to Cognitive Tool." *Action in Teacher Education* 17(4): 74–78.

Riel, Margaret, and Linda Harasim. 1994. "Research Perspectives on Network Learning." *Machine-Mediated Learning* 4(2–3): 91–113.

Roszak, Theodore. 1986. *The Cult of Information.* New York: Pantheon.

Rouzie, Albert. 1995. *The New Computers and Writing Course at the University of Texas at Austin: Context and Theory.* ERIC Document Reproduction Service, No. ED 384 895.

Silva, Marcos, and Alain Breuleux. 1994. "The Use of Participatory Design in the Implementation of Internet-based Collaborative Learning Activities in K–12." *Interpersonal Computing and Technology* 2(3): 99–128.

Sommers, Elizabeth. 1995. *Women Collaborators: Breaking the Rules and Learning How to Win.* ERIC Document Reproduction Service, No. ED 371 370.

Sommers, Elizabeth. 1996. *Humanities Educational Leadership Program (HELP).* San Francisco: http://www.sfsu.edu/~humanity/helpsite/ (25 Oct., 1997).

Sommers, Elizabeth, and Sandra Lawrence. 1992. "Women's Ways of Talking in Teacher-directed and Student-directed Peer Response Groups." *Linguistics and Education* 4(1): 1–36.

Vygotsky, Lev. 1962. *Thought and Language.* Cambridge, MA: Harvard University Press.

Whitehead, Alfred N. 1933. *Adventures of Ideas.* New York: The Free Press.

Appendix A: Sample Course Materials

Electronic Research and Writing

Course Prerequisite: English 214

Introduction: Participants will learn to use a wide variety of computer tools—SFSU library databases; World Wide Web search engines; e-mail; SFSU's Conference on the Web (COW); H.E.L.P. (Humanities Educational Leadership Program); Daedalus Integrated Writing Environment (DIWE). We will simultaneously explore DeLillo's *White Noise* and Roszak's *The Cult of Information*, works that examine and critique the convergence of technology and the humanities, while studying both computer-mediated research methods (e.g., Campbell) and theories about musical, artistic, and linguistic abstractions in relation to computers (e.g., Holtzman). Students will focus on their own research projects in the sciences and/or humanities, guided by the course questions (below) and sharing information, knowledge, and discoveries with the group.

Print Sources Needed:

Required Texts (All at SFSU Bookstore):
Campbell, Dave, and Mary Campbell. *The Student's Guide to Doing Research on the Internet.*
DeLillo, Don. *White Noise.*
Holtzman, Steven. *Digital Mantras.*
Roszak, Theodore. *The Cult of Information.*
Other Materials: Floppy disks for your work.

Course Requirements:

1. Class participation (10%). More than three absences will affect your final grade by 5% per absence. In addition, you must submit all three Working Project drafts on time to work in online peer response groups. If you fail to do so, you will be penalized as absent and will need to submit proof of peer response (a tape, an Interchange session, notes) with the final Working Project.
2. Conference on the Web (COW) (10%). Three kinds of out-of-class COW participation are: (1) You'll take a turn as a discussion leader of readings (to be explained); (2) You'll give a COW Presentation and lead a discussion of one of your Working Projects; (3) You'll actively discuss readings, Working Projects, and Course Questions each week.
3. Three Working Projects (about 5 "pages" each in print terminology) (50%). Original interpretations of technology and the sciences, humanities, literature, cultural phenomena, first submitted electronically in draft form for peer review. These works can take many forms: hypertext form, essays, Web sites. All three can be linked into one larger project or each can be separate. One of these Working Projects can be done collaboratively if you wish. If possible, please submit all final Working Projects both on disk and in paper form.

Both early drafts and final papers must be submitted by the deadlines written on the syllabus or will be considered late. Late papers will be penalized half a letter grade per weekday. Everyone, however, will receive a voucher allowing him or her to turn in one late piece of work (either a draft or a final working paper) with no penalty, no questions asked, and no explanations required.

4. Weekly readings with assignments with your written responses (10%). Four unannounced reading quizzes will be given.

5. Weekly computer workshops (20%): obtaining an e-mail account; using the e-mail program PINE; conducting a Boolean search; research using SFSU library resources; research on the World Wide Web; use of H.E.L.P. (Humanities Educational Leadership Project); CLIP Tutorial; DAEDALUS local area network discussions; hypertext programs (Hypercard, Storyspace) to develop computer research expertise. Proof of completion of Library Requirement is due by ____.

Grading: To receive credit for NEXA 365, you must complete/fulfill all of the course requirements. The percentages after each of the above course requirements is the amount of credit you will receive for that portion of the work.

Guiding Course Questions:

• What is the difference between information, knowledge, and wisdom?
• What constitutes "knowledge" in the sciences? In the humanities? What is "convergent" knowledge?
• How do human beings think, know, and feel? Does the computer affect human cognition and perception? If so, in what ways?
• What role can/should/might computers play in the making of meaning in a given field or fields?
• How can you use computers most effectively for research in your field(s) and/or for creating art, music, or literature?

Course Journal: As you read the course material, please keep a journal (online or on paper) of questions, thoughts, reactions, disagreements, opinions, points of interest. I'll seldom if ever collect this record, but we'll usually use these texts to begin discussing the readings. You may well find the seeds of your three Works in Progress here as well.

Appendix B

Elizabeth Sommers, Associate Professor of English
Electronic Writing and Research
An Early Collaborative Discussion in Small Groups

Consider the four books we're reading for Electronic Research and Writing (both individually and as a group):
Digital Mantras by Holtzman
White Noise by DeLillo
Student's Guide to Doing Research by Campbell and Campbell
The Cult of Information by Roszak

1. What meanings do each of these books have for you so far (1) individually and (2) as a group? Do they have a collective meaning yet?
Time: 30 minutes
2. Prepare to discuss your answer to question 1 with the entire class.
    a. appoint a spokesperson
    b. provide that person with the group's view
3. After each group has reported, we'll have an open discussion.
Time: 30 minutes
Total time: one hour

Appendix C

Elizabeth Sommers
Electronic Research and Writing

Week 5: Readings and Computer Work

1. In *White Noise,* Heinrich says "the real issue is the kind of radiation that surrounds us every day. Your radio, your TV, your microwave oven, your power lines just outside the door, your radar speed-trap on the highway. For years they told us these low doses weren't dangerous."
    Why is Heinrich saying this to J. A. K. and Babette, "massaging the data" as Roszak would say?
2. What is the significance of the mysterious Dylar? Would Langer consider it a sign or a symbol?
3. According to Roszak "every piece of software has some repertory of basic assumptions, values, limitations embedded within it. In no sensible meaning of the word are these 'information.' Crude as they may often be, they are ideas about the world, and like all ideas, they must be kept in clear, critical view" (p. 118).
    What are the basic assumptions, values, and limitations of a software program you often use—a spreadsheet, a word processing system, communications software?
4. Roszak also writes (p.120) that ". . . the ideas that govern the data are *not* information; nor are they sacrosanct matters of mathematical logic. They are philosophical commitments, the outgrowth of experience, insight, metaphysical conviction, which must be assessed as wise or foolish, childlike or mature, realistic or fantastic, moral or wicked."
    What ideas is Roszak talking about? How do *you* evaluate them?
5. Writing about a computer trying to ascertain whether it is raining (p. 125), Roszak sounds to me as though he is describing Heinrich. Do you agree? Do Heinrich's massive amount of data and his unwillingness to accept "common sense" make him seem computer-like, a possessor of artificial intelligence rather than the real thing? If so, why do you think Heinrich decides to deal with the world in this way? Is he right and smart or wrong and deluded?
6. Roszak writes that "knowledge is a status conferred upon an idea by [a certain broad] consensus." What do we "know" in our late-twentieth-century North American society? What are our criteria for "truth"?

7. Yuhara's conception of the future of artificial intelligence (p. 133) sounds like science fiction to me. Roszak explains that "Yuhara believes the human body possesses sensors that can act as electrical transmitters. These might be connected to computers by way of a magnetic link. The result would be "the ultimate modem": the extrasensory powers of the human psyche integrated in some ethereal way into the global telecommunications web."
What do you think of this vision? Why?
8. According to Langer (p. 105), when does language begin? And why do we as humans begin by *naming*?
9. What does Langer mean when she quotes Sapir that "the tendency to see reality symbolically" is the real keynote of language?
10. Finally, can you think of any metaphors or faded metaphors (in the sense that Langer defines them) that seem to be common among computer users?
11. During computer workshop tonight, do one of the following:
    a. Telnet or FTP to a distant computer, exploring a field in which you are interested.
    b. Explore SFSU gopher's services. What's most valuable to you as a researcher? Why?
    c. Look up the e-mail address for a BBS, a LISTSERV, or another online resource and join this group.
    d. Get caught up on the COW, maybe examining the questions above in more depth.
    e. Play with Netscape, seeing if you can find a meaningful path through images and Internet sites.

Appendix D

Elizabeth Sommers   Your Name:

Electronic Research and Writing
Week 8: Readings and Computer Work

This week again both in and out of class I'm asking you to demonstrate both that you have read the readings and that you know how to use the tools Campbell and Campbell have discussed. Please fill out this sheet and/or put answers on the COW, following the directions below. This sheet is due to me *next Monday*, as are the COW responses (to be placed on COW). After some initial freewriting and group talk on Monday, everyone can work at his or her own rate, with a partner or alone. I will help you.

In Class Talk and Writing:

1. Which of Roszak's ideas did you find most interesting this week? Which did you find most troubling, untrue, or questionable?
2. Freewrite: What do you know for sure you don't want to research? Make a list of topics that bore you.
3. Tell some lies you enjoy even if (or especially because) they are lies.
4. Pretend you could make a lie come true because you're talking to someone who usually believes everything you say but seems a bit skeptical in this case. What sort of arguments will you use to convince him or her?
5. Why does J. A. K. start throwing everything away (p. 223)?
6. Do you agree with J. A. K. that "fear is self-awareness raised to a higher level"? With Philosopher Suzanne Langer, who wrote that "fear is the driving force in the human mind"? Why or why not?

COW, Internet, and Web Work:

1. Go to the library (virtually) and explore Investigator Plus, Galenet, and the Encyclopedia Britannica. On the COW, report on one interesting piece of knowledge or information (and tell us which it is).
2. Use Harriett Talon's award-winning hypertext program on library resources, CLIP, which she designed at SFSU. If you bring a disk I'll give you a copy of this freeware.
3. What's a Usenet group? Find one that's useful to you and join it, or tell us about one you already belong to.

Campbells, chapter 9

4. What are the humanities? Do you agree with their definition?
5. Critique one of the following areas, finding the best sources for your own work and explaining why on (you guessed it) COW:

> art sources
> journalism sources
> language resources
> photography
> music
> religion

Campbells, chapter 10

6. Teach us something about accounting, the law, business, or another Management School resource that we'll find useful during this tax season and election year.
7. Have some fun on the Internet and ask yourself the question again: What's the difference between work and play?

Appendix E

Elizabeth Sommers, Instructor
Electronic Research and Writing

Working Project # 3 Ideas

1. Take one of Roszak's master ideas—for example, the concept that God is the creator of the universe—and analyze how it plays out in a cultural context. What do Christian fundamentalists do with this concept? Evolutionists? Darwinists? Madonna? (All of this would be too much; you'd have to select from among the ideas.)
2. Take two ideas that you feel strongly about—say Holtzman's idea that computers can be artists and might not "condescend" to speak with us in the next century—and offer an argument for or against the ideas. Base your arguments on the texts we've read, your own opinions, the ideas your peers have given you in the class and any other books you are reading.
3. Write a play with various authors—Holtzman, Roszak, DeLillo—having a discussion about what they've learned from reading one another's work.
4. Take a small topic—a very small topic—and do an Internet research essay on it. Here are some possibilities:

   a. Find a favorite author. What else has he or she written? What do critics say about the author? What does he or she say about his or her work? Finally, why is the work so important to you? Can you write a convergent answer, explaining why these ideas are important, for example, both as literature and as fact?

   b. Think of something you always believed when you were a child. Find out from the Web whether or not it's true. If not, think about the cultural and societal forces that led you to believe this idea. If it IS true, think about why adults would tell children such a thing. Was it to socialize you, to scare you, to interest you, to make you good? Was it an effective belief, one that made you behave in the ways others wanted you to?

   c. Find out about children's fairy tales on the Web. Interpret them in an adult cultural context, your own or any other you know well. If you have space, write about the differences between fairy tales on the Web and in books. Do any stand out?

   d. Can the great apes talk? If so, do they teach each other? And if they can talk and pass talk on to their offspring, what does this say about the differences between animals and humans? Some scientists used to think the ability to learn and use language was an important difference between animals and humans. If this is no longer true, do such important differences exist? If so, what? (Note: Rob's site is a gold mine here.)
5. Start your very first Web site. Think first of what you want to say and to whom. Then look at a lot of sites to get ideas and information. Rob and I will help you to get it on the server when you're ready, but you don't have to have a finished product by May 27th. (Web sites are NEVER done, in my experience.)

6. Think about anything you're curious about—your family history, the Kennedy assassination, the recent events in Peru, the murder rate in South Central Los Angeles during 1996, the lives of homeless San Franciscans—and explore this topic on the Web and in print sources. Once you have information, use the guiding course questions to synthesize this information into your own point of view. What does it mean, for example, that many of the homeless in SF are war veterans? Why would this be true from a sociological, scientific, psychological, or historical perspective? Make sure to document your sources as you go along.

7. Take a traditional term paper you are writing for another class and use it in an entirely different way for this class. For example, turn it into a hypertext document using Storyspace or Hypercard. Or make it into a Web site. How does form affect content?

All of your final projects should in some way address the guiding course questions, though they don't have to deal with the specific books we read in class. Good Luck!

6 Surfing the Net: Getting Middle School Students Excited about Research and Writing

Jean Boreen
Northern Arizona University

I walked around the lab, noting how industrious my eighth graders looked as they slouched over their computer keyboards and "hunt-and-pecked" their way through the second draft of their first computer-generated paper of the year. They were doing exactly what I had asked them to do: use the computer to compose and revise a "how-to" paper. They had peer-conferenced and provided thoughtful suggestions to each other on how to make the papers better. But as I moved from student to student, I was still troubled by one thing: they didn't seem excited about using computers for their writing task.

Not that I expected them to be thrilled and turn somersaults whenever I mentioned that they would be allowed in the computer lab. But I had read articles that suggested that computers sparked more creative work from students, that they encouraged students to take greater chances with revision and their writing in general (Lucking and Stallard 1988; Selfe, Rodrigues, and Oates 1989; Standiford, Jaycox, and Auten 1983). So where was the excitement? The intrinsic motivation? And what would happen when the novelty of working on the computers passed? What was I doing wrong?

As time passed, I realized that I really wasn't doing anything *wrong*. But let's be realistic. Why is sitting in front of a computer doing word processing necessarily more interesting than sitting down with a sheet of paper and writing down one's thoughts in a logical manner? For many students, it's not. I realized that I needed to find ways to enhance the computer work I was asking my students to complete.

"Surfing the Net: A Writing Workshop for Kids"

I now teach at the university level in an English Education program and consider it one of my responsibilities to prepare students for using technology to teach the writing process. Consequently, I developed a course called "Surfing the Net: A Writing Workshop for Kids" with the intent that it would provide concrete ideas for teachers on how to make computer work in the classroom more meaningful for secondary students. Offered during one of our five-week summer sessions, the course provides university students as well as veteran teachers with an opportunity to work one-on-one with a group of middle school—fourth through ninth grade—students in a computer-mediated classroom. Middle school students (who attend class the middle three weeks of the five-week session) have the chance to spend one week researching topics off the Internet before turning their attention to the various stages of the writing process. And adult students can experiment with how computer technology can be used to motivate and encourage enthusiasm in students as they work through the writing process.[1]

In this paper, I describe how the members of the class—middle school students, university students, veteran middle school teachers, university instructors—constructed and reconstructed various aspects of the course in order to meet the needs of all involved. Through this sharing of ideas and approaches, I hope to give classroom teachers more options when it comes to creative uses of technology in the classroom.

Challenging the Potential of Computers

We all work to make the writing *process* routine for students; the real challenge for teachers who have access to computer technology may be how to keep their students interested. Using the Internet as a research tool can be one of the most effective ways not only to heighten student enthusiasm for computer use itself but also as a way to influence how students explore and conceptualize what they want to accomplish with their writing. The exploratory nature of the Web is addressed by Heba (1997) who notes that "the experience of multimedia is more chaotic and, perhaps, appeals more to a rhetoric of exploration where the boundaries and destinations of the discourse are not always clear" (22). Students, from this perspective, can become engaged in a multitude of rhetorical activities without being restrained by a closely defined concept of "writing."

Connecting Computer Technology with Rhetorical Choices

One of the issues we dealt with in our "Surfing the Net" course was how to integrate process writing with computer technology in a manner that seemed natural and interesting to the middle school students. While a number of books and articles (Cotton 1996; Hawisher and LeBlanc 1992; LaQuey 1993; Merseth 1991; Reinhardt 1995; Sheingold and Hadley 1990) discussed the theoretical and pedagogical aspects of using computer technology in the classroom, it was not until the university students read texts like Nancie Atwell's *In the Middle* (1986) and Regie Routman's *Invitations: Changing as Teachers and Learners K–12* (1994) that they were able to conceptualize how to develop classroom writing and thinking strategies offered by this union of writing and technology.

Research Using the Internet

When I first taught this course in the summer of 1996, the offerings on the Internet were only adequate at best. For every site we found, there were typically two that we couldn't access or that simply didn't exist anymore. One year later, a search for information on "writing," for example, would give us anywhere from 50,000 to 1.2 million sites depending on the search engine—Lycos, Yahoo, Excite, Infoseek—chosen. So what do we as teachers do with this wealth of information as we plan instruction for and with our students? And how do we best prepare ourselves to work on this vast information highway?

Preparing the University Students

Many of the university students had never "surfed the Net" and were unclear as to what is offered on the World Wide Web. To give them a basic education on the use of Internet technology, our technology instructor, Fred Ducat, previewed for the university students much of the work they would be doing with the middle school students. For example, the students were instructed how to direct a "Key Search" on, as noted earlier, writing. The varied number of sites produced by the searches, based on the different search engines, exemplified for the university students just how much was available on the Web and how difficult it might be for their students to handle the huge amount of information and sites available. After all, when one has 50,000 sites to choose from and only a limited time to consider a small number of those, it is important to consider how these choices may affect individual students' creative processes.

Preparing the Middle School Students

One of the most motivational ways to help students become familiar with the World Wide Web is to ask them to go on an Internet treasure hunt. Working in pairs (or groups of four if one has a large class and few computers), students hunt out different sites and then look for specific information found on the site (see Figure 6.1).

This search technique is an excellent way for students to become acquainted with a variety of sites that may be of interest to them as they begin their own topic research. As this "hunt" list illustrates, students were asked to look for famous people, animals, authors, etc. Student comfort level with the Internet increases significantly as students become very adept at initiating key searches, typing in addresses, and quickly scanning for information. Once familiarity with the Net is established, students are more than ready for the next step: beginning the research for their writing project.

"I Want to Write a Mystery": Using the Internet for Source Material

When I asked my middle school students to "do research," I expected them to find information on specific topics and incorporate what they had found into short I-Search papers (Macrorie 1988) or persuasive essays. In giving these assignments, I hoped that students would take their facts, descriptions, and statistics and develop compositions that showed an understanding both of format and of the rhetorical choices possible when writing these types of essays.

During "Surf the Net," we found that using the Internet as a research tool could offer students additional ways to approach writing, especially in how the middle school students considered their rhetorical choices. Specifically, a student might begin research on a topic, a situation, or a place with the intent of writing one type of paper—informational essay, short story—and change her mind because of the wealth of options provided by the sheer volume of information found during prewriting.

Debbie loved mysteries. She also knew exactly what she wanted to accomplish during her three weeks: write a mystery in short story form. What she didn't have figured out were the specific details connected to the plot machinations she had in mind. Debbie began with a Net search on Carlsbad, California, a place she had once been on vacation. As she and her university teacher, Mark, scanned sites, they found a picture of a flower field with a windmill in the middle of it.

Scavenger Hunt

The object of this scavenger hunt is to allow you to become more comfortable with the Internet and to see how it works. By the end of this hunt, you should have a better sense about the Net and what it can do.

Let's begin!
1. Find **Net Search** and click.
2. Choose **Info Seek** and click.
3. Choose the **Kids and Fun** selection and click.
4. Select **Silly Jokes.**
5. Scroll down the page until you can find **Kaitlyn's knock-knock jokes and riddles.**
6. Once you are at Kaitlyn's page, choose either **Knock-knock jokes or Riddles** at the middle of the page.
7. Now feel free to look at the whole site. Also, write down your favorite joke or riddle you find at this site.
8. Once you are done, click on the picture of the **house** at the top of the screen. Doing this will bring you back to where you started.
9. Now you should be back where we started.
10. Select **Net Search.**
11. Choose **Excite** this time.
12. Choose **Entertainment.**
13. Find and choose **Cartoons (editor's review).**
14. Choose **Peanuts—The dog house** under today's cartoons.
15. Read the comic strip and then choose **Sunday Strip.**
16. Read the comic strip and go ahead and view other strips by selecting any date in the box at the bottom of the page. Write down the date of your favorite strip.
17. Once you are done, select the **Home (picture of the house) key.**
18. Here we go on another search. Choose **Net Search.**
19. Choose **Yahoo.**
20. Choose **Games.**
21. Choose **Puzzles**.
22. Choose **Tic Tac Toe.**
23. Choose **Steve's Tic Tac Toe.**
24. Play a few games to see if you can beat Steve. To play your "O", just click on the space where you would like to place it.
25. Once you are done, select the **Home key** and prepare to take one more journey on the Net.
26. Now we are going to try something different. At the top of the screen by the home key is a long box and the word **location**. There is an address already there but we are going to put our own address in the box. Take the mouse and place the cursor after **location** and click. You should see a blinking line. Now type in the address http://www.blacktop.com/coralforest.
27. After a few minutes, you should be at the coral reef. Go through this site and explore and find all of the different features this site has. Also, look at all the pictures of the sea. After you are done exploring, write down your favorite picture or your favorite place you visited on this site.
28. Choose the **Home key.** Congratulations! You have successfully completed the hunt!

Hunt created by Heather Nebrich and Ali Henderson

Figure 6.1. Internet Scavenger Hunt

Debbie decided that this was where the main action of the plot would be. From there, she pulled up the "America's Most Wanted" site and looked for the kind of face she wanted her murderer to have; this sight proved too intriguing, though, as Debbie and Mark spent two full days reading the background blurbs on each case pulled from the site. As Debbie's experience shows, students can get bogged down easily and become frustrated while surfing the Web. A possible solution to circumvent information overload is to ask students to step back from their research and reconsider their writing strategies based on the data gathered. In our example, Debbie reconsidered and decided to re-outline the action of her story. Instead of packing the first chapter with physical characteristics of the protagonists and antagonists, she created a more action-filled beginning and let the characters show more of themselves through their interactions. Then, using the Internet information she had found, she began to contemplate how later chapters might look.

The Novelty of Interactive Sites, or "Meet the Spice Girls!"

Interactive sites have the potential to be highly motivational for younger students who are visual learners. Much like the educational games developed for younger children, interactive Web sites can present—with sound, pictures, and voice-overs—how a scientific concept like the bonding of molecules was conceived and then illustrate how the individual molecules are drawn together, how they bond, and what the resulting molecular structure might look like (http://www.nyu.edu/pages/mathmol/). The possibilities of what may be seen and heard on interactive sites is only limited to the imagination of the person who developed the site.

Allan bounced—literally—into class on the first day; we should have suspected then that he would be a student who would look for a high-energy topic to research and write about. Allan was an ardent "hip-hop" fan, and the English band the Spice Girls was one of his favorite groups. The first site Allan found as he and his teacher, Samantha, looked for information about the band was an informational site that had a picture of the five band members and a short bio on each one. Allan dutifully bookmarked the page but clearly was less than thrilled at what he had found. On his second try, a blast of music took the entire lab by surprise. The slightly glazed look in Allan's eyes was replaced by an excited gleam as other students rushed over to see what he had found. On the screen, the Spice Girls danced as their mouths moved almost in sync with the music coming from the computer's speaker (http://www.serveyou.com/spice/songs.html). From that moment on, Allan was hooked, and he spent the rest of research week looking for similar exciting sites. One cautionary note: Samantha found out very quickly that if she let him, Allan would simply bounce from site to site unless something unique caught his attention. What teachers can do to avoid indiscriminate surfing is to make students read the information on each site thoroughly, then jot down a few notes or bookmark sites that had a great deal of information. In this way, students have to consider each site not only for its entertainment value, but also for its informational worth. This type of evaluation lends itself to the kind of critical thinking we want all of our students to embrace. Students need to read, evaluate, and choose information based on an understanding of why certain facts or ideas are more important within a specific assignment or in their search for enlightenment on a topic.

Conversation Anyone? E-mail and the Adolescent Researcher

For many of us, e-mail has become the correspondence of choice because of the speed and efficiency of the interchange. Like the use of personal interviews when students are creating I-Search papers, e-mail conversations allow questions and answers to move between inter-viewer and interviewee at a fairly rapid pace. However, we found that e-mail correspondence could offer additional rhetorical options that we hadn't even considered.

Amanda and her teacher Jody were having a hard time deciding which topic to choose for Amanda's writing project. Amanda's attitude about the topics she was researching reminded me of the old Lays' potato chips commercial—"You can't choose (eat) just one!" Shortly after her group decided that they wanted to put their writing in a newspaper format, Amanda found an interactive Web site on Edgar Allan Poe that included an obituary and a picture of the author's grave in Baltimore. This was Amanda's epiphany. "I'm going to create celebrity obituaries," she announced to her group.

Amanda decided that she would conduct searches on three or four of her favorite (living) authors. In the middle of her search on Danielle Steele, she realized that not one of the sites she had accessed listed Steele's age, a necessary ingredient in a successful obituary. As I listened to Amanda's plight, I noted that the site she had just pulled up listed an e-mail address for the author. At my suggestion, Amanda wrote to Steele, explaining the project, asking for her age ("Please be honest," Amanda wrote) and any other information Steele might want to offer about being a writer. Days passed without a response. Amanda became irritated with Steele and decided that the author would come to a "darker" end than she had originally intended: she would have her murdered by an unknown person, maybe a disgruntled reader.

As Amanda worked on the obituary, she became so intrigued with the mystery she was creating around the author's death that she decided to create a link between all of the obituaries. In a series of mysterious accidents, Steele, Beverly Cleary, and Stephen King all came to unusual ends, victims of Raymond, the "serial author" killer.

As this example shows, e-mail correspondence can create new venues for the middle school student. Whether authors write back or not, students can use their e-mail experiences to reconceptualize their writing task. Amanda might have been content to write the simple obituaries; however, her creative juices pushed her to write an article more intriguing and inventive. Furthermore, in order to make her piece more interesting, she had to look at police logs in newspapers and decide how to recreate the same tone.

Creating a Homepage: Yes, Middle School Students CAN Do This!

One of the adult student groups decided that they would like to help their students create a homepage as part of their group writing project. Middle school teacher Logan Bennett, "the female version of Bill Gates" (according to a classmate), convinced me and her teammates that the research and process writing that were part of the class objectives could naturally lead to Web page development. Because of my own experiences putting together a homepage, I was willing to let Logan and her team (Lee and Whitman) help the students develop sites as long as they didn't scrimp on the writing and research aspects of the course. They decided to divide the workload among groups of students: Lee handled the research and informational writing, Whitman worked on the creative writing aspect of the class, and Logan taught the students how to use html, find clip-art, use Adobe Photoshop and Graphic Converter, and so on. The adult teachers' hope was that the opportunity to work on a homepage would increase student motivation and encourage a greater willingness to hone skills related to the production of written work that would appear on the Internet.

Like the other groups, the homepage team and their students began by prowling around the Internet looking for sites that excited their imagination. As they surfed, they looked not only for interesting topics but also for innovative sites or clip art they found interesting. Moving from teacher to teacher, the students alternately took turns producing their creative work (a poem on Edgar Allan Poe or a song), detailing the information they wanted to use on their individual Web pages and fashioning the Web page itself. While the students were willing to make the creative effort, it was the Web page that caught and kept their attention. Similar to the writing process, Web page design needs to progress through various stages: students need to search for an interesting topic, decide on a specific topic, work on planning the Web page (text, background, graphics, etc.) and publish their information (upload to the Web). In the case of the students involved in this class, personal interests in Edgar Allan Poe, snowboarding, and bass guitar players became dynamic representations of the interests of each student. To access the student pages, go to

- http://www.nau.edu/~jmb5/initial/students/lucky/edgar.html
- http://www.nau.edu/~jmb5/initial/students/ryan/ryan'swebpage.html
- http://www.nau.edu/~jmb5/initial/students/wes/goodpage.html

Publishing on the Computer

Publishing student work, in many cases, increases students' enthusiasm for the task at hand. For this course, publishing took the form of a student booklet that would be shared with the other members of the class and their families and friends on the last meeting day for the middle school students. And, of course, we had the Web pages our three students put together. In this sense, the computers offered us another use, a different outlet for student creativity that went beyond the simple word processing aspect most of us take for granted. In case students do not have their own Web site, the Internet offers a number of sites that allow students to put their work online and receive feedback from others who also choose to access these publishing sites:

- KidPub: http://www.kidpub.org/kidpub
- Book Nook: http://www.i-site.on.ca/booknook.html
- Ace Kids: http://www.acekids.com/bkground.html

Final Reflections

In this final section, I would like to consider what conclusions we can draw for teachers who are trying to integrate the writing process and technology in their own classrooms.

Wedding Writing and Technology

As most of my students realized fairly quickly, this joining of approaches is not always the easiest to accomplish. As Lee noted toward the end of the first week with the students,

> We took the kids down the hall to talk about each other's progress. This was supposed to be the time where the three of us talked to the students about how they were coming along with their projects, and it ended up being a time where we spouted off our ideas for the individual deadlines for their work. I was interested in the structure they would develop for the research part of the project, Whitman was concerned as to the ideas they planned to use for the creative aspects of their writing, and Logan wanted to know what they wanted to use from their research and creative work on their Web pages. We were acting like the three activities were mutually exclusive.

Once they realized the interconnectivity of these activities, however, using the Internet became integral to the writing process.

Impacting the Stages of the Writing Process

The addition of the Internet component for research adds possibilities and frustrations to the prewriting and drafting stages of the process. The potential for motivating excitement about conducting research is enormous with the Internet because of the immediacy and variety of the information. As Leah, one of the adult students, noted,

> I saw this [class] as an opportunity to spend quality time with a student teaching useful information that he would be able to utilize the rest of his days. Sam [the student] was a joy to be around. He needed little instruction to be off and running with this writing project. As a matter of fact, I found it difficult to let him work independently. It is always a goal of mine to get my students to claim personal responsibility for their education, but I found in this situation how difficult it was to keep my hands off and let him write. I felt that I should be actively participating in his education. But then I realized that I could model time spent reading and writing for him even as he was spreading his wings with his own story telling/writing.

Leah, in this excerpt, is aware of the added dimensions created by using the Internet as a research tool. However, once she realizes the importance of letting her student explore his own writing process, she is able to modify her own "traditional" teaching behavior.

Using Student Ease with Technology to Extend Educational Parameters

Many students who have grown up with computers in their homes and classrooms easily embrace their computer work. They have little fear of the technology itself and often find it easier to "pull" information from the Net than from card catalogs or the *Reader's Guide to Periodical Literature*. Our middle school students found that the Internet made much of the information they needed more accessible. And they were able to use the time they may have "saved" to think about how the data they had found could be incorporated into their writing.

Creating New Experts: Letting Students Take Charge of Their Own Education

In addition, the use of the Internet in the classroom becomes a learning experience for teachers, especially in the way they can allow their students to become experts. Logan noted two things about her experience with Web page development. First, Wes, who created "Wes' Hippy Juicer Web Page," was so "into" Web pages that he eventually surpassed Logan's knowledge of Web development. Wes then began helping his classmates, as well as other adults in the class, with their Web site preparation. Second, for herself as teacher, Logan commented that

> I was extremely proud of the kids and myself as I had never taught Web page design before. I like the idea that one can do something active, actually create from scratch a *working* piece of writing you might say. I am glad you gave us the freedom to push that envelope and expand the writing process in the area of design. I now know that I can teach students to make a working page from scratch and get up on the Net.

Integrating Web-based research skills can promote student and teacher learning if we are willing to allow for new and innovative approaches to teaching with and about the Web. Most school districts have noted the importance of student fluency with technology, so teachers will need to continue to look for opportunities to connect computer technology with the everyday aspects of student education. Using the Internet as a research tool may be one fairly time-efficient way of accomplishing this goal.

Note

     1. For many reasons, this course attempted to accomplish more in three weeks than most of us would in ordinary teaching situations. The middle school students were with us for one hour and fifteen minutes for twelve days, and one of those was devoted to the publishing party we held during our final meeting with them. That meant that our young authors had to prewrite, research, draft, peer conference, revise, and edit in only eleven days. And while many of the adult students had taken a mini-institute on the writing process and how to teach it effectively through the Northern Arizona Writing Project, there were some who had little experience teaching writing but were curious about using the Internet in a research capacity. In addition, the university students worked within three- to four-person teaching units as they planned daily and weekly lessons for their particular middle school students based on the various writing projects the groups decided to create. Combined with this was the reality of how challenging computer technology can be, especially in lab settings.

Works Cited

Atwell, Nancie. 1984. *In the Middle: Writing, Reading, and Learning with Adolescents*. Portsmouth, NH: Boynton/Cook–Heinemann.

Cohen, M., and M. Reil. 1986. *Computer Networks: Creating Real Audiences for Students' Writing*. Technical Report No. 15. San Diego, CA: Interactive Technology Laboratory, University of California.

Cotton, Eileen. 1996. *The Online Classroom: Teaching with the Internet*. Bloomington, IN: ERIC Edinfo Press.

Hawisher, Gail, and Paul LeBlanc, eds. 1992. *Re-Imagining Computers and Composition: Teaching and Research in the Virtual Age*. Portsmouth, NH: Boynton/Cook–Heinemann.

Heba, Gary. 1997. "HyperRhetoric: Multimedia, Literacy, and the Future of Composition." *Computers and Composition* 14(1): 19–44.

International Association for the Evaluation of Educational Achievement. *Computers in American Schools, 1992*. Minneapolis, MN: USA IEA. http://www.socsci.umn.edu/%7Eia

LaQuey, T. 1993. *Internet Companion*. New York: Addison-Wesley.

Lucking, R., and C. Stallard. 1988. *How Computers Can Help You Teach English*. Portland, ME: J. Weston Walch.

Macrorie, Ken. 1988. *The I-Search Paper*. Portsmouth, NH: Boynton/Cook.

Merseth, K. 1991. "Supporting Beginning Teachers with Computer Networks." *Journal of Teacher Education* 42(2): 140–47.

Mike, D. 1996. "Internet in the Schools: A Literacy Perspective." *Journal of Adolescent and Adult Literacy* 40: 14–21.

Reinhardt, A. 1995. "New Ways to Learn." *BYTE* (March): 50–71.

Rogers, A. 1992. *Linking Teachers and Students around the World.* Bonita, CA: FrEdMail Foundation.

Routman, Regie. 1994. *Invitations: Changing as Teachers and Learners K–12.* Portsmouth, NH: Heinemann.

Selfe, Cynthia L., Dawn Rodrigues, and William R. Oates, eds. 1989. *Computers in English and the Language Arts: The Challenge of Teacher Education.* Urbana, IL: National Council of Teachers of English.

Sheingold, K., and M. Hadley. 1990. *Accomplished Teachers: Integrating Computers into Classroom Practice.* Special Report. New York: Center for Technology in Education.

Standiford, Sally N., Kathleen Jaycox, and Anne Auten. 1983. *Computers in the English Classroom: A Primer for Teachers.* Urbana: ERIC Clearinghouse on Reading and Communication Skills and the National Council of Teachers of English.

7 Foreign Language Resources on the Web: Cultural and Communicative Wealth on the Wires

Jean W. LeLoup
State University of New York College at Cortland

Robert Ponterio
State University of New York College at Cortland

Rationale

People studying a foreign language (FL) use language and cultural knowledge to make connections with other cultures and people in other lands. This idea of communication in an FL is a central and anchoring goal of the national Standards for Foreign Language Learning:

> In order to communicate successfully in another language, students must develop facility with the language, familiarity with the cultures that use these languages, and an awareness of how language and culture interact in societies. Students must apply this knowledge as they express and interpret events and ideas in a second language and reflect upon observations from other cultures. (National Standards 1996, 35)

How do teachers develop this facility in their students, and how do they provide them with "ample opportunities to experience the second language as it is spoken and written in the target cultures" (National Standards 1996, 35)? Certainly, the World Wide Web can become a means of making learning interesting while at the same time meeting the requirements emphasized by the Standards.

By accessing the WWW, FL teachers have a direct connection to any target language (TL), country, or culture; they also have a nearly inexhaustible source of authentic materials related to their focus of study. Hundreds of current online newspapers and magazines are readily available in many languages. Materials are not limited to text, however. Graphics, sound, quicktime movie snippets, and interactivity give Web pages their pizzazz and make the WWW a truly unique multimedia resource. Tourist information on thousands of foreign destinations is plentiful, fairly accurate, and amazingly extensive. The following Web sites feature easily accessible information:

- http://www.lashayas.com: provides photos of a luxury hotel at the end of the earth in Ushuaia, Argentina, gives a description of facilities there, and also allows you to make a reservation.
- http://pathfinder.com/@@bJLifAYAukdSw*q1/Travel/maps/ BANDARF.html: provides a detailed street map that will lead to the king's palace in Bandar Seri Begawan, Brunei, to the United States embassy, or to the Churchill monument.
- http://www.arctic.is/urval/Kot/NE1.html: enables you to rent a cottage in the Eyjafjördur valley in northern Iceland for a week.

It is also possible to hear live TL radio or television broadcasts of news, music, or cultural commentary. Two examples of news locations for FL teachers offer an idea of what is available:

- http://www.sv.vtcom.fr/ftv/: the television station France 3 provides a video of the evening news (national and local) each day along with the written text of the broadcast
- http://ondacero.adam.es/index_0.htm: lets you tune into a live radio broadcast from Spain

These sites provide streaming audio or video files that can be accessed by using RealAudio or VDOLive software, which can be downloaded from the Internet.

Clearly, using authentic FL resources on the Web can make the TL come alive for the students in the classroom as never before. They are exposed to TL input from a myriad of media, and they can experience the language in meaningful contexts. This is especially important because contextualized material can be more easily assimilated by the learner's cognitive structure than disconnected bits and pieces of information (Ausubel 1978; Omaggio Hadley 1993).

"How To's" of Using the Web

A wide variety of educational and technological settings can lend themselves, albeit in different ways, to the integration of WWW materials into the curriculum. Either the teacher or the student can access the Web individually as a source of information to be used in assignments or as a source of authentic materials to be brought into the classroom and shared. Groups of students can use this resource cooperatively, teaching each other about the technology and helping each other to comprehend the language that they encounter. A teacher may encourage students to use the TL to communicate among themselves as they work on Web projects either in class or out of class. Web-based teaching modules can even attempt to make the WWW the primary focus of an independent assignment or distance learning module. Whether the Web supports a presentation by the teacher or students, independent student home-work, or group work of any kind, techniques for accessing the desired materials must be easy enough that the medium does not distract from the principal goal of language learning.

To prevent the technology from getting in the way, the wise teacher will always have a backup plan for the inevitable times when the machines do not work. WWW pages can be printed ahead of time on paper or transparencies. Library books, magazines, brochures, objects, photographs, and other realia collected abroad are still valuable authentic materials that complement the use of the computer and should be available to replace electronic media when the inevitable happens and something doesn't work. There is a wide range of possible methods of Internet access in the American classroom, and the disparity between the electronic haves and the have-nots remains pronounced in spite of so much talk about the importance of ensuring access for all of our children. Yet, almost any situation can allow a creative teacher to exploit the power of the Web to connect students to exciting up-to-date resources.

A teacher with Internet access from school or at home can bring materials from the Web into class on paper or transparencies. Nevertheless, when Web pages involve sound or user interaction in addition to simple display, paper won't do. Programs exist (e.g., WebWhacker or FreeLoader) that allow easy capture of a complete page to a diskette, and then the page can be used by simply opening the html file on the disk from within any WWW browser. Browsers do change and behave differently from one another, so the exact details of how to capture a Web page will vary from machine to machine. A computer with enough storage space or ancillary removable media (Jazz or Zip drives) enables the teacher to store pages and have them readily available in the classroom. Live connections can be unreliable, so local storage can be a good idea. Access can be made easier by using bookmarks or by preparing a special WWW page for each class including direct links to pertinent resources. Of course, any time direct Internet access is used, teachers should be aware of the potential for students to waste class time accessing inappropriate materials and should always keep the students focused on the task at hand. All schools need to have clear Internet policies in place, reflecting the input and the collective responsibility of teachers, parents, administrators, and the students themselves.

Integrating the Web into Your Own Curriculum

The possibilities for using virtual authentic materials in the FL class-room are as limitless as the teacher's imagination. A key factor in determining optimal use of WWW materials, however, must be the relationship they have to one's own curriculum.

To determine the usefulness of the Web for your class, you might first gain some familiarity with the FL resources available on the Web. Without guidance, this can be a very time-consuming process. One initial resource can be found at the FLTEACH (Foreign Language Teaching Forum) homepage at http://www.cortland.edu/www/flteach. Many direct links to TL resources can be found there as well as numerous links to collections of FL sites that others have compiled. You do *not* have to reinvent the wheel. Take some time to peruse various sites so that you have a general understanding of what resources exist on the Web. Next, take a close look at your own FL curriculum and focus on how it aligns with the national standards. Then, select a set of objectives that especially parallels a goal area of the standards or a particular standard and review how you have presented the related material in the past. Finally, consider the resources on the Web: are there sites and information that would significantly enhance your mode of instruction for particular objectives? If so, brainstorm ideas for using these newly discovered materials to your advantage; then design an activity that will concomitantly facilitate your students' learning and add to their enjoyment. Some sample activities or projects are discussed below.

Sample Projects

Museum Visit

This French Museum Visit project asks students to plan a visit to two museums in Paris using information located on the WWW. This activity was part of a college-level distance learning class in French civilization, but a previous version of the project description was originally designed for the high school level. The course module can be found online (http://snycorva.cortland.edu/~ponterior/civ/dev7.html). The students were French majors preparing to become teachers. The objectives were numerous and were designed to support specific standards (see Appendix A): learning about getting around in Paris (2.1, 2.2), finding information about specific places through their online sites and interpreting the culture through this online information (2.1, 4.2), using search engines to connect to specific information about the TL culture (3.2), connecting with the TL community by writing letters of inquiry and dealing with responses (5.1), coordinating library materials with electronic materials (1.1, 1.2), communicating summaries of information both in writing and orally (1.3).

Students worked individually and had access to the Net through open computer labs on their campus. This was one of a number of online projects completed for the course, so students were already expected to know something about searching the Web for specific information when they began this activity.

The students received specific information about the circumstances of a trip to Paris for which they were responsible for organizing an outing to the Musée d'Orsay and the Musée du Louvre:

1. Discover information about the museums, about using the subway to get get to the museums, about the weather, and about places to eat.

2. Find an e-mail address for the museum and write a request for additional information.

3. Use the library to research an aspect of the online material that they discovered.

Paris WWW Visit

Tu vas faire un voyage à Paris avec ta classe de français entre le dimanche 28 avril et le jeudi 9 mai. Il y aura 20 élèves entre 15 et 17 ans et 3 adultes. Tu dois chercher des informations au sujet du Musée d'Orsay et du Musée du Louvre pour aider la classe à décider quand y aller. Le groupe voudrait visiter les deux musées le même jour.

1. Surfer le WWW pour trouver des informations afin de préparer les deux visites. (métro, musées, météo, restaurants)
2. Préparer puis envoyer un EMAIL à un des musées pour leur demander d'envoyer une brochure. (outline, first draft, final copy)
3. Chercher des informations supplémentaires à la bibliothèque. (bibliographie)
4. Ecrire un rapport d'une page dans lequel tu présentes ton projet pour la journée et ton raisonnement. (outline/ first draft/ final copy)
5. Présenter ta proposition à la classe (5 minutes). Apporter un support visuel (cartes, posters, images).

Figure 7.1. Paris WWW Visit

4. Write a one-page report of their findings.

5. Present their findings orally with visual support.

For use with less advanced and perhaps less motivated students, the same activity would require more detailed instructions, breaking tasks down into smaller components. For example, in a previous version of the activity designed for intermediate level students, the first task listed above was presented as a series of eight questions to be answered by students. Specific Web sites where the information could be found were listed so that the students' searching activities would be easier and more focused.

1. Où se trouve le musée? Près de quelle station du métro?

2. Quand est-ce qu'on peut y aller? A quelle heure? Quels jours? Quelle est la meilleure solution pour la visite?

3. Combien faudra-t-il payer pour le groupe?

4. Est-ce qu'il y a un numéro de téléphone ou une adresse électronique pour obtenir d'autres renseignements?

5. Y a-t-il des dispositions particulières dans ces musées pour un élève malvoyant et un autre qui est en fauteuil roulant?

6. Combien de temps faut-il pour aller d'un musée à l'autre? de l'hôtel aux musées?

7. Où est-ce que le groupe pourra manger?

8. Qu'est-ce qu'il ne faut pas manquer dans ce musée?

By thus adjusting the tasks to make them appropriate to the students' language abilities, the same authentic materials can be useful for language learning activities at different skill levels. Most students engaging in Internet-related projects for the first time will need a significant amount of support to ensure their success and to reassure them of their ability to handle both the computer and the real-world language use they will find on the Web.

Web-based activities tend to be rather open-ended, making evaluation an essential component of the instructions presented to students. For this project, the students were given rubrics inspired by sample rubrics developed by Wade Peterson, a teacher at Hampton-Dumont High School, Hampton, Iowa (see Appendix B).

Daily News

This activity/project was designed for an Intermediate-level Spanish class at a United States service academy. The average class size for this course was twelve to fifteen students; all had either taken the prerequisite language courses at the academy or had placed directly into this course based on language ability. Each student had a computer with Internet access available in his or her dormitory room. The primary objectives of the course were for the students to improve their language skills with a particular focus on their communication abilities and to gain knowledge about the history, politics, and culture of countries of Latin America. Two texts were used, one purely a grammar handbook and the other a reader with articles on Latin American countries, societies, and cultures. While both texts were adequate in their own right, the instructors felt that the course could be enhanced by utilizing Web resources. The goal was to have students draw on authentic materials from the Internet to increase their TL cultural knowledge and to provide them with information for various projects undertaken in the course.

One such project or regular activity was the "Daily News." Students were divided into groups of three at the beginning of the course; this grouping was their news team for the semester. Each news team was assigned dates for their "broadcasts" throughout the course on an alternating basis. On assigned days, the team gave a brief (around five minutes) news broadcast on a different country each time. The broadcasts were also "interactive" in the sense that the audience could request clarification and ask questions of the interlocutors; this also had an impact on the length of the broadcast and frequently depended on the controversiality of the topics treated as well as the vocabulary used. Each broadcast had to include three different subjects (one per person) and could include such topics as weather, politics, sports, social commentary, and entertainment. All topics for a particular broadcast had to pertain to the country chosen for that day by the news team. The format was flexible, and each group decided on the manner of presentation for their specific days. Generally, each news team member presented his or her news item for the day and pointed out why this might be of interest to the class. The "viewing audience" was then able to query the news team if they had difficulties understanding them.

The students found their information on the Internet and made sure it was as recent as possible. They accessed TL newspapers, magazines, weather, and tourist sites to gather data for their presentations. Examples are:

- http://www.mediainfo.com/ephome/npaper/nphtm/online.htm: this site—"Editor and Publisher Online Newspapers"—is a comprehensive listing of online newspapers from around the world. As of November 8, 1996, this site listed 1449 online newspapers on the WWW.

- http://www.vtourist.com: this site—the "Virtual Tourist"—is another good stepping-off point for FL students.

Students also learned to use search engines on the WWW effectively; there are many engines such as Altavista (http://altavista.digital.com), and they are quite powerful. The students enjoyed the "Daily News" activity immensely and often used it to showcase their creative talents as well as their language abilities. They were pleased that they could readily use authentic materials, and confidence in their language abilities greatly increased. The mini-presentations were frequently humorous, always original, and held the attention of their peers.

Evaluation of this activity was relatively simple. The news team received an additional participation grade for each day they gave a broadcast. Because the groups rotated days, this averaged out evenly over the course of the semester. A slightly more detailed and individualized evaluation could be effected using a rubric for each newscaster (see Appendix C).

The instructor can also evaluate listening skills on the part of the rest of the class by noting down one item from each portion of the broadcast and asking a brief question about it at some other point in the lesson. This mini-evaluation can be part of a participation grade or a small component of a larger listening skills evaluation. The instructors also noted egregious TL errors made by the newscasters as well as the viewing audience in the presentations and interchanges, and these grammatical points were addressed during later lessons when and where appropriate.

An activity such as "Daily News" is an excellent example of the effort to align one's FL curriculum with the national standards. The various components of this ongoing project—searching for information on various TL countries, using authentic materials as resources, presenting this information in a formal manner (i.e., the broadcast), discussing implications of the message in the broadcast, recognizing, comparing, and analyzing cultural differences—address many of the standards directly. Standards under the general goal categories of Communications (1.1, 1.2, 1.3), Cultures (2.1), and Connections (3.2) (see Appendix C) are exemplified by the different activities involved in researching, preparing, presenting, and discussing the "daily news."

Conclusion

The WWW is a tremendous resource for FL teachers in search of authentic materials, cultural information, and contextualized TL practice that can enhance their instruction. By designing and implementing activities that parallel the FL curriculum, are standards-based, and maximize the direct connection to TL cultures that the WWW provides, teachers make FL study a realistic and meaningful task for their students. Many of the most common concerns have been addressed above: ease of access, Internet supervision, evaluation of Web-based activities. Gaining the necessary technological acumen is not as daunting a prospect as it would seem to many. Several articles specifically written for FL teachers detail the information necessary to begin Internet exploration (cf. LeLoup & Ponterio 1995a, 1995b). A time investment is necessary, both to learn the technology and then to make it work well as an adjunct to FL instruction. In weighing the pros and cons of using Web-based activities in the classroom, the caveats are outweighed by the carats.

Works Cited

Ausubel, D. 1978. *Educational Psychology: A Cognitive View.* 2nd ed. New York: Holt, Rinehart and Winston.

LeLoup, Jean, and Robert Ponterio. 1995. "Basic Internet Tools for Foreign Language Educators." In *Virtual Connections: Online Activities and Projects for Networking Language Learners,* ed. M. Warschauer, 393–412. Honolulu, HI: University of Hawaii Second Language Teaching and Curriculum Center.

———. 1995. "Addressing the Need for Electronic Communication in Foreign Language Teaching." In *Technology,* ed. Richard Steinfeldt, 39–54. New York: New York State Association for Computers & Technologies in Education.

Omaggio Hadley, A. 1993. *Teaching Language in Context.* Boston: Heinle & Heinle.

National Standards in Foreign Language Learning Project. 1996. *Standards for Foreign Language Learning: Preparing the 21st Century.* Lawrence, KS: Allen Press, Inc.

Appendix A

Standards for Foreign Language Learning

Communication

Communicate in Languages Other Than English

Standard 1.1: Students engage in conversations, provide and obtain information, express feelings and emotions, and exchange opinions.

Standard 1.2: Students understand and interpret written and spoken language on a variety of topics.
Standard 1.3: Students present information, concepts, and ideas to an audience of listeners or readers on a variety of topics.

Cultures

Gain Knowledge and Understanding of Other Cultures

Standard 2.1: Students demonstrate an understanding of the relationship between the practices and perspectives of the culture studied.
Standard 2.2: Students demonstrate an understanding of the relationship between the products and perspectives of the culture studied.

Connections

Connect with Other Disciplines and Acquire Information

Standard 3.1: Students reinforce and further their knowledge of other disciplines through the foreign language.
Standard 3.2: Students acquire information and recognize the distinctive viewpoints that are only available through the foreign language and its cultures.

Comparisons

Develop Insight into the Nature of Language and Culture

Standard 4.1: Students demonstrate understanding of the nature of language through comparisons of the language studied and their own.
Standard 4.2: Students demonstrate understanding of the concept of culture through comparisons of the cultures studied and their own.

Communities

Participate in Multilingual Communities at Home and around the World

Standard 5.1: Students use the language both within and beyond the school setting.
Standard 5.2: Students show evidence of becoming life-long learners by using the language for personal enjoyment and enrichment.

Appendix B

Paris WWW Visit Rubrics (100 pts)

Inspired by Wade Peterson, Hampton-Dumont HS, Hampton, Iowa

	EXCELLENT	GOOD	NEEDS IMPROVEMENT	POOR
Class Time Management:	Self-directed, always on task, has all necessary materials, all deadlines met. 20 19 18 17 16	Usually on task, has necessary materials, all deadlines met. 15 14 13 12 11	Frequently not on task, often missing materials, one deadline not met. 10 9 8 7 6	Wastes time in class, does not bring necessary materials, some deadlines not met. 5 4 3 2 1
Content / Research / Organization/ EMAIL & Report:	Exceeds minimum requirements of task, material accurate and current, all significant information given, variety, clear & logical presentation. 20 19 18 17 16	Meets the majority of task requirements, material accurate and current, most significant information given, some variety, generally logical presentation. 15 14 13 12 11	Meets some of the task requirements, errors in accuracy, significant data missing, lack of variety, haphazard organization. 10 9 8 7 6	Does not fulfill the minimum requirements, inadequate quality of materials, insufficient data, monotonous, no coherent organization. 5 4 3 2 1
Presentation / Delivery:	Knows appropriate material well, shows self-confidence, is attentive to audience, is convincing. 20 19 18 17 16	Knows appropriate material while referring to notes, shows some self-confidence, is generally attentive to audience, presents valid arguments/ information. 15 14 13 12 11	Relies heavily on notes, lack of self-confidence/unprepared, not aware of audience comprehension or lack there-of, presents unconvincing arguments/information. 10 9 8 7 6	Inadequate knowledge of information, serious lack of self-confidence because of lack of preparation, ignores audience, does not stimulate interest. 5 4 3 2 1
Presentation Visuals:	All visuals accurate and attractive, appropriate selection to highlight presentation. 20 19 18 17 16	Most visuals accurate and attractive, appropriate selection to highlight presentation. 15 14 13 12 11	Visuals have flaws in accuracy, lack appeal, are not carefully prepared, inappropriate selection to highlight presentation. 10 9 8 7 6	Visuals are inaccurate, lack appeal, are sloppy indicating lack of preparation, inappropriate selection to highlight presentation. 5 4 3 2 1
Language Accuracy/ EMAIL & Report:	Uses well-formed sentences, excellent vocabulary choices, no grammatical errors. 20 19 18 17 16	Generally well-formed sentences, good vocabulary variety, few grammatical errors. 15 14 13 12 11	Numerous weak sentences, limited vocabulary variety, many grammatical errors. 10 9 8 7 6	Generally weak sentences, poor vocabulary, many grammatical errors. 5 4 3 2 1

Appendix C

Newscast Oral Evaluation

Newscaster _____   Date _____

Fluency	1	2	3	4	5	_____
Comprehensibility	1	2	3	4	5	_____
Listening Comp.	1	2	3	4	5	_____

                                                           _____
                                                            /15

                                                           Total

Definitions for Scale Intervals

Fluency
1 Speech halting and fragmentary; long pauses, utterances left unfinished
2 Speech very slow, frequently jerky; some short or routine sentences completed
3 Some stumbling, but able to rephrase and continue
4 Speech generally natural and continuous; only slight stumbling and few pauses
5 Speech natural and continuous; no loss for words

Comprehensibility
1 Nearly incomprehensible to a native speaker of Spanish
2 Mostly incomprehensible; some phrases comprehensible
3 Fairly comprehensible but many errors
4 Mostly comprehensible but many errors
5 Nearly completely comprehensible to a native speaker of Spanish; occasional words incomprehensible

Listening Comprehension
1 Newscaster does not understand question or comment from instructor or audience; needs and asks for repetition
2 Newscaster understands a few words but misses entire point of question or comment; needs and asks for repetition
3 Newscaster understands half of question or comment but does not grasp full content; may not ask for repetition
4 Newscaster understands most of question or comment; does not ask for or need repetition
5 Newscaster understands question or comment completely and answers

(Adapted from Omaggio Hadley 1993)

8 Building a Web for Literacy Instruction

Sarah Rilling
Colorado State University

Enikö Csomay
Eötvös University, Budapest, Hungary

[handwritten margin note: Step-by-step developing skills for accessing / evaluating electronic information]

Over the past few years, we have integrated computer-mediated communications and the World Wide Web into our classroom practices and developed an innovative approach to disseminating course information, conducting class discussions, and encouraging student autonomy in research and project development. Researchers interested in the application of computer-mediated communication have already explored and described the benefits of the new technologies (Gruber, Peyton, and Bruce 1995; Kern 1995; Warschauer 1997). Furthermore, the Web has been outlined as an important teaching tool in the sciences, especially for activities focusing on teaching scientific processes (e.g., dissecting a frog) (Bungay and Kuchinski 1995; Kinzie et al. 1996; Singh 1996). Computerized interactions and Web-based research are being incorporated into classroom practices in a number of contexts as the Internet continues to become more user-friendly and more available in schools (Allen 1996; DeLoughry 1994). However, designing meaningful learning tasks and materials for use on the Internet is a challenge which may require some technical support, but it is a challenge many are embracing as classroom dynamics change, allowing for communications and access to information at a distance.

In this essay we introduce two class settings in which computer resources are woven into classroom practices: a university first-year composition course in the United States and an advanced university English as a foreign language (EFL) writing course for teacher education in Hungary. We address how we are incorporating computer-mediated communications (CMC) and Web technologies into class practices to meet course goals, including

a. promoting English literacy skills,

b. developing collaborative learning experiences,

c. developing technical skills, and

d. fostering learner autonomy.

Rather than allowing the computer to dictate how we teach our classes, we have woven CMC and the Web into our courses to meet established program goals. While attaining literacy skills, our students are learning to do independent and collaborative research through our computer-enhanced curriculum. At the same time, they learn or enhance their technical skills, which is useful for future job competitions.

Our Teaching Contexts

Both the first-year composition program in the United States and the teacher education writing course in Hungary have clearly defined curricula, so our computerized activities enhance established peda-gogical practices. In the first-year composition program at Northern Arizona University (NAU), a mid-sized public university in the Southwest, we are using computers to augment library research instruction in all sections of the introductory composition course. The Web site created specifically for the composition program highlights library resources specific to conducting research at our institution (http://www.nau.edu/~comp/library.html). In addition to utilizing online library resources, the computerized sections of composition at NAU (currently 12 sections of 49, or approximately 20 percent) include computerized discussion groups (through a local area network, Internet newsgroups, or Web-based discussion groups) for students to report on their research progress, to discuss texts assigned for this class, to exchange search tips, and to receive input and feedback from peers and teachers.

In Hungary, teachers in the second-year intensive writing course at the Centre for English Teacher Training (CETT) at Eötvös University in Budapest have been experimenting with a collaborative learning approach to the development of critical literacy through Web-based research and CMC (http://jan.ucc.nau.edu/~ec23/acwrite.html). In this teacher preparation program, students build their English as a foreign language (EFL) reading by exploring the Web. Students further build critical literacy skills by evaluating newspaper and journal articles, and by considering artifacts of the target pop culture located on the Web. Online writing centers and other Web resources are visited by CETT students to help them improve their writing as well. Through CMC, our student teachers develop "interactive competence" (Chun 1998, 70) in their foreign language—English. In addition, the CMC component builds a sense of community in the classroom as students interact about their research projects and research processes.

We feel that adding computer resources to our teaching practices has enhanced our courses in a number of ways. In our programs, students

- gain access to content materials, and they gain practice in evaluating these materials;
- develop opportunities for collaborative communications among themselves and with us, which increases a sense of community in the traditional classroom as well (Rilling 1998);
- increase hypertextual reading skills and appropriate CMC behavior through guided practice;
- learn technical literacy skills and gain confidence in using computers for communications and as research tools;
- demonstrate autonomy in locating appropriate sources and resources for completing writing assignments accurately.

Our Course Goals

NAU First-Year Composition

At NAU, we familiarize college students with the process of conducting library and/or Internet research by incorporating Web-based searches into our composition program. Each student writes a series of essays, culminating in a critical appraisal of several research articles or essays surrounding one theme chosen by the student. Most of our students have limited experience with library research at NAU, and indeed many have not worked with computerized library resources at all. To help students, NAU's library site describes important concepts for library and Web research, such as specifying topics and accessing appropriate databases. Rather than replacing instruction provided in the classroom, this site serves to (a) repeat and emphasize key research strategies, (b) point to local resources and processes, and (c) provide links to search tools on the Web and in NAU's Cline Library.

Computerized sections of first-year composition at NAU meet for half of their class sessions in a computerized classroom where instructors can directly teach students how to access and navigate the library and other Web sites in order to locate materials for their final critical essay. Furthermore, students discuss their topics and research processes via local area or Internet newsgroups. In these asynchronous computerized class discussions, students exchange ideas about their research projects and give each other tips on fruitful resources. Follow-up discussions take place in the traditional classroom, where teachers create connections between research, reading, and writing, and between evaluating and reporting. Most instructors and students express satisfaction with the use of the computer for research practice and communications. Furthermore, reference staff at our library report that composition students are better prepared to conduct autonomous library and Internet research.

Advanced EFL Writing at CETT in Hungary

The Centre for English Teacher Training (CETT) at Eötvös University in Budapest, Hungary, offers a B.Ed. in TEFL (Teaching English as a Foreign Language) in a three-year fast-track program. During the first year of our program, students take courses to help them improve their English and to begin professional training as teachers (Brown 1995; Medgyes and Ryan 1996). During the second year, students participate in a two-semester-long, advanced writing course which supplements the students' professionally oriented courses in English teaching methodology and classroom studies. Our intensive writing course prepares students for a final, practical research project conducted during the third year of the program. We have integrated computer technology into our second-year writing course in order to complement the general program goals—fostering critical reading and writing skills, and preparing students to conduct efficient library and Internet research. The CETT prepares students to become competent English teaching professionals and lifelong learners. There are three basic aims underlying all courses in the program: (1) to develop English literacy skills, (2) to develop critical thinking, and (3) to foster learner autonomy. We have further specified these goals for the computerized version of the second-year writing course:

- to improve critical reading and thinking skills;
- to develop fluency in writing;
- to broaden research skills with library resources on and off campus;
- to give an orientation to general academic expectations with an emphasis on writing conventions (e.g., applying APA documentation style);
- to improve computer literacy on various levels (e.g., word processing; accessing databases on the Internet; using e-mail for basic communication; using the Web for research purposes).

These goals converge in the students' final writing projects for the course, emphasizing a literature review on a pedagogical topic and a preliminary report on observations and classroom-based research in preparation for their third-year practicum placement in English language classrooms. These project papers are meant to demonstrate proficiency in English as well as reflect critical thinking and research skills on a topic related to the students' professional interests. Our writing courses at CETT take place both in a computer lab and in traditional classrooms. Traditional class activities are grouped around discussions of critical reading tasks, writing processes, and peer revision. In the computer lab, the Web is used to teach research skills (e.g., locating information on a chosen topic and using proper writing conventions). Additionally, students discuss their topics and research processes through Internet newsgroups. In this way, participants can share research tips with one another and receive individualized feedback from the instructor.

Course Goals in Both Programs

In both programs, computers are assisting us in other ways as well. Through the Web, we are distributing course assignment sheets and other course-related information, thereby reducing the number of hardcopy printouts we give our students. In addition, we have been able to conduct our courses remotely so that we can attend professional conferences or take a working-maternity leave.

Using the Internet to Enhance Literacy Instruction

Background

In order to teach effectively with computers, we considered what resources are available on the Web in terms of technology at our own institutes. We also considered how users interact with the Web so that we could design tasks which would move our students toward independent research and writing. In conducting effective research, we make use of media (radio, newspapers, television), library holdings (books, microfiche, journals), and interactions with colleagues and classmates. The Internet provides a forum for combining these resources into one package. Vast quantities of information are available via gopher and ftp sites, and the Web provides easy access to many of these as well as to sites produced for the Web. Unlike other computerized information access systems, many of which incorporate complex and opaque commands, Web browsers generally provide an easy-to-use, point-and-click graphic interface, facilitating information retrieval of texts, audio bits, and visual images (still or moving). Furthermore, CMC is facilitated at many educational institutes through local area network software or Internet newsgroups. CMC interfaces have also become easier to use and are more accessible, and discussions through CMC support research and writing.

Interacting with Hypertext Environments

Discussion of literacy development through computerized instruction raises issues of how we interact with hypertext, or Web-like, environments. Research on how readers process traditional linear texts and hypertext (Dillon 1996; Foltz 1996; Watkins 1996) and how readers navigate hypertext systems (Dee-Lucas 1996; Gray 1993; Horney 1993; Spoehr 1994) indicates that successful use of hypertext depends on the task the user is trying to accomplish. When the task is to learn about a topic in general by using the Web, a search using key words to locate information about the topic can be followed by general browsing through associated links. When using a Web search engine, however, two conditions must be met: (1) the search must be narrowed sufficiently for the user to find the specific information, and (2) the search terminology and parameters must match the terminology and parameters used within that particular search engine. For example, if students looking for information about how Affirmative Action policies affect university admission policies use the key words "affirmative action" to search for readings on the Web, they are likely to find thousands of sites unrelated to the educational context. Students need to know how to narrow the search (e.g., add the word "education") as well as how to operate the search engine using appropriate commands (e.g., does the search engine use Boolean terms like "and" or "or" to connect search words, or does the search engine require special menu features to operate a multiword search?). The programs at NAU and the CETT provide such direct instruction to students in conducting their searches efficiently using Web browsers available at our institutes.

In a hypertext environment such as the Web, information overload can become a serious problem. As one student in the Budapest context commented, "I was very worried about this whole computer and Internet stuff in the beginning because I didn't know anything about it. I found that I couldn't do even the half of the tasks. . . But anyway, I got it at last!" This student's concerns support our claim that assistance is needed to become a skilled computer user. As students in our courses use the Internet, they receive technical support from us and their peers, and they receive support in conducting effective research. We developed tasks to move our students from specific searches to more independence in research. Information overload is alleviated through our task-based approach, as we provide students with specific step-by-step instructions and a safe environment in which to experiment.

Many instructors attempt to avoid the problem of information overload on the Web by creating self-contained Web environments. In a self-contained environment there are links only to other documents within that environment rather than to external sites on the Web. In the composition program at NAU, we integrate the self-contained information and materials at our site with guided external searches on the Web, since the only external links include Web search engines and local library databases. By providing specific information with few external links, our site provides students with practice in navigating hypertext while supplying information about conducting research. Students save time using self-contained sites as they learn to use the technology. NAU's site provides students with explicit instruction in conducting research in online environments, which facilitates the acquisition of critical literacy skills needed to succeed in an information age (Myers 1996).

Tasks Development

Our students need direct instruction on accessing and evaluating electronic information so they will be better prepared to meet the increasing demand for technical literacy (Blair 1996). We identified the following skills essential for using the Web to conduct research, and we have developed tasks around these skills: (a) visiting a site with a known URL (uniform resource locator, or Web address); (b) conducting focused searches without known URLs; (c) browsing with a purpose; (d) evaluating Web resources; and (e) downloading or saving information.

Students focus on the research processes of clarifying topics, seeking relevant information, analyzing the information they find, and creatively and accurately producing independent research projects. In addition to technological research skills, we also focus on:

- locating sources of information relevant to a given topic,
- taking notes,
- organizing diverse information,

- arranging information and ideas in a logical order,
- becoming aware of bias (Hester 1994).

Because of the varied nature of the materials on the Web, we have found it invaluable as a resource for developing critical reading and writing skills.

To get students started using the Web for research in Budapest, where students' general computer skills varied from none to highly proficient, a series of task-based assignments were prepared in which students summarize a news item accessed from a newspaper available on the Web (see Appendixes A and B). Students first visit a news site, which requires them to link to a known URL. Students then browse to find articles of interest. After they have read an article, they write a summary of it. During the process of writing the summary, students do focused browsing at online writing centers (see for similar applications Li and Hart 1996). The online writing centers serve as resources that these student teachers can use in the future as well.

At NAU, our library research Web site contains information on locating articles in periodicals and on the Web, and guided practice using this site enhances students' understanding of research processes and Web navigation skills. A brief one-page discussion addresses the differences between magazine articles and journal articles, thus assisting students in identifying the potential audience for articles they will find. The NAU library site also contains links to research tips (e.g., the merits of evaluating an article before reading it). All pages linked to the NAU library site are presented in index form, which enables students to review different sections easily. By accessing information on the research process through the Web, the students are actually practicing many of the research skills they will need in using other databases and online library resources.

At NAU and CETT, the students critically review information published on the Web. Through CMC and traditional classroom discussions, students are encouraged to evaluate and explain how the information they found on the Web is relevant to their research topic and how to analyze the viewpoints that the Web sites present. Through this research process, students learn how to select, analyze, evaluate, and synthesize various perspectives; formulate new insights through interactions with others; and experience intellectual growth (Kenny 1993).

The Internet as a Site for Collaborative Communications

Through the Internet, teachers can create alternative learning environments in which students' research can be shared and discussed through cooperative learning groups. Dörnyei (1996) claims that cooperative learning is a "highly effective classroom intervention, superior to most traditional forms of instruction in terms of producing learning gains and student achievement, higher-order thinking, and positive attitudes toward learning" (482). Collaborative learning tasks—including the use of study groups, learning teams, discussions, and jigsaw exercises—are effectively incorporated into our classroom practices. Careful task design utilizing the Web encourages students to learn not only from the resources they access on the Web but also from their experiences in exploring that information together with other students. Group discussions related to their Web searches assist students in understanding multiple ways of processing the same information. In short, our students learn from each other.

In both the NAU and Budapest contexts, we introduce Internet newsgroups or local area software to facilitate discussions with our classes. Internet newsgroups are similar to professional listservs in that all participants can post and read messages asynchronously through e-mail. Local area software, or software located on a computer network (often in a computerized classroom or lab), can also provide a forum for listserv-like asynchronous discussions as well as chat-like synchronous discussions. These CMC tools enable our students to discuss their research experiences, including the use of the Web as a research tool.

Advantages for using the Internet to extend class discussions about student research include the following: (a) learners are encouraged to be cooperative with peers rather than competitive; (b) learners acquire social skills by interacting with their instructor and peers online; (c) the teacher can accommodate individual differences effectively; (d) teaching can take place through inquiry; and (e) class discussions can continue beyond the appointed class hour. Our students are given the chance to cooperate and collaborate in new ways, irrespective of time and space. According to Hester (1994), "team learning begins with dialogue, the capacity of team members to suspend judgment and enter into genuine 'thinking together'" (5). Students' socialization processes and learning can be furthered by "thinking together" about their research projects through CMC.

Developing Learner Autonomy

One goal of our instruction is the development of independence in learning. We hope that students can apply what we teach to new contexts they will encounter. To create lifelong, autonomous learners, we need to encourage the exploration of new learning strategies as well as to enhance students' current learning strategies (Dixon-Krauss 1996). By conducting Internet research and discussing their findings through CMC, students learn not only how to be more independent, but they also acquire various learning strategies from their peers. Our tasks promote the students' gradual involvement in decision making concerning both the content of their research and their methods for conducting that research.

In Budapest our tasks move the students gradually from a highly controlled search on the Web to an independent search (see Appendix B). The first in this series of tasks requires our students to visit a particular Web site. Next, the students browse for relevant information in order to develop specific writing skills (e.g., paraphrasing and summarizing). Students then conduct focused and nonfocused browsing for resources related to their professional research topic. Finally, the students synthesize library and Web resources in a research paper. By introducing Internet research incrementally, the instructor can model appropriate research strategies. Moreover, the instructor can troubleshoot computer problems, so students gain confidence in using the Web as a resource. Through this method of inquiry, students gain extended practice in using the Internet for research, and they can discuss implications for these technologies to their future teaching posts. By building confidence and expertise in using Web technology, we are preparing our students to be teachers in an information age.

The series of learning tasks for the Web used in Budapest is supported by Starko's notion that it is the teacher's responsibility to gradually build independence in learning through course-related tasks (1995). This requires us to cultivate autonomy in the students by "deliberately making choices into situations" (Stevick, cited in Kenny 1993, 432). In instructional practices, this means that we first model appropriate behaviors. We then give learners opportunities to be members of a team where their roles are equally distributed, exploring Web resources and sharing findings. Finally, through conducting independent research, students demonstrate their understanding of the processes of conducting effective research. By allowing students to make decisions during their research process, we build an increasing amount of autonomy into our students as researchers and teachers.

At NAU learner autonomy is fostered in our composition classes by allowing students to work together in teams to initiate research projects. The team begins by considering topics which the class as a whole has generated or additional topics the team develops. The team then assists each individual in the group in selecting a topic that he or she will pursue. The team works together to design a research strategy for each individual, based on the strategies they learned from the library Web site. This includes generating several key words to assist in each individual's search process. Students then independently choose which materials to pursue. CMC discussions provide a forum for the teams to share ideas and resources as their projects progress. While teamwork is encouraged throughout the project, more and more autonomy is developed as students learn their own strategies for undertaking research.

Through the process of building independent learners, we are emphasizing that students need to: (a) identify and formulate their own learning goals; (b) modify these goals as the development of the project warrants; (c) work collaboratively with others to reach research goals; and (d) use learning strategies to monitor their own progress. Placing decision-making responsibilities on students requires a decrease in teacher authority and an increase in student responsibility for learning (Dickinson 1995); using CMC for classroom discussions may also decrease teacher authority (Cooper and Selfe 1990) and build a classroom environment in which students work collaboratively to solve problems. We find that by allowing students to profit from each others' experiences, students reflect a higher degree of skill with and a more positive attitude toward the processes of conducting research.

Conclusion

The Internet has enhanced the learning environments we are providing in our writing curricula. We have found that five features of the Web are especially helpful:

1. learners can access information and resources at any time, re-motely when available;
2. collaborative learning is promoted through CMC;
3. the learners and teachers are members of a team striving to meet course goals of improving student research and writing;
4. learner autonomy is promoted through both collaboration and independent research processes;

5. teaching can take place via inquiry rather than via information transmission alone.

For our writing courses, we have also found the Web useful for encouraging exploration and development of other research skills. Through guided instruction in Web research, we have seen an improvement in hypertextual navigation skills. CMC has given us the chance to allow student exploration of research and writing processes with each other and with us. We generally observe heightened motivation in our students as a result of using these technological innovations, and we feel we are encouraging the transfer of Internet skills to new contexts. By teaching students to navigate and evaluate products of the Web and to communicate through computerized interfaces, we are training individuals to use a variety of technological skills which will serve them beyond the classroom walls.

As with any innovation, we have noticed caveats to the use of the Web and CMC. Not all students use technology appropriately. We have found that developing "acceptable use policies" (Day and Schrum 1995) for our classrooms in conjunction with our students helps to eliminate misbehavior in terms of visiting inappropriate Web sites or in using unacceptable classroom language and behavior in CMC. We have also had varied luck in terms of student access to computers. In first-year composition at NAU, students have adequate access to computers around campus, and many students are fortunate enough to have home computer access with Internet connections. On the other hand, students in our teacher preparation program in Hungary do not have as much access to computers as their American counterparts. We therefore must devote more class time at CETT to computer use so that students can complete the research and discussion tasks.

While we had not experimented with CMC located on the Web at the time this essay was written, we look forward to incorporating this technological advance. Technical support teams at many universities and software development labs around the United States have created Web development tools for self-contained Web sites in which the teachers can easily post course materials (little or no HTML needed) and manage classroom interactions. CMC tools for both synchronous and asynchronous computerized discussions are integrated into these Web interfaces, thus enabling various configurations for computerized classroom discussion groups. We look forward to continuing our own growth in incorporating technological innovations into our pedagogical literacy practices.

Note

We are indebted to Jená Burges, former Director of Composition at Northern Arizona University; the NAU library staff; and Zoltan Lenart, Director of Information Technology at the School of British and American Studies in Budapest. Thanks are also due to Jená Burges and Bill Grabe for commenting on earlier drafts of this essay.

Works Cited

Allen, N. 1996. "Gaining Electronic Literacy: Workplace Simulations in the Classroom." In *Electronic Literacies in the Workplace: Technologies of Writing*, ed. P. Sullivan and J. Dautermann, 216–37. Urbana, IL: National Council of Teachers of English.

Blair, K. L. 1996. "Microethnographies of Electronic Discourse Communities: Establishing Exigency for E-mail in the Professional Writing Classroom." *Computers and Composition* 13: 85–91.

Brown, J. D. 1995. *The Elements of a Language Curriculum: A Systematic Approach to Program Development*. Boston: Newbury House.

Bungay, H., and W. Kuchinski. 1995. "The World Wide Web for Teaching Chemical Engineering." *Chemical Engineering Education* 29(3): 162–65.

Chun, D. M. 1998. "Using Computer-Assisted Class Discussion to Facilitate the Acquisition of Interactive Competence." In *Language Learning Online: Theory and Practice in the ESL and L2 Computer Classroom*, ed. J. Swaffar, S. Romano, P. Markley, and K. Arens, 57–80. Austin, TX: Labyrinth Publications.

Cooper, M. M., and C. L. Selfe. 1990. "Computer Conferences and Learning: Authority, Resistance, and Internally Persuasive Discourse." *College English* 52(8): 847–69.

Day, K., and L. Schrum. 1995. "The Internet and Acceptable Use Policies: What Schools Need to Know." *ERIC Review* 4(1): 9–11.

Dee-Lucas, D. 1996. "Effects of Overview Structure on Study Strategies and Text Representations for Instructional Hypertext." In *Hypertext and Cognition*, ed. J. Rouet, J. Levonen, A. Dillon, and R. Spiro, 73–107. Mahwah, NJ: Lawrence Erlbaum.

DeLoughry, R. J. 1994. "Stamp of Approval, Major Higher-Education Group to Explore Technology for Teaching and Learning." *Chronicle of Higher Education* (May 11): A16.

Dickinson, L. 1995. "Autonomy and Motivation: A Literature Review." *System* 23(2): 165–74.

Dillon, A. 1996. "Myths, Misconceptions, and an Alternative Perspective on Information Usage and the Electronic Medium." In *Hypertext and Cognition*, ed. J. Rouet, J. Levonen, A. Dillon, and R. Spiro, 25–42. Mahwah, NJ: Lawrence Erlbaum.

Dixon-Krauss, L. 1996. *Vygotsky in the Classroom.* New York: Longman.

Dörnyei, Z. 1996. "Psychological Processes in Cooperative Language Learning: Group Dynamics and Motivation." *The Modern Language Journal* 81(4): 482–93.

Foltz, P. W. 1996. "Comprehension, Coherence, and Strategies in Hypertext and Linear Text." In *Hypertext and Cognition,* ed. J. Rouet, J. Levonen, A. Dillon, and R. Spiro, 109–36. Mahwah, NJ: Lawrence Erlbaum.

Gray, S. H. 1993. *Hypertext and the Technology of Conversation: Orderly Situational Choice.* Westport, CT: Greenwood Press.

Gruber, S., J. K. Peyton, and B.C. Bruce. 1995. "Collaborative Writing in Multiple Discourse Contexts." *Computer Supported Cooperative Work* 3: 247–69.

Hester, J. P. 1994. *Teaching for Thinking.* Durham, NC: Carolina Academic Press.

Horney, M. 1993. "Case Studies of Navigational Patterns in Constructive Hypertext." *Computers in Education* 20: 257–70.

Kern, R. G. 1995. "Restructuring Classroom Interaction with Networked Computers: Effects on Quantity and Characteristics of Language Production." *The Modern Language Journal* 79(4): 457–76.

Kenny, B. 1993. "For More Autonomy." *System* 21(2): 431–42.

Kinzie, M. B., V. A. Larsen, J. B. Burch, and S. M. Boker. 1996. "Frog Dissection via the World Wide Web: Implications for Widespread Delivery of Instruction." *ETR&D* 44(2): 59–69.

Li, R., and R. S. Hart. 1996. "What Can the World Wide Web Offer ESL Teachers?" *TESOL Journal* 6(2): 5–10.

Medgyes, P., and C. Ryan. 1996. "The Integration of Academic Writing Skills with Other Curriculum Components in Teacher Education." *System* 24(3): 361–73.

Myers, M. 1996. *Changing Our Minds: Negotiating English and Literacy.* Urbana, IL: National Council of Teachers of English.

Rilling, S. 1998. *The Language of Composition Classrooms: Teaching Diverse Students in Traditional and Computerized Classes.* Unpublished Ph.D. dissertation, Northern Arizona University.

Singh, R. P. 1996. "Teaching Food Science and Technology on the World Wide Web." *Food Technology* 50(3): 94–99.

Spoehr, K. T. 1994. "Enhancing the Acquisition of Conceptual Structures through Hypermedia." In *Classroom Lessons: Integrating Cognitive Theory and Classroom Practice,* ed. K. McGilly, 75–101. Cambridge, MA: MIT Press.

Starko, A. J. 1995. *Creativity in the Classroom: Schools of Curious Delight.* New York: Longman.

Warschauer, M. 1997. "Computer-Mediated Collaborative Learning: Theory and Practice." *The Modern Language Journal* 81: 470–81.

Watkins, S. 1996. "Effects of Overview Structure on Study Strategies and Text Representations for Instructional Hypertext." In *Hypertext and Cognition*, ed. J. Rouet, J. Levonen, A. Dillon, and R. Spiro, 73–107. Mahwah, NJ: Lawrence Erlbaum.

Appendix A: Student Handout for the Centre for English Teacher Training in Budapest

Preliminary Steps to Access and Copy Information from the Web

These tasks increase students' Web skills by helping them to: (a) access an address (URL) known to the user; (b) search for specific information without knowing the address and browse in general; and (c) download information.

(A) The First Steps: Accessing a Given Address in Four Steps

Step 1: Look for an icon that says "Netscape."
Step 2: Click on it twice.
Step 3: You are now at the Magyar homepage in Budapest. Notice the navigation buttons at the top of the screen: Back, Forward, . . . Images, . . . Open . . . Click on Open and type in the following URL address: http://jan.ucc.nau.edu/~ts7
Step 4: Once this site is loaded, you can go up and down the screen as you can go up and down in a word processing program. That is, you need to click on the little arrow on the right hand side, pointing downward or upward, or by pushing the keys saying "page down" or "page up." Congratulations. You have navigated your way to a Web page where you know the URL.

(B) Searching for Specific Information

The basic tool you will use is the NET SEARCH button. Click on it.

a) Browsing in general

When you have a specific idea in mind that you would like to find out about, you can use this strategy. For instance, if you would like to browse around, seeking information about English Departments in Australia where English might be taught as a Second or Foreign Language, you can start with the section in the search site on Education, Higher Ed, Language, Australia, etc. . . . You will arrive at a wide range of possibilities to achieve your goal. Another example is if you are interested in the latest books available published by Heinemann (you are particularly interested in one, but you know only the title of the book, *Changing Perspectives in Teacher Education*), you can browse around at the Heinemann site as you can in the library. First search for Heinemann, and then begin browsing. You can find out about your topic more efficiently through indexes (Yahoo) or via search engines (Magellan, Lycra). You can start searching via topic headings or via the search boxes.

b) Focused browsing

When you would like to know about one very specific topic, go to one of the search engines and/or indexes (see above), and type in one, two, or even more keywords to this topic in the little box provided. For example, you would like to know whether there is anything available on the Web concerning the APA documentation style. Type that in and see where to go from there. Or for instance, type in paraphrasing and see whether the information that the search engine provides you is relevant to your needs. Maybe it is! Follow links which seem promising.

Homework:

1. Find out about youth hostel accommodation in San Francisco.
2. Find the names of major state universities for a specific state.
3. Find the library holdings of a university library. Do they have a copy of a specific book that you are interested in? Can you access the book from Budapest?

(C) Copying Information from the Web

There are two ways to copy pages from the Web: (1) File/Save or (2) highlight, copy, and paste into a word processing program. Don't forget to properly reference information taken from the Web. A guide to citing electronic sources can be found at http://www.cas.usf.edu/english/walker/mla.html.

Appendix B: Web-Based Writing Tasks for the Budapest Context: Advanced Academic Writing

Task 1
Write a summary of an article in a general area of interest that you could find on the Web. Find a relevant article, copy it, read it, and summarize it. For an article, visit the following sites: http://www.sunday-times.co.uk or http://www.nytimes.com or http://www.cs.cmu.edu/

Web/books.html. This last site provides a reference list of electronic books, journals, and magazines.To help you write a summary, visit http://owl.trc.purdue.edu/introduction.html.

Task 2
Write a summary of two articles related to the profession (EFL, ESL) that describe the same topic from two different points of view. For further help on how to paraphrase, quote, and so on, please visit the existing Online Writing Labs (OWLs) cited above. If you have problems locating further resources in this area, please ask for references.

Task 3
Write an introductory paper that could serve as part of your literature review on your chosen topic. Refer to at least three different sources. The topic could be either the one you have defined in Task 2 or a completely new one. Ultimately, based on your readings, you should create a new conceptual framework about the topic itself. While exposing your audience to your own understanding of the topic, refer to the resources (i.e., quote or paraphrase the text you have read). Professional teaching resources on the Web include these sites:
http://www.aitech.ac.jp/~iteslj
http://math.unr.edu/linguistics/tesl.html
http://www.tcom.ohiou.edu/OU_Language/Language.html

explore

Task 4
Write a literature review on a topic you identified in collaboration with your methodology teacher. Use APA documentation style and be careful not to plagiarize. Your resources may include material from virtual and/or other libraries and discussions with fellow professionals via the Web. You need to have at least five sources to draw information from. Review and critically analyze these resources, putting the information into your own conceptual framework. Excellent starting points for further resources include:
http://math.unr.edu/linguistics/tesl.html
http://www.yahoo.com/Education/Languages/
    English _as_a_Second _Language and
http://www.pacific.net/~sperling/eslcafe/links.html

III Supporting Collaboration and Interaction

9 Changing Writing/ Changing Writers: The World Wide Web and Collaborative Inquiry in the Classroom

Patricia R. Webb
Arizona State University

In the coming decade, as electronic texts, hypertexts, and hypermedia texts proliferate and as our pedagogical practices add electronic discussion to the oral dialogues that have been the staple of the classroom, writing instruction can no longer concern itself exclusively with words on paper. Nor can writing instruction continue to ignore the ways tools implicate and are implicated in the power relations, or more broadly the ideologies, permeating reading and writing acts.

Nancy Kaplan, "Ideology, Technology,
and the Future of Writing Instruction"

Kaplan suggests in the above quotation that electronic writing is changing what we do in the writing classroom. Writing is always already collaborative in that we cite each other's work, derive our ideas from interactions with others, seek feedback on our writing from audience members, and often ask others to write with us. Often, however, students do not acknowledge the collaborative nature of writing; instead, they steadfastly defend the Enlightenment notion of the isolated individual writing alone (Brodkey 1996), a view which limits the kinds of texts they produce and the types of writing activities they participate in. Even when presented with descriptions of other writing practices that diverged from this mythical image of Writer, students defend the Enlightenment author (Webb 1997). After studying students' vehement critiques of alternate writing processes and having unsuccessfully encouraged them to see writing as always already collaborative, I realized that asking them to *theoretically question* their own narratives of authorship was not enough; instead, students needed to be offered opportunities that asked them to *engage* in other kinds of writing behavior. The Web can provide these opportunities by helping to shift the focus from a centralized text and a singular author to a view of writing and thinking as part of a dialogic process in which we are in continual conversation with others. In this chapter, I offer a brief summary of the Web-based assignments that I implemented in an advanced composition course at the University of Illinois at Urbana-Champaign and point to the results that these assignments had on students' conceptions of authorship.

Web Assignments in the Class

Rather than basing my class solely around the technology, I decided to carefully integrate the technology into my already existing course goals. I would not have chosen to include the Web in my class if it did not help me to better meet my pedagogical goals: collaborative inquiry. And while I understand that the technologies we employ in our classrooms change the shape of our instruction and have effects that we have not always planned, it was important to me that the course still be driven by my goals rather than by the technologies' goals and limits.[1] What I discovered as I integrated use of the Web into my classroom, though, was that the Web was only one part of the equation. Though the Web did prove useful in helping to challenge students' traditional ideas about authors and authorship, it needed to be situated in a classroom context which explored collaboration from a variety of angles (the Web could not hold the whole weight of collaboration). I also had to make collaboration—the reasons for it, the way the Web helped with those goals, and the problems with it—an integral part of the class discussion.

I designed the course around the topic of space and how it shapes our sense of ourselves and our relations with others.[2] The syllabus outlines the theme of the course in the following way:

> This course will ask you to think about the importance that place/space plays in shaping our relationships and interactions with others. It will focus on the ways in which our conceptions of place (home, school, etc.) determine what our experiences there will be like. It will ask you to analyze and think through many different aspects of place (architecture, ambiance, activities performed there, etc.) that shape how we view those places and how they shape us.

Around this theme, I devised four units:

Space/place

Unit One: Exploring/Comparing Real and Virtual Coffeehouses. The focus of this unit was to introduce students to the space of the Web and to compare the information provided on the Web about coffeehouses to the ethnographic information students compiled about coffeehouses on campus. After completing these analyses, students wrote collaborative papers that compared their online cafe experiences with their "real" coffeehouse experiences. They cited Web pages as well as their observations to support their contentions.

exercises

Unit Two: Researching Popular Culture on the Web. In the previous unit, students had examined and critiqued the space of the Web. For this unit, I asked students to use the Web for research and topic generation. As a class, we watched *Blade Runner* and then searched the Web for sources that would broaden and complicate our understandings of the movie. Students then collaboratively wrote papers which focused on a salient issue about the movie and used the Web as their sole source of research.

? Pop. culture

Unit Three: Creating a Collaboratively Written Web Page. Students were asked to use their experiences using the Web to help them collectively author a Web page that would serve as a newcomer's introduction to important campus places.

Web page

Unit Four: Critically Reflecting on the Project of Web Page Design. After collaboratively creating their own Web page, students wrote reflection essays which examined the process of collaborative writing/work and analyzed the Web page they produced.

Since the third and fourth units were the heart of the course (and actively asked students to collaborate through all stages of the writing process), I would like to discuss how I implemented these units and what the pedagogical results were. The third unit, which comprised the entire second half of the course and accounted for almost half of the students' semester grade, required students to study the places that make up the space of their university, to collaboratively write about key places, and to create a Web site which is intended to provide the audience—incoming students[3]—with a general overview of these places (http://www.english.uiuc.edu/webb/infocamp). The class divided itself into small groups of two and three. Each group was responsible for researching information about one specific part of the campus. I divided the campus into seven sections and assigned a section to each group.

do thu with school

check

Individual groups toured different buildings located in their designated areas. They decided what the key places of these areas were and how to divide among themselves the researching of these places. Their research entailed three main components: real tours of the place, interviews with key people who had a shaping influence on the places, and virtual tours accessed by scanning Web pages that related to the places and to the activities pursued there. I provided them with questions to help them critically evaluate Web sites. Then, as a group, they compiled all of this information, wrote a section introduction which explained the basic theme of their space, found Web sites that should be linked to their descriptions, and presented this information to the class as a whole. The class suggested revisions and raised questions during in-class presentations and on out-of-class response forms. The individual groups were then responsible for revising their sections based upon their peers' comments. (The review process was threefold: Their fellow group members responded to each other's descriptions; I responded to everyone's descriptions; and the class as a whole responded to all the various groups' descriptions.)

Throughout this unit, we also collectively toured two sites on campus. We then discussed how we would portray one of those places—Krannert Center for the Performing Arts. I asked each student to list the key parts they would include in a description of the Krannert Center. Then, as a class, we looked at their individual responses and discussed how we would frame the portrayal, keeping our audience in mind as well as the demands of the space in which we were going to be posting this information. Writing about these places for a Web page requires different sorts of choices about language, tone, and structure than for a standard informative essay about the same topic. Many key issues arose during this discussion: space limits, focus, and purpose. The students argued that if we had a lot of space that we should definitely explain not only the five different theaters housed in Krannert Center, but should also explain the architect's motivation behind each of the theaters and their structure. One student[4] suggested that the Center be presented in much the same way as our tour was presented—from the founders' perspective. Others claimed that it would be more useful to our audience if we discussed Krannert's purpose rather than focusing on the founders' choices of marble and teakwood. Another student contended that since we were trying to reach first-year students, we should frame our discussion of Krannert around a "space-for-all" kind of philosophy so as to illustrate that anyone could go to see a play or listen to music while wearing jeans.

This discussion of how to present descriptions of places on our Web page opened many useful avenues of inquiry. Students began to realize how different writing situations require different writing practices. They began to see that the purpose of this class was not to teach them how to write once and for all; rather, the purpose was to illustrate that writing is contextually situated and socially defined. Far from writing alone in their garret, students were required to negotiate with each other during each phase of the writing process. One particularly interesting class discussion which highlights these negotiations focused on the concept of voice. Questions raised during this session included the following: Should the Web document appear to be written in one voice, or should it include multiple voices? Who exactly should be responsible for this document? How should the authors of this text be identified? Should the page adopt a purely informative tone, or could it also be persuasive? All of these questions led students back to issues of purpose and audience, two important topics that are often hard to explain in concrete ways in classroom-sponsored writing situations. I have tried in previous semesters to encourage students to write for a specific audience, but this discussion was by far the most engaged conversation about audience I had ever had with students. That they were newly familiar with the medium in which they were going to write and that they had critically analyzed its component parts, its focus, its possibilities and limits (in the first two units of the course) prepared them to have an in-depth discussion about how to write for this audience. As a new technology, the Web offered an avenue for us to have a conversation about audience that was grounded in specific, concrete space—students could point to exactly where their work was going to be published and used, and students had clearly and specifically defined their audience.

This discussion was richer because students had a conception of not only who was actually going to be reading their work but also why it was important for them to be writing it. In subsequent discussions about how to shape our page to meet our audience's *needs* and *expectations* (which may or may not be the same), students began to collaboratively explain why this writing task was important. When they were first-year students, they had no clue what all the buildings on campus were, and they often heard terms thrown around—the Orange, the Six Pack, etc.—but did not know where those places were, did not understand the use of the terms or the campus lore about those places. By including these things in their descriptions on the Web page, my students were providing incoming students with information that they wished they had had. They were sharing their expertise about this place with those who were inexperienced but desperately wanted to fit in.[5] Thus, writing was being undertaken not so much to fulfill a class assignment (though that is still very much a part of anything we do in the classroom), but more to fulfill a perceived need that they identified. They were more vocal about how to present this information once they recognized its importance, to them and to their audience. There was also a sense that they knew that their writing was going to be published and that others would read it besides me, the teacher, which seemed to encourage them to assume a sense of accountability toward it that I have not always seen students assume. I have not been able to achieve these kinds of discussions in classes where I only taught the essay.

When each group finished their revisions, we then came together as a whole class and decided in what order we wanted to present these various sections on our Web page, what links were viable ones to include, what areas needed more links, and which interviews to include and why. Once we as a group made these decisions, we enlisted the help of computer programming students to help us design the page to our specifications. After the Web page had been constructed, the class responded to the page in writing, and each group was responsible for soliciting feedback from our actual audience about the page. We then used the class's responses and the audience's suggestions to revise once more. After the actual construction of the Web page, I asked students to write an analysis paper in which they reflected on the process of describing the space of the university in this format. What had gotten left out? What dominant view of the university had we presented? How might other groups view this university differently? How had their positioning as insiders—students who had access to most of the spaces on campus (though some students had a problem with gaining access to some buildings and had to gain access through people)—shaped what they wrote? The two key articles we had read during the semester[6] had not only described places, but had addressed the stories behind the places, and had explained how the shape of the places excluded certain people while inviting others in. In what way did our descriptions of the places on campus replicate that? Did we find the campus to be a public space? A private one? And how was this reflected in our descriptions? In what ways did our descriptions—which were, in a way, meant to promote a favorable view of the campus—hide some of the social, political, cultural aspects of the university? In what ways could we have incorporated those aspects into our page? Who is the author of this page? How will people who hit our page know who the author is? What different ideas of authorship does the construction of this page suggest? This paper encouraged students to think critically about the project that they had just completed and to examine not only what they learned about the topic, but also what they learned about writing.

Before embarking on this kind of assignment—one which requires the instructor as well as the students to learn how to produce a Web page—instructors should consider how much institutional support they can get for completing such assignments. Are training classes offered? Are Web-savvy colleagues available who will share their knowledge? Is the instructor the type who can read a manual about something and self-teach? I was fortunate that I had had experience with other new technologies and knew that they could be temperamental but also very rewarding. I was also fortunate in that the university at which I worked had wonderful resources for learning about these technologies. SCALE (Sloan Center for Asynchronous Learning Environments) offered many technology demonstrations and workshops. Further, the computer services office on campus offered hands-on support. Including the Web in a syllabus does require extra work and expertise, but it is well worth it when its inclusion opens up new avenues of discussion, assists students with their research, and helps them to challenge their traditional conceptions of writing and authorship by encouraging collaborative inquiry.

Benefits and Problems

So, did the Web help me to achieve the pedagogical goals that I laid out at the beginning of the semester? Did the Web help students to engage in collaborative inquiry? Yes and no. As I noted above, including the Web in my class and asking students to write for the Web opened up engaging discussions about audience, writing, and texts. In past semesters, I have tried to frame discussions around these areas, but until these abstract concepts actually mean something to students, they will not engage with them well. Collaboratively researching and writing on the Web seemed to cause students to question their basic assumptions about writing and to bring to the forefront the tacit decisions they made while writing. But in order for the Web to have this kind of effect on my students' inquiry, the technology had to be situated in a classroom environment which encouraged collaboration in multiple ways. The Web proved to be an important part of my strategy to encourage students to question traditional assumptions about writing, but it was only one part of a whole class dynamic that emphasized this critical questioning. So, no, the Web did not accomplish my goals all by itself, but it helped. How did I determine that the Web did, in fact, help my students to achieve the goals I had outlined for them? I turned to students' reactions to the Web and the collaborative writing they produced to evaluate the effectiveness of the inclusion of the Web in my classroom. What I found was that while students had mixed reactions to the Web, their collaborative inquiry skills did improve.

Some students understood the connection between our use of the Web and the course goals. In a journal entry in which I asked them to reflect on the usefulness of the Web to their work so far, Greg[7] wrote

> I think I finally realized in class last Tuesday the reasons we have done the things we have done. I originally thought that all this World Wide Web review was worthless. I realize now how everything was leading up to what we are doing in this final project. That in order to write a web page one must be able to evaluate one. One must know what is valuable to the reader, and what is pointless. I am glad I devoted an effort to all these things which I thought were of no use, because I would have been lost if I hadn't. Now that I see how important it was for us to learn how to evaluate space, the web, and even in the context of the film, I am prepared to work on the final project and do it well.

For this student, my pedagogical plans began to fall in place, and he understood how the elements of the class built upon each other. At first he completed the Web assignments because they were required; as the semester progressed, however, he began to see why the assignments were important. He also identified the connection between analyzing the Web as a text and producing text to be published on the Web. Another student, Susan, commented that

> the World Wide Web has been useful to me in that it has shown me a whole new "world" I did not know existed. I had never used the Web before this class. I found it amazing that almost anything can be found on the Web. It was particularly interesting to see that there were coffeehouses on the Web. I found that I can use the Web to look up various information on many different subjects.

For her, the usefulness of the Web as a research tool extended beyond my class into other arenas in which she may be asked to research information. She remarked in an earlier journal entry that she had always heard about the Web, but had never tried it. Once she tried it, she saw how useful it could be for her research.

Yet, some students resisted the Web and argued that it did not add anything useful to the class. Susan, who recognized the Web's potential in the above comment but failed to find it adequate for some of her work, wrote that "I did not find anything useful that I could use for my paper on *Bladerunner.* Sometimes I was unsure of exactly why we were using the Web sites for class." Though she found the Web to be an exciting new place, Susan was still unsure of how to use it in her academic work. She, unlike Greg, could not correlate the reading of the Web with her own writing. Jean likewise expressed dissatisfaction with the Web: "I have struggled a bit with the assignments that deal with the Web. I don't use it much and I certainly have become more familiar with it through this class. But I still never seem to find anything really helpful. I think I just need to be more patient and more willing to experiment with it." Jean admits that the Web has not helped her writing very much, but she, unlike some of my other students, was not willing to give up on it. These students were among the ones who saw that the Web had potential to help them, but were still unsure of how to integrate it into their writing practices. Both Susan and Jean expressed disappointment with the Web as well as a willingness to try it again, hoping that they would unlock its potential. For these students, then, my class introduced them to the Web and provided them with some grounding even though I did not completely eliminate some of their doubts about it.

Other students were not as generous about the Web's potential. These students explained that they did not like the Web because it interfered with their usual writing practices, highlighting that this new technology asked them to include a foreign element into their practices and thus made them examine exactly what their practices were and why they liked them. Although this was exactly what I had hoped the inclusion of the Web would accomplish, some students did not see this effect as beneficial. Damon's response to the Web was particularly condemning: "The WWW has been a pain in the ass. I can't stand using it. I would much rather look the stuff up in a book. I enjoy reading and collecting books and find something appealing in the physicalness of a book. The web is so unreal. It's just 0's and 1's when you get down to the bottom of it." Thus, because the Web is not like a real book to him, he resists it and wishes he could return to the older technology of print for his research.[8] Adding to this theme of the Web's disruption of usual writing habits in harmful ways was Brenda's comment:

> The WWW has not really been much use to me. I do not like to rely on it as one of my sources. I guess this comes back to my formula way of writing papers and it has never previously been one of my sources. So, I think that I am one of those people who

> has troubles with change. This is what the WWW is to me: change.
> It also has not been useful to me in my thinking about the topics
> so far because I never really found one site that I had in mind that
> would help me tie everything together. I kept thinking that there
> would appear this site that I had been "searching" for. But of
> course, that never happened.

Brenda's comment highlights the desire for the Web to be the end-all answer to her research problems (which it is not) as well as her fear of adopting a new research method. Since the new method is not perfect and is very different from the library, she is uncomfortable with it and prefers to fall back on her formulaic writing procedure. As Brenda's and Damon's comments suggest, the Web *does* have a disruptive effect on students' perceptions of their writing process, which is, contrary to these two students' responses, not necessarily a bad thing. While these students expressed a dislike of the Web, they both used the occasion of its introduction into the class to think about their own writing practices and to define them specifically.

The Web supported collaboration and helped students to question their usual assumptions about writing, but the Web could not have done all the work itself. I also chose to focus class discussions on collaborative work. For example, before we began the Web page unit, we discussed the benefits of and problems with collaboration. I offered them Lunsford and Ede's (1990) characteristics of a good collaborator. Then I asked them to think about problems they were having with collaboration and had them decide which of those key characteristics was missing. I discussed explicitly what I meant by "collaboration" for each unit: Sometimes it meant that they actually sat at the computer and wrote the paper together. Sometimes it meant that they relied upon each other to provide research material. I also had several discussions with students during my office hours and through e-mail in which they expressed frustration with a certain collaborative practice and asked for solutions. I would then take these concerns and suggestions back to the class as a whole and we would discuss them. So, yes, the Web did help but not without student resistances and not without a whole classroom structure which emphasized collaboration.

Practical Suggestions

From my experience with using the Web in my class, I have identified a number of salient issues that other teachers may want to keep in mind as they prepare Web assignments for their own classes. In order to effectively integrate Web technologies into our classes, we need to:

- Introduce students to the technologies by demonstrating them in class. If the classroom is not a computer lab, then perhaps the instructor can schedule a tour of a computer lab on campus and have the lab directors or monitors demonstrate the Web to students. If at all possible, it is important to schedule class time for students to use the technology in the classroom. This demonstrates that the instructor prioritizes it (what we focus on in class gets our seal of approval), and it can also provide a workshop environment in which students can ask questions and can show how they are learning to incorporate the Web into their work.

- Integrate the use of the technology into our course goals. We should not try to make technology the sole focus of the course; rather, we can use the technology to support our own pedagogical goals. We will certainly want to discuss the technology and how it is shaping students' writing, research, etc., and to make those experiences a part of the class discussion, but to focus the class around the technology rather than around pedagogical goals seems self-defeating.

- Clearly explain to students the purpose for using the Web. We should make explicit the ways in which the projects we are having them engage in are questioning the traditional notions of authorship, authority, etc. Whatever goal we have set out to accomplish, we need to inform our students of the reasoning behind our choices. Galin and Latchaw (1998) raise interesting questions about this: "What is the nature of the course? Why is the technology being introduced? What can the computer do that cannot be done in other ways? What implications, consequences, and results might be expected in the computer-facilitated course?" (8). These are important questions for instructors to consider before incorporating any new technology into their classroom, including the Web, and they could be very useful questions to address with students as well.

- Determine students' level of expertise with Web technologies and adapt lesson plans to accommodate where they are. I devised a simple questionnaire sheet which I distributed at the beginning of the semester to survey their computer knowledge. I then used their responses to guide my teaching. For example, I found that most of my students were computer literate, but that many of them had never used the Web before or did not feel comfortable using the Web. So, I incorporated several days into my syllabus which allowed them to try the Web early in the semester, *in class*. I demonstrated the Web for them using an overhead projector, to give them a feel for the technology. I also devised a simple, clearly stated handout that summarized the instructions I had presented in class about how to use Netscape. They had a handy guide, then, when they went to explore the Web on their own.

[margin handwritten note: Collaborative searching]

- Ask students to work together—they can figure out the technology together and they can draw from each other's expertise. I often assigned Web site evaluations to be done collaboratively.

- Identify a number of textually rich sites which you can offer to your students as examples. Some of these sites should actually pertain to the topic you are discussing in class, but some of the sites should also help them answer writing questions. For example, I directed my students to our Writers' Workshop homepage (www.english.uiuc.edu/cws/wworkshop/writer.html).

[margin handwritten note: N.B.!! link for web page]

- Require that students critically evaluate Web sites so as to help them get past the "Wow!" response to the sites.

- Always have alternate lesson plans in case the technologies are "acting up." For example, during one class period I had hoped to use a multimedia cart to demonstrate on an overhead screen how to log on to the Web and to point students toward a couple of Web sites. On that particular day, the multimedia cart would not connect to the Internet, so I had students use the computers at their desks and I guided them through the same discussion. I also made overhead transparencies of the pages I wanted to show them, just in case of technical difficulties.

- Expect delays. Andrew Ross (1991) offers readers this humorous warning about technology and its tendency to break down: "Warning! This machine is subject to breakdown during periods of critical need . . . Never let anything mechanical know you are in a hurry" (1). While our computers may not be sentient beings who know when we need them the most and deliberately break down during those periods, they can indeed fail us when we need them the most. Again, plan ahead.

- Train ourselves. We should attend workshops to learn how others on our campuses are using the technologies that are available. A number of books offer suggestions about how to use Web technologies in our classrooms and also how to create a Web page.

Keeping these suggestions in mind and being aware of the available campus resources will help instructors better implement Web technologies in their courses.

Notes

1. For an in-depth description of how computer technologies and software embody certain ideological goals and limits, consult Paul LeBlanc's (1993) *Writing Teachers Writing Software*. In this work he examines the ways in which

the programmer's goals have a direct effect on how writers will use the technologies. And though he does not specifically address the World Wide Web, his concerns can be extended to this arena. Readers might also want to look at Ellen Ullman's (1997) *Close to the Machine,* in which she maps out the ways in which programmers' assumptions about users are built into the technologies' interfaces.

2. I recommend that instructors adopt a syllabus with a simple focus, especially if they are using Web technologies for the first time in their course. Keeping the topic of the semester simple not only provides students with an opportunity to explore one issue in depth rather than jumping superficially from topic to topic through the semester; it also helps to provide continuity when they introduce the complexification of the Web.

3. Although I knew that we could not control who would "hit" our page (i.e., access it), I wanted my students to have a clear sense of who their audience was so that they could practice adjusting their writing and their research to that audience.

4. All students discussed in this chapter gave me written permission to use their comments and writings.

5. This was the students' perceptions of their audience, which they drew from their own experiences as first-year students.

6. We read Sharon Zukin's (1995) "Whose Culture? Whose City?" and Elizabeth Grosz's (1995) "Bodies-Cities."

7. I use pseudonyms throughout my chapter when I refer to students. Again, I have received written permission from the students to use their writing here.

8. Damon's negative response to computer technologies was persistent throughout the semester. He emphatically denounced the Web's usefulness in his journal entries and disrupted our Interchange discussions by constantly questioning the usefulness of talking to each other via a machine.

Works Cited

Brodkey, Linda. 1996. *Writing Permitted in Designated Areas Only.* Minneapolis: University of Minnesota Press.

Ede, Lisa, and Andrea Lunsford. 1990. *Singular Texts/Plural Authors: Perspectives on Collaborative Writing.* Carbondale: Southern Illinois University Press.

Galin, Jeffrey R., and Joan Latchaw, eds. 1998. *The Dialogic Classroom: Teachers Integrating Computer Technology, Pedagogy, and Research.* Urbana, IL: National Council of Teachers of English.

LeBlanc, Paul. 1993. *Writing Teachers Writing Software: Creating Our Place in the Electronic Age.* Urbana, IL: National Council of Teachers of English.

Ross, Andrew. 1991. *Strange Weather: Culture, Science, and Technology in the Age of Limits.* London: Verso.

Ullman, Ellen. 1997. *Close to the Machine.* San Francisco: City Lights.

Webb, Patricia. 1997. "Narratives of Self in Networked Communications." *Computers and Composition* 14(1): 73–90.

10 Using the Web to Create an Interdisciplinary Tool for Teaching

Aijun Anna Li
SouthEast and Islands Regional Technology
in Education Consortium

Margery D. Osborne
University of Illinois at Urbana-Champaign

Greg typed "Whales" in the blank box and clicked the "SEARCH" button on the Web page before him. "It will take a while," Greg told his partner, Ben, sitting with him watching the "comets icons" coming down behind the big "N" at the corner of the screen. Greg and Ben were using the Web browser Netscape to look up some information. They waited patiently for the search results. About five minutes later, the search returned with more than 15,000 indices. "My goodness, how could we have time to go through all the pages?" Ben exclaimed. Ben and Greg skimmed through the first page and didn't find much information on white whales. "Let's try 'White Whale' this time," Greg suggested. This time the search resulted in forty indices. They quickly scanned through the list and clicked on the ones that seemed right. Finally they were able to find a picture of a white whale and a couple of articles, and they saved them for their HyperStudio project.

Given the recent impetus to connect schools to national, state, and local information infrastructures, teachers need a clearer vision of the impact network technologies will have on student learning and their everyday classroom practices. Why should teachers use the World Wide Web in classrooms? What does it do for them that wouldn't otherwise happen? We often observed scenarios like the one above in Mr. Ramme's fifth-grade classroom in Broadmeadow Elementary School. Greg, Ben, and their classmates learned to use Netscape and to research their questions. They created exciting multimedia documents which they shared with classmates, parents, and anyone else they could. The Web became an important tool that the students used daily. In particular, Mr. Ramme and his students used it to further pedagogical goals such as

- community building and collaboration
- researching and organizing ideas
- publishing and sharing multimedia products
- integrating subject areas and integrating these with writing
- critical thinking

The Web as a new technology—and one being publicly advocated for use in school classrooms—is being experimented with by many teachers. These teachers are aware that it is an information resource and communication tool as well as a teaching and learning space, but they find it difficult to actually integrate the Web into preexisting curricula and pedagogies. In fact, we would argue that the use of such technology involves a rethinking of curriculum goals and teacher and student roles. Research studies suggest that computer technology supports project-based authentic learning (Means 1995), collaborative learning, community building, critical thinking, and interdisciplinary teaching and learning (ACOT 1995). In this essay, we describe the means one teacher used to integrate multimedia HyperStudio projects into his classroom. We provide an overview of Mr. Ramme's pedagogical goals and how he was able to enact them as he and his students worked to integrate the Web into their curriculum. We discuss Mr. Ramme's perceptions of the Web and how he worked with the restrictions imposed by access to technology and limited classroom time.

The Setting

Mr. Ramme teaches at Broadmeadow Elementary School. It is located in Rantoul, Illinois, two hours south of Chicago and fourteen miles from the University of Illinois at Urbana-Champaign. A native of Rantoul, Mr. Ramme has never left his hometown and has been teaching in the same school for the past thirty years. During the time when we were there, the school had 256 students from kindergarten to sixth grade. About 40 percent of the students qualified for free lunch. In August 1995, Mr. Ramme was assigned to a new class of twenty-seven students who had some experience with Apple IIs but no experience with Macintosh computers. The classroom is equipped with six computers sitting along the wall behind students' desks: three Apple IIe computers and three Macintoshes, with one Mac connected to the Internet through a 14.4 K modem.

The Foundation: Equip Yourself

The first step Mr. Ramme took in integrating the Web into the curriculum was to become familiar with the Web himself. He learned what was available and what was possible to do. Mr. Ramme took every possible training opportunity he could in the preceding five years. Giving up his summer work painting, he spent all his break taking computer classes and going to workshops. Finally, in experimenting with developing a Web page himself, he found guides on the Web that described step-by-step ways to design a page. He also found rich information sources such as museums, libraries, science centers, and many lesson plans and educational resources.

In the Classroom: Preparing Students

With pedagogical goals and an idea of how he could accomplish them in mind, Mr. Ramme began to train his students. He started with small steps and was amazed at how fast his students picked up new skills. In fact, some of the students became so knowledgeable about aspects of the Web and hypermedia that they became leaders and helpers in the classroom—a role which fit in with many of Mr. Ramme's pedagogical goals. Mr. Ramme helped students to learn basic computer skills, become familiar with the Web, and develop Web pages.

To prepare students with the basic skills to use the Web and other computer software, Mr. Ramme installed Mac Tutorial and Mario Typing on the three Macintosh computers. He demonstrated to the class how to use the Tutorial and the typing tutor. Then the students were encouraged to learn and practice on these two pieces of software during their spare time. The tutorial was written in HyperCard and emphasized basic skills such as using the mouse to navigate and operations such as pointing and clicking.[1] These skills can also be reinforced by using word processing or any productivity programs.

In Mr. Ramme's class, he combined students' word processing activity with developing the Web page. Mr. Ramme had designed a preliminary class Web page in the summer when he was taking a Web publishing class at the University of Illinois. Now he wanted to involve his students in redesigning the Web page together, taking ownership as a class for the page.

To experience the community-building and information-sharing functions of the Web, Mr. Ramme provided his students with a template that described a biography profile called "Getting to Know Me." Every student was given a disk. Mr. Ramme showed them how to use Microsoft Word and how to copy files and save a file on a disk (see Figure 10.1).

This template served several functions. In addition to learning how to use Microsoft Word and how to save and copy files to disks, the students got to know each other within the class: they exchanged ideas about their favorite books, sports, and movies. Furthermore, statements such as "I know a lot about _____", "I am really good at _____", and "One thing that people like about me is _____" prompted students to think about themselves and their values. The exercise mimicked some of the qualities of the Internet and Web by allowing the children to create facsimile "homepages" and share these with a larger audience.

The next step involved actually using the Web in the classroom. This involved learning two important Web tools: bookmarks and search engines. Mr. Ramme started with his own homepage and the bookmarks he had created. The children learned to follow those and construct their own. Mr. Ramme emphasized that it was important to

---

Hello, my name is _____. I was born in _____(city), _____(state) on _____(month) ____(date), ____(year). I'm in the 5th grade and I attend Broadmeadow School in Rantoul, Illinois. The following information is for you to get to know me better.

      One skill I have is _____.
      I know a lot about _____.
      I am really good at _____.
      One thing that people like about me is _____.
      I am best at _____.
      One thing I like about myself is _____.
      When I don't know what to do, I _____.
MY FAVORITE:
      Game is _____.
      School subject is _____.
      Sport to play _____.
      Sport to watch _____.
      Food is _____.
      Place to visit _____.
      Television Show _____.
      Animal _____.
      Kind of Book _____.
      Hobby _____.
      Singer _____.
      Athlete _____.
      Season _____.
      Holiday _____.
If you would like to be my key pal please send e-mail to: meadow@life.uiuc.edu.

Figure 10.1. "Getting to Know Me"

establish the concept that the Web is a resource and learning tool (his bookmarks included sites such as NASA rather than DisneyWorld). As students discovered topics of interest and questions to pursue, they learned how to navigate search engines.

The Last Preparatory Step: Join a Class Project on the Web

Finally, Mr. Ramme had his class join an ongoing Web project: GeoGame. He felt this was necessary so that the children did not view the Web solely as an information searching tool but also as a tool that provided a space for creating projects. At GeoGame, each participating class is required to complete a questionnaire about their own location, including information about latitude, typical weather, land formations, nearest river, time zone, points of interest, direction from capital, and population. The coordinator of GeoGame collects responses from all the participating sites, scrambles the information, and returns the data to participants as puzzles for the classes to solve. Students, with help from maps, atlases, and other reference materials, match the description of each location (based on the questionnaire) with the name of the corresponding city. The pedagogical goals of this contest are to help students develop critical thinking skills, improve their ability to organize information, and search for information, as well as have opportunities to communicate and work with students at other locations and develop leadership skills acting as project coordinators.

The Goal: Develop a Multimedia Project

Mr. Ramme had been thinking of a way to help his students make connections between different subjects: reading, writing, science, social science, music, and art. He also wanted parents and the community to become involved and to know what the students were doing in his class. For these reasons, he decided that his students needed to make a multimedia presentation using HyperStudio. While Mr. Ramme wanted his students to design Web pages to publish their own work, he hesitated for two reasons. First, the classroom only had one modem (14.4 k) connection to the Web server, and transferring files between the server and the computer was very slow. It was physically impossible for twenty-seven students to work simultaneously on the homepage. Second, he did not want his students to be lost in HTML scripting. Instead, he introduced HyperStudio, a multimedia authoring program.

Like other multimedia authoring software, HyperStudio offers the ability to bring together text, sound, graphics, and video. It provides

[handwritten margin note: NB: What, if you don't have good connections?]

its own accessible approach to collect data from the Internet, create and edit QuickTime movies, import images with AV Macs or the QuickTake camera, and use graphics and sound that can be imported or created within the program. Students can research a topic, gain knowledge, organize what they learn, and represent their knowledge as they actively create a project. The activities also help students to achieve goals that include developing higher-order thinking skills and interpersonal skills, learning content by engaging multidisciplinary (interdisciplinary) subjects, developing technical competence, and increasing media literacy (Agnew, Kellerman, and Meyer 1996).

To train all twenty-seven of his students on HyperStudio with seven computers (Mr. Ramme added his own laptop) was a daunting task. As an example, Anna observed Mr. Ramme train his students on "adding a sound button" on the computers. He paired the students up and gave each pair a copy of the HyperStudio tutorial. Mr. Ramme patiently took the students step by step going through the tutorial. Partners helped each other, one reading the steps from the tutorial and the other trying to follow on the computer. Ben and a few other students figured out how to add sound cards and went on to learn how to add video clips. Within two weeks, all the students were trained. "It was really amazing that the students could learn so fast. Now they even know more than me," Mr. Ramme told us proudly after the training was finished.

The students were very interested in the special features and possibilities of HyperStudio. They used animation, movie, sound, and graphics, and they chose their own topics and identified research that interested them. Mr. Ramme also told them that they were to present their individual projects not only to the class but also to their parents and the school board. Most students quickly decided what they were going to do, found their own partners, and set out to work enthusiastically. The students searched for every source they could find to obtain the information for their projects. They searched both the school library and local library, bookstores, and the Web. The Web was their major and favorite source of information. This multimedia production proved to be a design and technical challenge as well as substantive in individual project content. Students had to organize the information they had gathered, choose what to include in their projects, and decide the form of presentation. Finally, they had to grapple with the technology needed. When they designed the buttons, they discovered that they could make buttons which would play sounds or a piece of music; they could also make an animated character dance across the screen. They became immersed in figuring out such technical problems and work-able solutions in the context of creating their presentations—a dialectic process of mediation between the real and ideal inherent in all designs.

For example, Ben was very fond of jets. He already had collected pictures of all kinds of jets, and had an aviation journal too. Wanting to integrate his personal interest into this project, he found Keegan to work with, and together they read much information on jets in order to write their story. In addition they found pictures and sound files on the Web. To create the animation of a jet taking off, he and Keegan integrated these files, experimenting with buttons and reading through the tutorial several times. Finally they were able to use seven cards to make the effect of a jet taking off. Ben, a quiet boy, emerged as the HyperStudio expert of the class.

The children's projects formed and emerged as their skills using HyperStudio and the Web improved. The activity helped "to motivate kids that don't experience such success in another area," Mr. Ramme commented, "because even though some students might be very quiet and shy in the class, they can develop a sense of accomplishment and a sense of success. They feel good about themselves because they might be able to help someone else on the computer . . . while someone else might be good in sports or good in music, they might be good on the computer."

The HyperStudio project was a success. The projects were presented as planned to parents and the Rantoul school board. Students' enthusiasm and commitment were evident throughout the project. The boundaries between traditional subject areas—science, writing, reading, social science, health, and spelling—disappeared when the Web and HyperStudio were used. The students learned to be active learners. They asked their own questions, designed their own projects, learned problem-solving skills, and they proved to be very responsible. Mr. Ramme's role changed from instructor to facilitator and manager. As Mr. Ramme said, "They know that you don't really have to know everything about something as long as you know where to find the answer. They know where they can go and how to find the answer."

Reflections and Recommendations

Mr. Ramme, a fifth-grade teacher in rural Illinois, has found creative ways of using the Web with limited classroom resources. In the past two years, we have had experience observing and working with teachers such as Mr. Ramme at different schools from the Southeast to Midwest. We conclude with some recommendations from the words and experiences of Mr. Ramme for integrating technology and the Web into the classroom in complex and creative ways.

Prepare and Equip Yourself

"Teachers have to make themselves ready, find time to get the training," Mr. Ramme said. Teachers are the ones who oversee what is happening in the classroom, and their enthusiasm will definitely affect the students. It takes a commitment from the teacher to see beyond the inevitable problems which accompany innovations. Teachers who want to integrate the Web into their curriculum have to make a commitment to learn how to use the Web themselves both in preparation and as the classroom project unfolds. All problems cannot be anticipated. Teachers may go to a workshop or learn from a colleague or their own students. To be open-minded is the key.

Be Flexible in Terms of Classroom Schedule

Usually Web-related multimedia projects take longer blocks than forty-five minutes. As Mr. Ramme was teaching in a self-contained classroom, he had the advantage of being able to have a flexible schedule except during those times earmarked for P.E. or music. As for teachers who might be concerned with not being able to "cover the curriculum" and teach all the units, Mr. Ramme commented, "You cannot be so concerned and so obsessed about achievement test scores and coverage. A lot of pressure is being put on us teachers to make sure that we are accountable, that the students have obtained so much knowledge before they are passed on. I don't want to undermine [this goal] and say that it is not important. [. . .] You use flexibility in your teaching. When the students are engaged in learning other activities, the gaps will be filled . . . learning gaps will be filled. These kids are taking the knowledge [and] it is rounding their education more."

Take Small Steps and Build on Them

Suppose you have your computers, Internet access, and your new group of students, where do you start? "You would want to start with a program, maybe a software program that is compatible with what you are [planning to do]. A lot of times there are math games, there is spelling software, where the students can tie in to where their curriculum is and spend time on that. And then from there the person would want to be comfortable with a word processor, Microsoft Word or other word processing program where the students can type. You can start simple with some simple software and let the kids build on that. . . . Begin simple and then as we build on that, show them the Internet things. Then we are building into the HyperStudio."

Use Bookmarks and Assignments to Guide

Giving students assignments to look up specific information gives the students a starting point. Let students have some experience searching for information using reference software such as Compton Encyclopedia or Encarta so they understand what a keyword search is. GeoGame, which Mr. Ramme used, sets a specific and clear task. Some good locations for such sites are found at http://www.citynet.com.

Changing Pedagogy and Teacher's Role

If a classroom already uses collaborative groups and learning centers, integrating the Web will be an easier transition. It takes collaboration between students and the teacher to produce multimedia presentations and design Web pages. The teacher's role is no longer as authority since the purpose of such activities is to enable the child, in process and substance, to articulate and solve problems. As Mr. Ramme discovered, the teacher becomes a facilitator involved in and promoting student learning.

Note

1. If using a Windows machine, it might be a good idea to start students with a tutorial on Windows. Microsoft has put on the Web some good tutorial materials for some of the Microsoft programs such as Microsoft Word. These materials can be accessed through the Microsoft homepage: http://www.microsoft.com.

Works Cited

Agnew, P. W., A. Kellerman, and J. Meyer. 1996. *Multimedia in the Classroom.* Needham Heights, MA: Allyn and Bacon.

Dwyer, D. 1994. "Apple Classrooms of Tomorrow: What We've Learned." *Educational Leadership* 51(7): 4–10.

Means, B. & Olson, K., (1994) "The Link between Technology and Authentic Learning." *Educational Leadership* 51(7): 15–19.

11 Alewives

Katherine M. Fischer
Clarke College

A lewives, the small fish of the Great Lakes, have always been a distasteful, nearly repugnant topic of conversation among the shore dwellers of Lakes Michigan, Superior, and Erie. Alewives are not large or tasty enough to serve at those wonderful fish frys so traditional in the villages dotting the inland coast, but it is not until they die that they become a serious problem. Nonetheless, I've always had an affection for these cast-offs. As a child growing up along Lake Michigan dunes, I used these fishies as spoons to stir my sand cakes and their stiffened bodies served as flags for my castles. Although my mother and father tried to teach our dog Rusty to refrain from leaving dead alewives on the doorstep, I silently cheered his offerings and slipped him treats to reward his doggie appreciation of the finer things in life.

As I see it now, the main problem most people have with alewife carcasses is that they fail to perform like live fish. Toss them in a water tank and they sink to the bottom. When dead, they stink, smelly beyond even a hound's indulgence. And to see them stiff on the beach with vacant eye sockets is more than most people can humanely tolerate (thinking more about the fish than the gulls, of course). Now, if they had been alive, if they had acted like the fish we were "used to," those that pleased us by surfacing to feed, or gathering in schools darting in and out of the seaweed, well, that would have been an entirely different story altogether. But unlike those who found them bothersome and repulsive, Rusty and I did not expect them to act like alive things. We appreciated them for what they were and for what they were *not*.

My first dives into using the Web with students remind me of how most people regard those postmortem alewives. I approached the beach with the wrong expectations. Going to the Web with students was like going on another fishing trip to just another great lake of information. Granted, the water was warmer, students *liked* surfing the Web more than they *liked* surfing the library stacks or the *Reader's Guide to Periodical Literature*, but I had the sneaking suspicion I was trying to make carcasses swim when, indeed, the Web has wonderful properties all its own which we were ignoring. I directed students to search the

Web as a fancy sort of encyclopedia, much as I required them to search the college library—for information retrieval which could be used either as background in literature classes or in writing classes where students could easily access subjects using simple keyword searches. We went for the wrong reasons. Although they did not take advantage of the Web's fuller capabilities, these were worthwhile experiences.

Working now with first-year composition classes with access to the Web, however, I move beyond this level and suggest that students take advantage of ways the virtual environment allows and encourages their interaction. Why use the Web if all it does is poorly replicate what other sources and media already do well? Of course, some say that the main reason to use the Web with our classes is motivational: it holds students' interest. Although there is some merit to this belief, given that many of our students belong to a generation that cut its teeth on MTV, I believe there are far better reasons to incorporate Web technology. Whether for literature or composition classes, Web sites that invite readers to add information, to comment on the sites, or to e-mail authors seem to offer students a more profound ability to interact with information than does print. While students may write the author of a book or phone the writer of a journal article, chances are that the effort and cost will prevent most from doing so. And without the easy capacity for immediate response available in today's electronic writing environments, it is unlikely that learners would receive a timely response to their letters or phone messages. As much as the Web has to offer students and teachers in writing classes, it is the classes outside this skill area, however, where I found the most need for appreciating the properties of fish that do not swim like other fish.

In my first literature classes using the Web, students located search engines that led them down colorful corridors full of slick presentations mixing text, video clips, and sound bits with the enticing language of the advertising world with their topics, but we really were not using the medium in any significantly different ways than how we used print sources and their counterparts (microfiche, Dialog, First Search, and ERIC).

Quite by accident, my students in the upper-division science fiction class and I stumbled upon the more interactive features of the Web. The group researching *Slaughterhouse-Five* found not only reliable and up-to-date information on Kurt Vonnegut (http://www.duke.edu/~crh4/vonnegut/s-five.html, http://www.duke.edu/~crh4/vonnegut/chronology.html), but also chanced upon a link that led them to the Web pages of senators involved in legislation regarding the Vietnam

War. Through a flurry of e-mail exchanges between students and senators, students began seeing the case of Billy Pilgrim as being more than just the stuff of literary study. Literature was no longer merely an academic subject; it had become a social and political involvement for students in this course. Given my own goal that the study of literature be an energetic undertaking that relates strongly to our lived existence, I came to see the Web as a powerful tool in bringing to life the texts on the page, even those written decades and centuries ago.

More recently, my students and I began swimming upstream by focusing on using the capabilities unique to the medium. Our required introductory class, Approaches to Literature, is composed for the most part of first- and second-year students. Clarke College is a small school with tidy classes of twenty to twenty-five students and a great deal of student-teacher interaction. It is an informal place; everyone in the college from the president to administrative staff to faculty to maintenance crew to students is on a first-name basis. Students in this class study poetry, drama, and fiction through a thematic approach.

I teach literature with two considerable and unmovable biases. One is that the class is successful only if the literature "breathes" for the students. Only if it rises off the pages of that heavy inky textbook and whispers some siren call to each student am I satisfied. Dan Morgan (1993) refers to this as a "humanistic, student-centered approach" (495) which encourages students new to the discipline of literary interpretation to analyze, comment, disagree, initiate, and fully respond to readings. Although I remind students constantly to return to the text for evidence for their assertions, I want them to move beyond the nearly biological dissection of a piece, the subtraction and addition of parts into neat sums of literature. I encourage them to see that although we may dissect the fish, we will never put it back together quite the same way because in the dissection, we will add something, we will see something, we will *feel* something.

The other bias is my persistent belief that students need to write a great deal in a literature class in order to interact with the text and to reflect on what meaning readings have, what impact there might be on their own lives. As Charles Bazerman (1994) suggests, writing is central to learning and key to students being involved in knowledge-making within a course of study. As I considered designing an assignment connecting the Web with the first thematic unit of literature, no longer satisfied with simply repeating on the Web what we had already done with traditional sources, I focused on those characteristics I found unique: (1) the immediacy the source offered—new information can appear instantly and old can be modified without going through the physical obstacles facing information in print formats; (2) the multifarious ways of leading readers/viewers to more associative thinking than to linear first-to-last ways of reasoning; (3) the immense potential for interaction with text and with Web authors. It was the last characteristic that I found particularly attractive given my two biases. This one, I was sure, would afford students the opportunity to write more and to write to a "real" audience. Pinocchio and the Velveteen Rabbit would have nothing on them, I hoped. They would be able to feel the literature inhale and exhale.

I wanted to keep the assignment very open so that students could follow where the medium led them in their searches and resulting essays. (Only later did I realize that this was the wrong bait.) I asked them to consider the literature of the first unit, which focused on the theme of family and self-identity. In class we brainstormed issues found in readings like Edward Albee's "The Sandbox," Amy Tan's "Two Kinds," Theodore Roethke's "My Papa's Waltz," David Michael Kaplan's "Doe Season," and Lorrie Moore's "How to Talk to Your Mother, (Notes)," all selections from our anthology (Kirszner and Mandell 1994).[1] Students listed topics including treatment of the elderly, coming to terms with one's gender, sibling rivalry, child abuse, the immigrant family experience, and so on. I handed out guidelines for the paper: (1) The thesis idea of the essay should situate the literature and themes of the first unit in the context of 1990s "real life"; (2) Students were to select two readings from the unit which would serve as the basis of their essays; (3) They were to use three to five Web sources that related to these two selections in a way that linked them with current events or 1990s advances in the field; (4) The project must include at least one interactive Web activity in the process. This last requirement was crucial to the project, I felt.

Marshall Gregory (1997) suggests that one of the most important outcomes of literary studies is that readers undergo "vicarious experiences of the human condition far vaster than any of them could ever acquire on the basis of luck and first-hand encounters" (54). With the capability for interaction with Web writers and creators, I wondered if students might move beyond "vicarious." They were fairly good and specific guidelines when coupled along with the specifications of page length, format, and so on, I thought. So why did the project nearly fail?

Bring on the Carcasses

I knew early that we were in trouble when one student showed up at my office door frustrated because "the stuff I found on the Web is awfully chauvinistic." She was attempting to deal with gender identity within the context of the family, but her Web sites, mainly the products of fundamentalist and conservative groups, supported raising children according to stereotyped gender roles. "I just cannot find any reliable sources," she said, echoing the words of my colleagues who had pronounced the Web a poor place to fish for information because they expected it to taste like print sources used in traditional research. I realized that students educated in one main way of using information, i.e., as a basis for logical thought and proof, were hard-pressed to deal with sites that wouldn't swim like live fish. In this student's immediate case, we talked about using the Web information in her paper more as primary research, that is, as corroborating evidence of how people often stereotype gender even in the 1990s. We also discussed using different search words, acknowledging that various browsers indexed sites in far more haphazard ways than did traditional indexes for sources in print. She returned to the Web. I returned to thinking further about alewife cadavers.

I borrowed the advice of colleagues in my online writing and teaching group. I was asking students to see connections between apparently disparate things, they pointed out:

> Students are almost never asked to do this in academia. They take courses that are separated by many dividers—faculty who teach, the departments that offer them, genre, time periods. We teach students to put things in the proper place in their notebooks, which separates their knowledge into units. And you are asking them to make connections between things that are even more re-moved because at least one of them, the Web site, is non-academic. (Steve Newmann, personal communication)

I realized that regardless of course or subject area, students needed to be taught new thinking skills in order to deal with the Web. In order to help them make such associative connections, I asked students to consider two news articles appearing on the same page. One was about the thirteen-year-old daughter of a New York tycoon who had been missing but was found in a sleazy hotel on the lower East Side dead from an overdose of drugs. The other was about Oregon's change in legislation making possession of drugs a misdemeanor rather than a felony. Students quickly realized how the two articles, appearing side by side, resulted in a sort of editorializing about drug legislation.

Furthermore, I modified an exercise from the *Universal Traveler* (Jim Bagnall and Don Koberg) in which students listed attributes of their literary selections and issues at the core of their essays. They made another list of attributes of the Web sites they had found and then began connecting the two by looking at alternate and embedded qualities. Finally, I asked them to move on to "invention" where they began making connections between the two.

With these two activities aimed at helping them envision the ability of the Web to stir ideas and associative thinking—just as dead alewives may be used to stir sand and water—came a broader understanding of the task before them and the ways using the Web would never smell quite like using other sources. And I suspect such strategies may be advisable in any literature class using this technology. But there were other problems.

Blame It on Carrion

"What do you mean by 'interact'?" they grilled me weeks into the project. I advised that they look for links on Web sites which would allow them to add their opinion, to ask questions, or to e-mail the author of the page. Even the best students claimed they could find no such options at the various sites. I realized this was a visual problem. Students new to the Web were unaccustomed to recognizing that highlighted text indicated button links. Although these students were engaged in e-mail discussion groups, e-mail was still so new to most of them that they did not pick up on the cue that "@" signals an online address. By the time I informed them of these protocols, it was too late for them to receive any response. In my current literature and writing classes, one of the first things I introduce students to is how to recognize and read the Web.

Although the essays that resulted from this initial use of the Web were disappointingly like the essays my past students had written about literature, where sources serve merely as underpinning for background information, this first project did serve as a good exercise in clarifying what was possible and how using the Web as a source could be significantly different from writing about literature without it. In classes I have taught since this first one, I share the papers of former students from later in this course which successfully use the interactive features of the Web in their writing alongside anecdotal information. These models make clearer the ways that electronic space is different from print research. But I am not sure—given the homogeneous and limited nature of how students are taught to use sources throughout their education prior to Web work—that a first project within a course can necessarily be any more successful. The process may require trial and error.

In our second attempt in the same class, we focused on literature thematically arranged around the topic Making Peace, Making War. Now more savvy to the Web's various kinds of sites and its ways of stinking and linking differently than other sources, students in class easily listed a greater variety of keywords to use in browsing. This time essay assignment guidelines were as follows: (1) the paper had to focus on examining two to three readings from the unit where the images of peace or war contrasted; (2) students had to find Web sites which similarly revealed contrasting images; (3) the thesis idea for this paper had to bring texts and images from both the Web and from their literature anthology together; (4) students were to correspond with several sites since it was likely that some would never respond; with four weeks until the due date, they also needed to begin this interaction early in the project. This time, less hesitant to lure them with better bait, I gave them a short list of URLs (see Appendix A) with multiple links on subjects such as pacifism, the Vietnam War, and the psychology of violence to get them started. We met in the computer classroom and began searching together, exchanging successful "hits." From the errors of our earlier attempts, we learned firsthand the advice of "observability and trialability" (Madigan, Spirek, and McIntyre 1996) crucial to successful implementation of technology in the classroom. Why did the project succeed this time?

Discern It as Denizens of the Deep

Now with greater awareness of the unique capabilities of the Web and of ways of using it differently from print sources, students were much more confident. Michael[2] reported in first, excited that he had found Web sites focusing on how war affects those left behind at home. He began seeing links between these sites and Amy Lowell's poem "Patterns" and Richard Lovelace's "To Lucasta." And he made connections closer to home by interviewing his mother, who had stayed in the United States when his father had been drafted into the Vietnam War. By writing veterans through e-mail addresses given on the Web, Michael was put in contact with others—wives, husbands, girlfriends, children, brothers, and sisters who had stayed home while those close to them went to the Persian Gulf and Vietnam wars.

In his essay Michael saw the literature of even the seventeenth century as being pertinent to modern life. He examined possible reasons that homefront lovers and relatives reacted differently to war-related absence and the threat of death. Later in e-mail, Michael wrote me to let me know "this was a really cool project, Katie. When I first read those poems for class and when we discussed them in class, I thought, 'oh, how boring.' But they are not boring. When I saw how they related to all those real people who wrote me in e-mail and then saw my own mom cry in the kitchen when we talked about the war, I learned things about literature I didn't ever realize before." Michael's epiphany was similar to those of most students in this class.

In previous literature classes studying similar thematic units, students easily sidetracked into two distinct and polemic camps—pacifists and those who believed the road to peace was through waging wars that "settled things." Although these conversations are crucial to students in internalizing readings and in making future decisions, I found students became embroiled in issues and abandoned the stories and poems. In short, they would turn from interpretation of texts to debates over them and lose sight of characters, plots, and other literary devices altogether. As they came into contact with veterans, war protesters, politicians, and writers through the Web, however, they were constantly challenged to return to the literature at hand.

I had a friend in town diagnosed with extreme Post Traumatic Stress Disorder (PTSD) due to his involvement in the Vietnam War. When I asked him if he might visit with students to give one veteran's perspective on the war and aftermath, he told me that as a result of the disorder, he "didn't go out much anymore," but that he'd be very willing to "meet" students on e-mail. Although I'd already realized the potent benefits of e-mail's "facelessness," his preference gave me a new appreciation. In writing him online, the students' growing attention to audience was obvious. Although Clifford Stoll and others claim that writing online may depersonalize communication, student e-mail was very attentive, gentle in allowing that some things may be "too painful" or "too personal" for this veteran to discuss. Politically and socially, this interaction stirred many students to broader possibilities in viewing war and its effects. They began to internalize more fully the literature and the topics of war and pacifism than had the students in the science fiction class. They began making connections between their own existence and the war behind pieces like Tim O'Brien's short story, "The Things They Carried."

For the first time in the unit, students came to discover who the characters in their literature are, these young soldiers who go to war, people who are very much like themselves:

> Jason: I was born two years after the war ended. I've always thought of going to war as just doing your patriotic duty. I never really thought about dying. I never really thought about having to kill other people and then living for years and years with the memories.

One of the veterans responded generously to such thoughts:

> The Vietnam experience for all of us was a rude awakening to what the world was like outside our warm and fuzzy existence. Keep in mind that, for the most part, the Vietnam soldier was young, maybe 20-22. Global politics such as the domino theory and World Finance were not parts of our vocabularies. Many of us joined more out of macho, male, lower brain functions than of some surreal agenda that we were going to save the free world from Communism. Before we went overseas, for many of us, it was a game like football. Yes, we knew people were getting killed, but we were young and indestructible. Look around you now, at your friends. Are there some of them that act like they cannot die, that they are indestructible? We were like that, like many kids today that speed down the back roads at breakneck speeds. We were no different. (Patrick Pavey, personal communication)

By being in contact with veterans' Web sites and by engaging with veterans from World War II, the Korean War, the Vietnam War, and the Persian Gulf War, these students untested and inexperienced in war-time realities came to better understand the fear and conscientiousness, the loneliness and pride of the literary characters they read about. Because interacting with the writers of the Web Vietnam literature was made easy by the medium, students gained more than just vicarious experience. They had to engage with the subject, with the writer, with the text. They had to respond.

For some students, searches and e-mail conversations took them into the practices and philosophy of pacifism. One student changed the original prescribed essay writing assignment. Instead, she rewrote one of our assigned short stories, considering how it would have been different if the characters had followed the principles of passive resistance outlined by Thoreau and Mahatma Gandhi. Although this may seem to be a far-fetched revisionist approach in a literature class, I applauded her efforts because she applied both critical and creative thinking and writing in finding the pulse of the literature. She not only had to attend to issues and themes, but she also had to analyze and imitate style, characterization, and setting in her revision. She went beyond the normal perimeters of reader response into the area of reader/co-author. In the process, she gained confidence in dealing with interpretation of a literary text, inside out.

Most memorable of student successes in this project, however, is Ellen's. A nursing student interning in mental health, Ellen made comments in class discussions noting possible diagnosis of characters suffering stress in times of war. Through Web sites and listservs of Vietnam Vets, she came in contact with many who suffered from PTSD. She viewed their real-life stories in connection with stories like "The Things They Carried" (Tim O'Brien) and "Kaiser and the War" (Simon Ortiz) and studied them from the medical practitioner's perspective. Freire's (Shor, 1987) suggestion that learning occurs best when situated within the student's environment was borne out in her project. Moving beyond on-screen encounters, Ellen traveled to one of the treatment centers in Iowa with some of her correspondents and saw firsthand the facilities and methods used in dealing with the syndrome.

She talked to members of the control group, those veterans who saw combat but who do not suffer from PTSD. She learned that the disorder had existed in previous wars, too, but had been labeled "shell shock." Writing veterans requesting "an insider's" viewpoint on PTSD, Ellen received e-mail from veterans who told her "Combat dirt never washes off completely. You live with it, you deal with it, and you die with it; no matter what war you were in" (Lou Rochat, personal communication). She was in contact with numerous ex-soldiers headed to "The Wall," the Vietnam Memorial in Washington, D.C., just days before Veteran's Day. And she heard from some who would not go:

> I cannot go to the Wall. I tear up at what seem like the most fool-ish things. But I like to call that being human and having feel-ings. I was not this way before Vietnam. I have not slept a full nights sleep since I was in Nam the first time in '65. The slightest sounds wake me up and I am fully awake/alert to everything. No bad dreams though. Very jumpy ever since '65. (Chris Christensen, personal communication)

Others gave her further insights into the personal havoc wreaked on their lives by the syndrome:

> As for leading a normal life? I would have to say yes, we lead a normal life for us. Those of us who suffer PTSD cannot imagine life any other way. It takes a long time and a lot of patience from our counselors and close associates to help us realize that most people don't get only two hours of sleep at a time. Or that most

people don't have to check and recheck the locks of the doors each night. Or that most people don't wake up in a sweat. Or that most people don't mind when a good friend stops by unexpected. Or that most people don't mistrust everyone except other vets. Or that most people don't think that they are wasting their time on the earth. Or that most people don't have to sit with their backs to a wall at public outings. Or that most people don't think that every task attempted must be accomplished perfectly or someone will die. (Robert Drury, personal communication)

Putting together these text-based interactions from veterans with the information she received at the PTSD sites and the literature readings she'd selected, Ellen developed her own Web page for the project instead of writing an essay. She linked passages from the literature multifariously with other pages—some detailing her textual analysis as a student of literature, others outlining diagnosis and treatment of mental health concerns embedded in the literature, and yet others linking to various "outside" sites on the Web from veterans' organizations which explained PTSD or offered poems and letters about war. In the final project, Ellen fully used the Web for its unique characteristics of immediacy, associative thinking, and interaction. She tossed her former ideas of research essay writing back into the tank in order to enjoy more fully Webfish glistening in the sun.

Our experiences, then, suggest the following guidelines in dealing with using the World Wide Web in subject-area classes:

1. Introduce the Web to students. Although future students may well arrive on our campuses knowledgeable about virtual environments, for now students need to be taught the basic principles and operations of the Web including button links, highlighted text, interactive features, search engines, the nature of associative thinking and linking, and those ways in which the Web both emulates and differs from print environment sources. It may be further useful to model reading the Web by verbalizing the choices you make when working through various button link options.

2. Rather than using the Web to replicate how print sources are used, capitalize on those features unique to the medium including its immediacy, its associative patterns of linking, and its interactive capacities. Work these things into student assignments (see Appendix B). If students have not yet used e-mail, plan on introducing this medium as well, including protocols like netiquette, listserv posting, lurking, and the like.

3. Recognize that students are unlikely at first to understand how using this medium will differ from using other sources. If models are available of student writing and interacting with the Web, offer these to students for examination. In discussing

Albee's *The Sandbox*, for example, I might take students to Web sites about geriatric care as well as sites about Dr. Jack Kevorkian; with these, we might brainstorm possible thesis ideas regarding the play, treatment of the elderly, physician-assisted suicide, or depression among the aged. Realize, too, however, that students may need one to groan on, i.e., an initial experience with failure. It may be wise to make the first writing assignments involved with Web searching small in scope and size so that students do not so easily lose heart.

4. Test the potential for sites and keywords by surfing the Web yourself in advance of classes. Offer URLs for the kinds of sites you are suggesting that students visit. Model verbally and in writing the juxtaposition of seemingly disparate sites and literary readings in order to broaden student perspective on how sites might be used in their thinking and writing.

5. Teach students to think critically and analyze closely the credibility of their Web sources, and thus, of the material they find. My students searching the Web for "Doublespeak" when studying George Orwell's *1984* came across some of the most racist, sexist, intolerant texts I have ever read. Taught to question the reliability of the source, they were able to use these materials in a way which called into question the misinterpretations of Orwell afloat in many areas of current pop culture.

In addition to these suggestions, realize the following precautions:

1. As students often remind me, "there's a lot of cool stuff on the Web." New users especially may find hours of time drifting away from surfing while losing focus of the hook they are searching for. If you have whole class periods in the virtual environment, realize too that students will inevitably wander off task at times to search out alternate sites or to read their e-mail, the electronic activity equivalent to tucking comics inside textbooks. Since our classroom permits access to student screens, I found instances of "fading out" were lessened as long as I kept strolling throughout the room.

2. The adventure will take more time than one might initially think. Since systems crash, since one group of students may catch on more quickly or more slowly, since the fish are not always biting, I now generally plot out twice as much class time on Web instructions as I actually expect it to take.

3. Always have an alternate plan for any class scheduled in the computer room. Again, since systems crash and since traffic on the Web can be tremendously slow, I always enter the room with my bait box filled with alternate lures—handouts of sample Web screens, overhead transparency overlays tracing button linking paths, and when possible, a brief video revealing the Web in action.

4. Although I don't share the current paranoia about abundant decadence on the Web infiltrating innocent minds, just as browsers in any library might come across unsavory images in books, there are many sites users can land on quite by accident which they may find objectionable. This may be particularly distressing to some students, and teachers need to be prepared to talk with students about such sites.

5. There are always issues involving student privacy. If students compose Web pages in fulfilment of writing assignments, students and teachers must negotiate whether or not they are "required" to publish these with active links on the Web. Furthermore, when students become involved e-mailing people listed on Web pages, they may be asked to give out their own e-mail addresses, thus opening themselves to receive text from strangers. Of course, this may seem similar to students sending letters in the post, but the ease and immediacy of e-mail makes unsavory encounters more possible.

Whether you prefer to think of the Web as carp carcasses or not, I leave it up to you. More than anything, I have come to disagree with the notion prevalent in the field of computer-assisted instruction (CAI) that computer technologies should be invisible, that we should use them to replicate as exactly as possible the activities, pedagogy, and philosophy driving pre-CAI courses. In doing so, we fail to take full advantage of the unique properties these technologies offer us in a learning environment. To do so is to expect dead fishes to swim.

Acknowledgment

Thanks to John Wozniak, OSF, for his support in advancing the exploration of computer-assisted writing and thinking in my earliest classes.

Notes

1. Subsequent references made to literature selections are from this text.

2. All names given for students are pseudonyms.

Works Cited

Bazerman, Charles. 1994. *Constructing Experience*. Carbondale: Southern Illinois University Press.

Gregory, Marshall. 1997. "The Many-Headed Hydra of Theory vs. the Unifying Mission of Teaching." *College English* 59(1): 41–58.

Kirszner, Laurie, and Stephen Mandell. 1994. *Literature: Reading, Writing, and Reacting.* 2nd ed. Ft. Worth, TX: Harcourt Brace.

Koberg, Don, and Jim Bagnall. 1974. *The Universal Traveler: A Soft-Systems Guidebook to Creativity, Problem-Solving, and the Process of Design.* Los Altos, CA: William Kaufmann.

Madigan, Dan, Melissa Spirek, and Susan McIntyre. 1996. "Five Considerations for Technology Use in the Classroom." *The Council Chronicle* (November): 6.

Morgan, Dan. 1993. "Connecting Literature to Students' Lives." *College Composition and Communication* 55: 491–500.

Senator Tom Harkin Biography. 1995, October. http://www.senate.gov/~harkin/about.html

Shor, Ira. 1987. "Educating the Educators: A Freirean Approach to the Crisis in Teacher Education." In *Freire for the Classroom: A Teacher's Sourcebook,* ed. Ira Shor, 7–32. Portsmouth, NH: Heinemann–Boynton/Cook.

Appendix A

War and Peace URLs

http://grunt.space.swri.edu/thepast.htm
"Remembrance"

http://www.mcc.org/ask-a-vet/index.html
Ask a Vet

http://www.ionet.net/~uheller/vnbktoc.shtml
"Images of My War"

http://members.aol.com/jimm844224/catext01/polloc03.html
"Vietnam Memoirs"

http://grunt.space.swri.edu/poetcrnr.htm
"From the Heart": Poetry by veterans

http://www.chronicillnet.org/PGWS/
Persian Gulf War Syndrome

http://www.powmiaff.com/
POW/MIA Freedom Fighters

http://www.tiac.net/users/write/vwlitlinks/vwlitlinks.htm
Vietnam War Literary Links

http://www.maui.com/~lesslie/gandhi.html
Gandhi Web site

http://www.pbs.org/pov/stories/
Re: Vietnam—Stories since the War

http://www.prairienet.org/vvaw/
Vietnam Veterans against the War, Inc.

Appendix B

Katie Fischer
kfischer@keller.clarke.edu

Sample Class Plan
Literature and the Web

To the Student: As a member of our literature class, you recently completed reading Kurt Vonnegut's *Slaughterhouse-Five.* You are aware that Vonnegut's novel deals with several wars—most obviously World War II and the Vietnam War. With this background in mind, please travel to the sites listed below:

Part I: During Class

1. First visit the Kurt Vonnegut homepage to find background information on how he feels about war and pacifism and to uncover what his own background might tell you about Billy Pilgrim's story. Make a list of those items from the novel which appear based on fact and those which seem more a created part of the fiction.
http://www.duke.edu/~crh4/vonnegut/chronology.html
http://www.duke.edu/~crh4/vonnegut/s-five.html

2. Return to the Web and search for information about Vietnam vets and POWs
http://grunt.space.swri.edu/thepast.htm

3. Visit Senator Tom Harkin's homepage and biography to discover how his political life intersects with POW concerns.
http://www.senate.gov/~harkin/about.html

Part II: Before the Next Class
(choose one)

1. Use one of the interactive links or e-mail addresses listed on the pages above and write the person involved responding to material you find at the site. Make sure your write-up attends to both the site and the novel. You might consider questions, comments, or other responses linking the two.

2. Consider Senator Harkin's political action in light of what the novel details about POW treatment and write about how these two events intersect.

3. Reviewing poetry or letters at the vet site, find evidence of responses to war that either agree or disagree with Pilgrim's reaction to his World War II involvement.

4. Develop your own written response linking the novel to any of the material you found at Web sites.

12 Writing Images: Using the World Wide Web in a Digital Photography Class

Anne Frances Wysocki
Michigan Technological University

The first reading I asked of the people in the class I am about to discuss is shown in Figure 12.1. When I teach digital photography, my goals are to help class participants learn to use image-manipulation software and to discuss the images they make with that software, so that they can increase their understanding of the rhetorical workings of images: how, for example, does a change in the focus or composition of an image change how others respond to it—and why? What can you achieve—and for whom—by tinting blue the faces in a photograph of a mixed cultural group or by combining a photograph of your now-dead father with your young son? How, in other words, do you combine technical skills with a sense of an audience in order to achieve an intended effect—with images? When the section of HU/FA331 I am writing about here ended in May, the people in class could do what I have discussed: they could use the software fluidly, and they had also discussed and written at length about how their images grow out of, make sense within, and have effects back on their particular time and place. When I constructed the syllabus from which the Web image above comes, I had hopes, of course, that we would achieve those goals—but I had no idea how much experimentation people in class would do, and how energetically and thoughtfully they would seek out and provide feedback for the many versions of images they made: my memory holds this digital photography class as one of the best classes I've ever had the delight to teach. In what follows, I'll present why and how I believe our class's use of the Web was necessary to our successes.

HU/FA331: d i g i t a l   p h o t o g r a p h y

Michigan Technological University
Spring Quarter, 1996

C O U R S E   D E S C R I P T I O N

This course is about how you take images that were originally produced by
means of some sort of camera, transfer them to a computer, and manipulate
them.

You can manipulate the images to "improve" them by "traditional"
photographic standards, or you can manipulate them to meet the standards
of... well, the class will be concerned with what those other standards
might be. I want to emphasize here that this is not simply a class in
technique: I expect you to work towards articulating, over the quarter, the
aesthetic and other concerns that motivate and worry and delight you as you
make your images.

We will therefore be emphasizing (through class demonstrations, discussions,
and projects you carry out) three things in this class:

- Techniques for manipulating photographic images on the computer

- What standards you use for judging the success -- artistic or
  otherwise -- of the images you create

- Questions about the status of photography now that any photographic
  image can be manipulated, made to look "life-like", and combined with
  any other image; this includes legal & ethical questions as well as
  aesthetic ones

Figure 12.1. Course Description

Decisions about Using the Web

As with any class, there were aspects over which I had no control: there was, for obvious example, the particular group of twenty-one engaging people who came and stayed, and there was also the Humanities Department computer lab where people from class did the majority of their work. The lab is a relaxed and bubbling place, set up with computers in pods rather than rows, with plants and stuffed animals and wall hangings and student-hung posters; there are almost always several conversations flickering around the computers, and students in the department often get to know each other well in the lab. The lab has been like this ever since I began my teaching at Tech, and its atmosphere certainly carried over into our class to contribute to the comfort and ease people developed in using the Web for their digital photography work—something I am happy to have had happen, but which I could not change, even if I so wanted. But regarding the aspects of class over which I did have control, it is the following four decisions I made involving Web use that I think contributed most to the pleasures and productivity of class:

- All class materials—syllabus, calendar, assignments—were available in one place on the Web from the first day of class.
- People in class published all their work on the Web.
- Class emphasis was not on achieving technical proficiency with HTML coding, but on creating pages that sought some particular intended effect.
- People in class had the freedom to set up their Web pages as they wanted, and could change their pages at any time.

Before I describe how these decisions worked themselves out in class, I'll describe why I made them.

Reasons for Using the Web as I Did

My reasons for the various decisions are not easily separable. For example, I decided to put all class materials on the Web, and to ask people in class to publish their work on the Web, for initially practical reasons, but also with expectations that there would be effects on class atmosphere and participation. So, to save on paper and copying costs—and to give the feeling that the class had a coherent structure from the start—I put the syllabus and class calendar on the Web, together with all class assignments. I decided that class participants would each make their own pages for displaying their images and their writings about their images: this would save them the (not insubstantial) costs of printing multiple versions of their images in order to get the kind of output they desired; in addition, images prepared for the screen resolution of the Web take up little hard-drive memory, and they process faster on the computers.

But I also hoped that the public nature of the Web would encourage people in class to be more aware of how others might respond to their work. To help with this sense of audience, I also decided that we would put our e-mail addresses on our pages—this would also allow us to use the e-mail capabilities of Netscape Navigator (our computer lab's browser of choice) to respond to each other's work directly while looking at it, as well as make it easy for people outside of class to respond. Class participants would do their individual work in the Humanities Department's computer lab (the Center for Computer Assisted Language Instruction, or CCLI), but when we met as a class we would meet in a room with a networked Macintosh connected to a projection system; this projection system, together with everyone's work being accessible through the Web, meant that when we met together we would be able to get to and see everyone's work quickly and projected largely—a format, I hoped, that would encourage group discussion. The effects of these various choices wove themselves throughout class, as I hope the next sections make clear.

How the Decisions Played Themselves out in Class

All class materials—syllabus, calendar, assignments—were available in one place on the Web from the first day of class.

On the first day of class we went through the class Web pages together. I showed class participants where to find the pages, how they were linked together, and what was on them. I made a total of sixteen pages for the class: syllabus, calendar, a page on which we would put links to the Web sites they would be creating, a sample Web page for class participants to copy and modify for their work if they hadn't made a page before, and pages describing visual and written assignments. The pages were linked in this structure (see Figure 12.2).

With all class materials and assignments before them on linked pages, class participants could thus (I hoped) not only "see the text"—Stephen Bernhardt's (1986) expression for how the visual aspects of a page help readers organize for themselves the structure of the information on the page—but they could also "see the class." For example, Figure 3 shows the course calendar page.

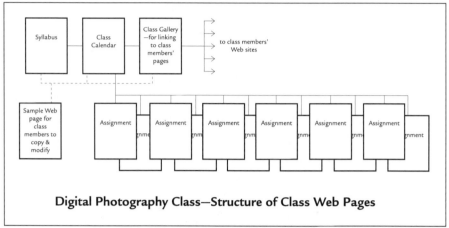

Digital Photography Class—Structure of Class Web Pages

Figure 12.2. Digital Photography Class—Structure of Class Web Pages

The calendar displayed how class would proceed from day to day and week to week of the quarter; in addition, it provided links to all assignments: when a class participant clicked "Assignment 1," for example, a page describing the assignment would come to him or her. In addition, this calendar page uses the same typefaces and colors, and a similar header graphic, as the syllabus and class gallery pages, so that these pages would visually cohere as the place where participants could go for general class information; the visual assignment pages used the same typeface but were of a different color with a different sort of graphic at the top, and the writing assignment pages looked like the visual assignment pages except that they shared their own header graphic. (To produce these assignment pages, I first made an HTML document that did what I wanted, then—for each new assignment—I modified a copy of the document by changing only the image and instructions; this kept the pages consistent and made the HTML coding a matter of simply replacing one assignment with the description of another). I was hoping that the consistent visible organization, repetitions and variations of illustrations, and linking of the pages would help class participants begin to see and understand not only how class was structured, but why I had structured it as it was, and how they would be adding to the structure.

These pages show more than structure, though: there are the graphics at the tops of pages, and the colors of those graphics and of the pages and text. I chose these elements to give a serious but exploratory tone to the pages and hence to class. The images also model what can be made with the software we were using in class; the visual assignment

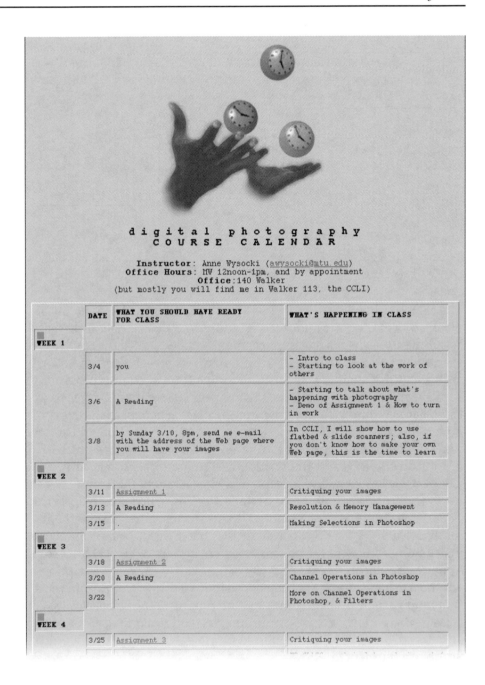

Figure 12.3. Course Calendar

pages, for example, each show the same photograph at the top, but with the photograph modified to suggest what the assignment asked.

Students can acquire such senses of structure and tone from paper materials as well, obviously, but Web materials can provide a sense of cohesion that is very different from that in a class in which all the materials are on separate pieces of paper, spread out over the quarter and in various notebooks and pockets. Because our class materials were together on the Web, they felt as though they existed in one place, which class participants could reach from any networked computer on our campus, at any time; because of this, students said that class seemed to them to exist, and persist, beyond our three weekly face-to-face meetings as well as outside the space of our classroom: people in class said they felt they could visit class any time to see who was at work, adding to or changing their pages, and that they could build onto class at any time, day or night. It was not just when they saw me in our classroom, then, that people thought it was classtime, or that they thought of the Web and the class as the same thing; instead, the persistent visual center that the Web provided, around which class participants built their own continually changing sites, contributed to a sense that class had a life of its own in the ongoing in- and out-of-classroom work.

Amidst the continual change, though, people in class were also giving careful thought and feedback to each other—in part, I think, because of the public nature of their work, which I will discuss in the next section, but also because of the length of instruction I was able to give them by using the Web. For example, here are guidelines—linked to the course calendar—for class participants to use to respond to each other's work at the end of the second week of the quarter:

> 3/18
> Responding to someone else's work
>
> In this piece of writing, you will respond—with a partner—to the work of someone else in class. There are two main reasons I ask this of you: I want you to further sharpen your abilities to think & write about how & why we respond to images in particular ways, and I want someone else to benefit from your observations.
>
> Please read the rest of this page all the way through before you start responding to the other people's work.
>
> What to do:
> With your partner, look at all the work for Assignment 2 of the two people whose names you drew in class. Then pick one image from each person (pick either of the two "combined" images that

were due in class), and write two responses, one for each image. Make clear in your response the image to which you are responding. Give your response the following form:

1. Describe your immediate response to the images. What do these images make you think/feel/want to do?

2. Describe the images in as much detail as you can muster. What is in the picture? What things do you see? Where in the picture are the things you just described? (Are they in the center? At the borders? At the top? At the bottom?) Describe the colors (are they warm, cool, saturated (intense?), soft, hard, light, dark?).

3. Now tie #1 and #2 together: how do you think what you described in #2 helped you have the response you did in #1?

In addition, if you can make suggestions for how an image could be stronger (whether because of technique or color or . . .) or if you can make suggestions for how someone's Web page setup can help you get to their images more easily or more clearly, please include such comments.

Please send your response as e-mail to the person whose images you are viewing, and cc: me (awysocki). Please try to write a minimum of 250 words per response. And as you are writing, please keep in mind the tone and tenor you would like other people to have as they respond to your work.

WHEN TO SEND OUT YOUR RESPONSES: Any time they are done, but no later than Tuesday night, the 20th.

If I had not been using the Web, I probably would have discussed these guidelines in class, but not given them to students in this length or detail. I would probably not have made them available in printed form because of the limited copy budgets in our department (I frequently use up my budget in the first two weeks of the quarter, copying syllabi and calendars and the first assignment or two). When I watched students working in the lab, they would frequently leave open the Netscape window containing the above guidelines so that they could refer to them as they composed their responses in Netscape's e-mail window. What follows are examples of the resulting response, from the third week of the quarter, when the assignment asked them to add words to images in order to learn techniques for doing this and to consider how the addition of a word to an image affects the image. (I have quoted the passages at length, to give you the fullest possible sense of how they were responding to each other; also please note that most of the following examples come from e-mail messages: the spelling and punctuation reflect the medium. In this particular message, the person to whom this message is addressed (who has the same name I do) had just been elected to a position in our university's student government; hence the comment in the last sentence):

Anne,

I decided to respond to your first image for this assignment, the "aero plain." My first response is that the words go very well with the image. The photo seems to me to be of some bureaucratic complex (like the pentagon or something), situated in a wide open spot (like a plain). But it is blurry, almost indistinguishable. It could be any of a number of building complexes. The effects you used on the text make my eye go to the word aero before anything else. I think this is because of all the white in the letters, it contrasts more than anything else with the background image. The text is very distressed; it seems to be dissolving into the photo, especially the word "plain." It also feels like the letters are sinking into the background—the overall effect is very flat. This is a result of several things: the squareness of the image, the straightness of the text frames the top and bottom borders, the saturated (dark) colors of the photo.

It's hard for me to say how you could make the image stronger, because as far as I know, your intention may have been to make a flat image. Flat, 2-dimensional could be a metaphor for government, and for bureaucrats. Which is interesting in light of your recent election victory!

Leia

Here is another response from another class participant to the same image:

Assignment Three Response:
The first image of "aero-plain"

I like the play of words Airplane—the chosen spelling of the word reminds me of the spanish (or any latin based language) word for air, "Aero." It is very global. On the other hand, the use of "plain" instead of plane reminds me of the flat midwest small town simple life. The letters of "aero" look like they are disintegrating while "plain" looks like it is made out of a very translucent glass. The word play is effective, it plays with how words can be used to doubel mean things just by fiddling with spelling, synonyms and latin roots.

I kind of have a hard time understanding the relevance of the overall design though. I am not sure why you chose the image of an airport, what is it's importance? What is the image saying? This particular airport seems very conservative and corporate, like it would be seen in a business report about investing. Maybe by altering the background in some way to provide more tension or contrast would give it a more complicated, witty effect.

. . .

Take care-
Emily

By my having put all materials on the Web from the beginning, then, I believe that people in class were able to see easily the structure of class; they also felt, as the quarter developed, that class didn't exist only at the time of our meetings in a room, and they were able to benefit from much thicker directions than I would have otherwise given.

People in class published all their work on the Web.

These are two results that I think grew out of my having decided to ask everyone in class to publish on the Web:

- People in class collaborated frequently on their work.
- The public nature and accessibility of the Web encouraged people in class to be particularly aware of how others respond to images.

I will discuss each of these points separately below, but woven within them is another result I cannot cut away from the others, as I hope you will see:

- Class participants responded carefully and thoughtfully to each other's work.

For this to happen, however, there was the first step of how class participants learned to create their own Web pages—which then leads into these results.

At the beginning of class, I linked to the class calendar a "mock-up" Web page that people new to HTML could copy and use as a template for their own work; slightly more than half the class had never made a Web page. At the end of our first week of classes, we met in the CCLI so that those who needed help could get a demonstration of how to start their pages. I made myself available at other times, letting students know they could ask me questions when they saw me in the lab. Others in class who were already quick-fingered with HTML were also pleased and proud to show what they knew and to offer help. The CCLI is conducive to such offers of assistance, as I described in the opening of this essay. Within this whole atmosphere, then, people in the Digital Photography class began their work, understanding (I think) that they were neither isolated nor without resources: they could turn to each other for help or could offer what they knew as they started their own Web pages for class.

This atmosphere worked in combination, I think, with the general excitement students still have about the newness and expansiveness and hipness of the Web to lead to and encourage the collaboration I mentioned above. Since new tools for shaping information on the Web are continually appearing, no one can claim any final expertise, and anyone who desires can find and figure out a new resource—and so considerable, and shared, experimentation went on in class. I had made it clear that, although we would be discussing how people presented their work on their Web pages, being a Webmaster was not the purpose of class, and I had no set expectations about how their pages would look. I encouraged them to go out looking on the Web for whatever resources they could find, whether those resources be related to Digital Photography or to the enhancement of a Web page. And so, whenever anyone in class (especially someone new to making Web pages) found a new way to make her pages work, she would be excited; someone else in class then might ask how he might go about getting similar effects, and soon two people would be working together at the same computer, figuring it out. There was lab time in class for such work to happen, but it also happened on its own, in the lab, while people were preparing for class.

The Web concerns that were the focus of such collaborations might be peripheral to the image-making and image-critiquing of class, but the working relationships people established in this way carried over into the central work of class: similarly to how they shared their Web excitements, people in class also started to share readily what they discovered while working on their images, whether it was an idea about image-making or a software technique. One class assignment asked two people to collaborate on image-making, but collaboration had been going on well before we got to that assignment; because people in class had already been working together, the results of that assignment were rich, and in their feedback at the end of class, people described how much they had learned from each other, and they suggested I give more collaborative assignments in the future. I believe that their working together in these ways—along with the explicit guidelines I gave them, as I described above—encouraged relationships that allowed them to see each other's strengths and curiosities, and so encouraged them to respond carefully and respectfully to each other's work.

I think they were careful toward each other also because of the public nature of what is on the Web. Before class started, I had thought that this aspect would affect class participants' sense of the audience for their work, and it did: one student was initially hesitant to publish her work in so open a space, but then proposed that she present her work under a pseudonym; early on, another student wrote in response to one assignment that:

Where is it more public than on the World Wide Web? I guess this
publicity of the images that I am creating in class makes it important for me to focus on the audience as much as on the art. What
kind of people do I want to look at this and go "ohh"? . . . I am
interested in the audience learning about me through my images,
so that they can get a sense of who I am.

Our class certainly provided one kind of audience: every Monday and
most of every Wednesday we spent the class time looking at and
discussing and writing about each other's work, sometimes projected
largely before us in our classroom, sometimes projected on the
individual computer screens of the lab, where I would ask people to
respond singly or in small groups to images made by others. But, in
addition to this, just about everyone in class also received unsolicited
feedback from someone outside of class who had somehow stumbled
onto their pages and was moved to respond. Class participants were
thus very aware that their work was affecting others, but I think that our
ways and places of working helped that vulnerability be an openness to
response instead of a turning away.

And so, as the quarter progressed, Mondays, when people would
present to class the images they had made for that week's assignment,
became days of nerves and excitement. When I would walk into class,
those there ahead of me would be gathered and chatting, describing
what they had figured out, waiting to be able to show their work and to
see what others had made. There was never a time when no one
volunteered to have his or her work displayed; instead, as the quarter
progressed, I heard more and more from students how much they
valued hearing from others in class, and the final class evaluations
included comments like "Let's have more looking at people's stuff in
class!" and "Feedback is creative fuel!" and "I love criticizm (even
though I do not know how to spell it)."

**Class emphasis was not on achieving technical proficiency with
HTML coding, but in creating pages that sought some particular
intended effect.**

**People in class had the freedom to set up their Web pages as they
wanted, and could change the pages at any time.**

I don't think I can describe separately the results of these two decisions.
These decisions played themselves out together in class, allowing, I
think, for these results:

- People in class experimented frequently and thoughtfully with
  how the elements of an image or a Web page create an overall
  effect.

- Class belonged to everyone, and not solely to me, the teacher.

By focusing on the rhetorical effects of a page rather than on the fineness or gadgetry of its coding, I think our class encouraged people to explore the possibilities of even the simplest HTML coding; they did not get caught up in becoming Webmasters in control of frames and CGI scripts. In addition, though, the explorations were certainly supported by the freedom people had to try whatever they thought might get the effects they sought. And because their pages were theirs to build and manipulate, I think they felt that the pages really did belong to them— and because the pages were so closely tied to class, class thus belonged to them, too: they looked to each other for response and suggestions and direction as often as they did to me.

In the beginning of the quarter, people's Web pages had tended to look alike: because over half the class had never made a Web page before, or had only made a rudimentary page with a graphic or two and some text, many people used the template page I had provided. As the quarter progressed and they explored Web resources and shared what they learned, participants' pages no longer looked like pre-fabs. People changed their pages because they saw something they liked while out examining the pages of others or because they were getting feedback from class (or outside) on how their pages worked to present their information: one quick e-mail message from one class participant to another, for example, said, "I found it very difficult to examine this image within that background. I tried but was force to load it by itself in order to make any sense out of it." Another communication between two other class participants included the comment, "I think you are a very thoughtful person and I would suggest to you to try and separate [signs of your campus] organizations (logos, text, etc.) from your images. I think sometimes it might limit you in what can be done."

But pages also changed because their owners increased their senses of what they could express. The following passage comes from one person's response to an assignment that, in part, asked the class to respond to the question, "What thought processes are you using as you move from a slide or a print to an image on screen?"

> I find myself thinking about the images I want to create—what moods do I want to evoke? what colors to use? how can I use filters to create the effects that I want? what images do I have at my disposal? and on, and on, and on. . . . In any case, there are things going on in my brain that I am not used to, and it's kinda fun!

Some of these thoughts concern my goals for this class. First, and naturally, I want to learn how to use the tools in Photoshop. Second, I want to create something of myself, let a bit of myself peek out onto the Web.

When I had been preparing for the class, it had not occurred to me to require students to stick to the template page, or to show their images on plain grey or white Web pages that had nothing on them but images, which would have been a rough equivalent of how traditional photographs would traditionally be displayed on mattes. Others might argue that the individualized and varied pages of our class detract from the images—and in some cases, as the participants' responses to each other quoted above showed, they certainly did—but the individuality of people's images and pages brought the question of how images are displayed into direct discussion in class.

More important to me, however, was that, as people in class made their pages more personal, their image work became more personal, and stronger: the control they felt over their pages—and the possibilities for experimentation—seem to me to have spread to their other class work. And while they usually did what an assignment asked, they often did more, by making additional images, or additional writing, or rearranging their pages in support of what they wanted to achieve. They started linking their pages together, too, so that (for example) a piece of writing arguing for a class participant's interpretation of her own work would use as support images on Web pages made by others in class: by linking their pages together in these ways, they began providing different structures not only for their own pages, but for the class pages all together.

By the end of the quarter, I think, none of us felt we were working in isolation from each other, or from the world outside our classroom. And while my words of response as teacher certainly carried their weight, no one in class looked only to me for response or encouragement. We had built for ourselves a place that gave us a center for looking—individually and as a class—out at the world and back in at what we were making.

Closing Thoughts

I have taught the Digital Photography class once more since I began this writing. Because of feedback from the first class, I gave more assignments that asked for longer written response and, also because of feedback, more assignments that asked two people to collaborate in image-making; I also used a book—*Electronic Highway Robbery: An*

Artist's Guide to Copyrights in the Digital Era by Mary E. Carter—that discusses the legal and ethical issues of the digital copying of images. But I didn't change how we used the Web: I hope my writing here has indicated how many non-Web-related practices and structures had to come together for this class to provide the pleasures it did, but also how necessary the possibilities of the Web were to those pleasures.

Works Cited

Bernhardt, S. A. 1986. "Seeing the Text." *College Composition and Communication* 37(1): 66–78.

Carter, Mary E. 1996. *Electronic Highway Robbery: An Artist's Guide to Copyrights in the Digital Era.* Berkeley, CA: Peachpit Press.

13 From Castles in the Air to Portfolios in Cyberspace: Building Community Ethos in First-Year Rhetoric and Composition

Elizabeth Burow-Flak
Valparaiso University

Since the mid-1990s, a groundswell of college and university courses have begun to incorporate World Wide Web (WWW) building into their curriculum. This trend not only demonstrates cost-effective dissemination of information, but also corresponds with the increasingly collaborative model of composition instruction that focuses on students as creators of knowledge.[1] For almost any course, the World Wide Web offers a convenient medium for posting documents such as syllabi and assignment sheets, and for linking to relevant material on the Web. In courses in which students participate in WWW construction of their own, either through creating their own hypertext markup language (HTML) documents, participating in Web-based discussion forums, or creating work such as essays or electronic discussion transcripts to be posted on the Web, WWW sites additionally enable an inexpensive means of publishing student work. Communally created course sites can thus become easy-to-update archives, online portraits of individual classes, and portfolios of entire classes' work. Particularly pertinent to courses in composition, World Wide Web building enables students to write for a real audience outside the classroom that can and will respond. For courses that value collaborative work, Web construction is particularly suited to group assignments; for courses that emphasize revision, Web building facilitates unlimited possibilities for editing, particularly on sites in which students can post and update pages themselves. At their best, student-constructed Web sites can yield an additional, equally important outcome: students who post material on the Web demystify that technology sooner than students who only frequent the World Wide Web as browsers and consumers. Moreover, students who create class Web sites are more likely to accomplish what popular critics of electronic communication such as Neil Postman and Sven Birkerts endorse: evaluating new technologies critically and establishing community not only in cyberspace, but also in the face-to-face undertakings of the classroom.

Although in even my earliest experiences incorporating Web construction into literature and composition classes students have overwhelmingly indicated that they value Web building as part of the curriculum,[2] that zeal has not always translated into visually coherent, technically competent, or rhetorically appropriate sites. Students who are inexperienced in WWW building, for example—and who thus lack the confidence or ability to sufficiently incorporate and edit images—tend to insufficiently attribute graphics they have borrowed, incorporate inappropriate images, or neglect to integrate graphics sufficiently into the design of their sites. This tendency differs little from that of writers of research papers who, unsure of how to handle quotations, tend to plagiarize, quote indiscriminately, or fail to integrate quotations sufficiently into their prose. Many students new to WWW construction, having prior experience with Internet communications primarily as the medium for chat rooms, may additionally equate all Internet communication with pseudonymous discussion of a temporary nature, rather than viewing Web construction as a more permanent presentation of material in which one's ethos as a student and the author of a site is central. Moreover, in classes that lack consistent structuring of WWW building as a communal rather than an individual activity, students commonly consider course sites to be more their instructors' projects than their own. Being assigned to contribute to a class site, in other words, does not always result in student investment in the project.

In order for a class site to succeed as a project in which students communally take ownership, students must first be able to imagine the breadth of an Internet audience, achieve proficiency in composition specific to the WWW, and assume sufficient responsibility in presenting their work for public readership. Only then can a truly communal class site progress from castles in the virtual reality of its designers' intentions to structures in the more solid reality of cyberspace.[3] To that end, this chapter details a sequence of assignments for a first-year writing course that integrates Web searching, evaluation of WWW sites, and ultimately, Web building while taking advantage of the collaborative, interactive potential of the WWW. This chapter also discusses variations on that sequence for classes that do not regularly meet in computer-assisted classrooms, concluding with evidence of composition students' growth through World Wide Web construction into a critically savvy community of writers.[4]

Building Up to Web Construction

English 306, the course in which I first implemented WWW building, is a first-year course in argumentative writing at the University of Texas at Austin. The course emphasizes critical reading, rhetorical analysis, and library research. In 1995–96, sections of the course that met in any of three computer-assisted classrooms (about a third of the roughly fifty sections of the course per semester) met in classrooms equipped with networked IBM 486 computers or Macintosh Power PCs, complete with Ethernet connections to the Internet and Web construction capabilities via HTML Editor or BB Edit Lite. The classrooms, which double as computer labs when classes are not in session, display the computers on tables around the perimeter of the room so that students face the wall when using the computers; when not working at the computers, students face each other and the instructor around a table in the center of the room. In this laboratory atmosphere that is literally decentered from the instructor, instructors of literature and composition in the University of Texas at Austin's Computer Writing and Research Labs (CWRL) have taught and conducted pedagogical research by facilitating class discussion via networked computers and by incorporating e-mail, newsgroups, and multiuser environments such as MOOs, MUDs, and MUSHes into the curriculum, in addition to incorporating activities that center on the World Wide Web.[5] This classroom setting and a medium—networked computers—that encourages interaction naturally offers practice in creating academic community from which communal Web construction can grow. The course's inclusion of evaluation in its focus on the modes of argumentation additionally lends itself to activities to which students can apply their experience with computers, for example evaluating InterChange (a real-time conferencing program via the Daedalus Integrated Writing Environment) as a mode of discussion, or discussing readings that evaluate Internet use (for example, a 1995 *Harper's* forum between Sven Birkerts, John Perry Barlow, Kevin Kelly, and Mark Slouka).

In English 306 and in subsequent composition courses that I have taught, I have not only encouraged reflection on how computers affect the ways that we write, collect information, generate ideas, and communicate as a class, but also have assigned a progression of assignments that include a "scavenger hunt" of academic and recreational WWW sites and an assignment to evaluate a Web site.[6] The scavenger hunt typically requires visits to online writing labs, the campus writing center, and resources on WWW building, as well as schedules of campus activities, seasonal and popular sites, library resources, and postings from civic organizations. (Although first-year students come to college increasingly practiced in browsing the WWW for entertainment, considering the Web as a source of academic and civic material is often nonetheless a new experience.)[7] Students conclude the activity by e-mailing or compiling a bookmark list of noteworthy Web sites that I later format into a recommended links directory on our class site. In addition to encouraging students to find material that interests them, the activity can also spark heated discussion among students (for example, whether sites that feature pin-up models or vulgar names of music groups are appropriate for a class site). The exposure to an array of WWW sources and the evaluation necessary for the conclusion of the scavenger hunt also feed into subsequent writing assignments on what constitutes a quality WWW site, and an evaluation of a specific site (one option within an assignment to evaluate a controversial place). My own links on the class site to archives on WWW building and to the "best" and the "worst" of the Web offer reference points for discussion.[8]

Along with implementing the above browsing and evaluation activities, teaching WWW construction early in the term—either by teaching HTML code, or by introducing students to an HTML automation program such as Netscape Composer, Adobe Pagemill, or Microsoft Frontpage—allows for more immediate contributions from students on the class site, avoids information overload later in the term as students grow increasingly busy, and offers students sufficient time to experiment with Web building before final Web projects for the course become due. (Particularly helpful for teaching WWW construction are textbooks that detail evaluation and construction of WWW sites such as Daniel Anderson, Bret Benjamin, and Bill Paredes-Holt's *Connections: A Guide to On-Line Writing* [1998], Carol Clark Powell's *Working the Web: A Student's Guide* [1997], and Wayne Butler's *Writing for the Information Superhighway* [1997]). One way to solicit student participation in the class site includes assigning what I have referred to as "housekeeping tasks": adopting synchronous discussion transcripts, a hypertextual e-mail directory, or portions of a class journal to maintain and format for the class site.[9] Students perform these tasks in groups of three at various points throughout the semester, account in writing for what they contribute to the tasks, and receive credit for a small percentage of their course grade for completing them. The tasks not only serve as a tutorial project in Web formatting and design, but also require dividing work equitably and encourage responsibility for group projects. In my spring 1996 class, in fact, many groups began to exhibit investment in the class site as they performed such tasks through individual and group "signatures" on their work: taglines that indicate who created specific pages and recurring images or motifs by which contributors identified themselves. (One group, for example, included images of members' favorite cartoon characters in its work; another consistently chose "retro" or psychedelic backgrounds, and a third included brief biographies of its members.)

Still another way to engage students in Web construction early in the term is to assign students to create personal homepages from which they link to writing assignments that they format for the WWW as the semester progresses. This strategy works particularly well in situations where students can post and update pages on their own accounts, as the students in my fall 1997 and spring 1998 Exposition and Argument classes at Valparaiso University have done. Often, in fact, students continue to polish and augment their work after the class ends. Either option—having students adopt portions of the class site or begin their own homepages as indexes of their work—lends itself well to peer review of growing sites and discussions of student ethos on the WWW.[10] In addition, both methods of Web construction benefit by students advertising their work and by inviting responses to their presence on the WWW. Students can index their work by topic in Internet search engines, incorporate keywords in the <meta> tags in their HTML formatting, include the addresses of their Web sites in the signatures of their personal e-mail messages, register their work in college or university-wide indexes of student sites, and submit the URLs of their work to appropriate newsgroups.[11] When possible, as well, student work should always include a mail form or a <mailto> command from which people who browse their work can contact them. Receiving e-mail in response to one's site is far more likely when the site is sufficiently advertised. Responses may not come overnight, but receiving responses, more than any other experience, solidifies for students the nature of their audience outside the class.

For either method of constructing a class site, moreover, the following strategies can enable more effective, responsible, and aesthetically pleasing sites.

Graphics

Concerning the integration of graphics into their work, students should be aware not only of copyright restrictions on many images in print and on the WWW, but also of acceptable and creative options for acquiring, documenting, integrating, and adapting images. Directing students to WWW or CD-ROM archives of images in the public domain (including graphic elements such as buttons, lines, and textured backgrounds, if desired) generally suffices for the early stages of Web construction. Encouraging students to scan in images that are in the public domain supports my objective of students contributing new material to the WWW. Should time allow, students may also, of course, request permission to incorporate copyrighted material into their sites. Graphics programs such as Adobe Photoshop or other paint, illustration, and scanning programs are also important for fully incorporating many images into a site's design, from sizing and cropping an image or deleting an image's background to artistically altering an image with filters and creating one's own logos, mastheads, or collages of images. Moreover, students who wish to enable graphics to function like hypertext can incorporate either of two strategies. For simple graphics, they may incorporate the <img src> tag and the name of the image that functions as a link in the place of the "hot," or underlined copy in a standard textual link. For multiple links within a more complex image, students can use image mapping programs to designate "hot spots" or coordinates within an image.

Text and Hypertext

Concerning formatting longer works for the WWW (such as multiple-page composition papers), students should also be aware that rhetorical standards for WWW documents have come to include frequent subheads, hypertextual links, short amounts of text, and ample graphics. Although such standards challenge conventions of traditional academic essays, the conflict need not be insurmountable. Students can, for example, post long, nonhypertextual documents on the Web from a more image-heavy front page that highlights their written documents and links to pertinent material on the WWW. Doing so replicates one form of cyberjournal or WWW archive of documents. In adapting traditional papers for the WWW, students may also concede to prevailing WWW aesthetics by breaking paragraphs into smaller pieces of text, making footnotes hypertextual, linking to WWW sources that they cite, and breaking long documents into shorter, interlinked papers (often with a menu in a lefthand, top, or bottom table or frame) or anchored subheads within a continuous document.

Presentations

Finally, concerning bridging the gap between WWW and oral presentation, instructors should be aware that WWW sites' capacity for infinite revision can make them more closely resemble an additional draft of a paper than a performance—an oral presentation—from which students can derive energy and immediate responses to their work. Requiring students to present drafts of their final Web projects and their essays therein to the class—an activity that works particularly well if one has access to an LCD projector—can help bridge the rift between oral and electronic presentation. Doing so encourages students to articulate to a more immediate audience—their peers—the reasons behind their written and design choices. Classmates who have previously reviewed the presenters' written and WWW compositions come prepared with a question or two to lead discussion. This activity that students generally enjoy can thus result in a productive exchange of suggestions on sites' technical, visual, and argumentative successes.

Alternative Web Construction

The above suggestions for evaluation of Internet (and particularly World Wide Web) communication; emphasis on the WWW as an interactive medium of conversation, rather than simply as a medium of publication; and attention to visual and technical as well as verbal ethos in Web construction constitute only some methods for forging community in the classroom and in cyberspace. One alternative or addition to full-fledged WWW construction is participation in a WWW message forum, which functions like an electronic bulletin board or hypertext-based newsgroup. Because students may converse proficiently via message forums with little or no knowledge of HTML, message forums are ideal for classes that never or infrequently meet in computerized classrooms (provided, of course, that students have access to computers and WWW connections outside of class). Composition students can use message forums to post research for class, such as a background report on an assigned reading, or to turn in assignments, such as journal responses, structured to generate conversation. Students might also use a message forum to converse with each other, students from other sections of the same course, or interested outsiders between class meetings. Message forums allow their users to submit interactive links to material on the WWW; students can use message forums, then, to submit links to sites relevant to course material. Message forums—especially if addressed to a larger group than the class—additionally provide an excellent vehicle for practicing "netiquette" and garnering input from beyond the university. (Message forum postings to a course that I have taught on banned books, for example, have yielded messages from instructors in whose classrooms books are currently being challenged, queries about the works in question from students from other universities, and replies from instructors who are teaching similar courses.) However integrated into the curriculum, message forums, once established, essentially maintain themselves, and can become vital extensions of group interaction.[12]

From Web Building to Critical Thinking

Beyond the product and production of Web communication, my students' experience with WWW construction over the past four years has yielded a benefit important to composition in general: the ability to view published works—and particularly Internet sources—critically, enhanced by firsthand knowledge of WWW production. One composition student, for example, wrote in a journal entry that making a Web site helped him demystify Internet technology, and knowing how Web publication works caused him to look for signs of authority such as institutional affiliation, documented references, or otherwise credible information in the WWW sources he previewed for his paper. Another student, in a journal entry on a paper he had just written, constructed the following ironic scenario:

> To: bflak@mail.utexas.edu (Elizabeth Burow-Flak)
> From: james14@mail.utexas.edu (James Anthony [Tony] Wann)
> Subject: Writing Log #4
>
> As far as research papers go, this was certainly one of them. That's not a complaint, by the way, but research papers have this strange tendency to grate on my nerves. . . . If you could just write the thing and not worry about who says what and why, and even how, maybe they would be a little more interesting. . . .
>
> Maybe someone should try writing a total bunk paper and post it on the almighty Web claiming that its contents can actually be supported by facts. Okay, not totally bunk, maybe just subtly bunk; facts just obscure and precise enough to camouflage

themselves into the unquestionable realm of lucid truth. After all, with the introduction we've had to the Web so far, this doesn't seem all that hard to do.

"Dr. James Walker claims that 53% of all newborns have the emotional capacity of a perfectly normal adult" suddenly appears in the "research" writings of thousands of students because some woman named Carol Rogers though it would be funny to play games with high school English students and naive college students alike. "How many of them are actually going to research my research," she thinks to herself. Or better yet, thanks to a pesky little editing error, Melvin L. DeFleur accidentally reports that 38% of children show direct effects of influence from televised violence. Whoops. That should actually say "83%". "Crap! The book's already gone to the publisher!" Suddenly Tony's research paper becomes an exercise in creative writing, or real-life inspired fiction at best. Not to say I don't value research papers, because we couldn't be an "information society" without them. They're one of the best darn ways to learn mediated truth that I know of. . . .

On one level, Tony's e-mail message, which distorts facts from one of the sources he used for his paper, reflects—however playfully—an anxiety over the precision of his work that is common to writers who have just completed a large project. ("Carol Rogers" deliberately misquotes Dr. Walker in order to mislead college students; worry over content, credentials, and medium "grates" on writers' nerves.) On another level, the message not only communicates a healthy skepticism of "the almighty Web," but also applies firsthand knowledge of error—typos—that occur in publication, whether in a research paper, a Web site, or a book. As Tony facetiously distances himself from his work (for example, by referring to himself in the third person), he also demonstrates a skill, enhanced by experience with electronic communications, of demythologizing the "almighty Web." In so doing, Tony demonstrates the same skill that Postman (1995), who is skeptical of computers' role in education, advocates: not blindly following the "god of Technology" whom educators believe "works in mysterious ways" (377). More ironically, Tony's experienced skepticism accomplishes what Birkerts (1994)—who characterizes refusing the "sorcerer of the binary order" alternately as comic attempt and as a crisis at the core of his life (211–13)—finds lacking in computer culture as epitomized by *Wired* magazine:

> The remarkable thing about *Wired* is that it presents a fully self-contained order, a closed circuit. Nowhere in its pages do we find any trace of the murky and not-so-streamlined world that we can still see outside our windows. No ice on the mittens, no fumbling

for quarters while the bus (late) toils toward us through morning traffic. Everything is as clean as a California research park. No sense of getting from here to there. (215–16)

In addition to articulating concern over finding reliable informa-tion on the World Wide Web (my students have needed little coaching on being critical of WWW sources), my students' experience contribut-ing to the WWW has additionally exercised interpersonal skills that Birkerts and Postman fear will atrophy with increased computer use. Students' hours working side by side in the computer lab constructing Web sites, discussion of Internet technologies in class, and presentation of their Web sites to each other demonstrate an alternative to the future that Birkerts predicts of spending "more and more of our time in the cybersphere producing, sending, receiving, responding, and necessar-ily less time interacting in a 'hands-on' way with the old material order" —a future in which we "establish a wide lateral interaction dealing via screen with more people at the same time and our sustained face-to-face encounters diminish" (215). Moreover, students' experience in the classroom, along with their material on the Web, demonstrate what Postman defines as one of the fundamental goals of primary and secondary education: to help students become "civilized people" who can function in groups, to "connect the individual with others," and to "demonstrate the value and necessity of group cohesion" (380–81). Lastly, students' participation in the culture of the WWW qualifies them not only as consumers—however informed—of electronic media, but also as creators of Internet communications who found and shape that information through their words, cognitive and hypertextual links to related material, visual presentation of their messages, and interaction as rhetoricians with others.

Notes

1. For recognition of collaborative learning in the writing classroom, see Lester Faigley's *Fragments of Rationality: Postmodernity and the Subject of Com-position* (1992), p. 165, and Jerome Bump's "Collaborative Learning in the Com-puter Classroom" (1996).

2. In addition to writing in course evaluations that they valued learn-ing to make Web sites, my students at the University of Texas at Austin in 1995–96 ranked their first-year writing course as exceptionally high in the categories "the course was . . . educationally valuable" and "the instructor increased stu-dent knowledge": an anomaly in a required course that students often resent having to take. I suspect that the reason for the high numbers was the inclusion of Web building in the curriculum.

3. In mentioning castles, I not only refer to the literary commonplace of castles in the air, but also play on the "enchanted castles" that Umberto Eco cites as emblematic of the hyperreal in the United States landscape. In *Travels in Hyperreality,* Eco defines hyperreality as a system of substitutes through the example of the neo-Renaissance Hearst castle. Such a "network of references and influences," according to Eco, eventually permeates the realm of history and high culture, and authenticates itself as real (quoted in Vitanza 1996, p. 53).

4. My own incorporation of Web building in composition courses is archived in the following sites: my fall 1995 and spring 1996 rhetoric and composition courses at the University of Texas at Austin (http://www.cwrl.utexas.edu/~betsyb/classfall95/ and http://www.cwrl.utexas.edu/~betsyb/classspring96) and my fall 1997 and spring 1998 exposition and argument course at Valparaiso University (http://www.valpo.edu/home/faculty/bflak/E100fall97/ and http://www.valpo.edu/home/faculty/bflak/E100spring98/)

5. For a plethora of class sites from Computer Writing and Research Labs at the University of Texas at Austin, refer to the following site: http://www.cwrl.utexas.edu/.

6. For suggestions on such a sequence, see Anderson, Benjamin, Busiel, and Paredes-Holt, *Teaching On-Line* (1996), and Butler and Condon, *Writing for the Information Superhighway* (1997).

7. For samples of such a document, see the course sites referred to in note 4.

8. For sites on WWW building and evaluation, see, for example, the Barebones Guide to HTML (http://werbach.com/barebones/), the Sun on the Net guide to Web style (http://www.sun.com/styleguide/), the Yale C/AIM Web style guide (http://info.med.yale.edu/caim/manual/index.html), Unplugged Software's site on Web design tips (http://www.unplug.com/great/), and—a favorite among my students—Jeff Glover's Top Ten Ways to Tell If You Have a Sucky Home Page and Sucky to Savvy sites (http://jeffglover.com/sucky.html and http://jeffglover.com/ss.html, respectively).

9. For suggestions on having students design, format, and maintain portions of a class site before undertaking large projects of their own, see Anderson, Benjamin, Busiel, and Paredes-Holt, p. 132. I am also grateful to Michele Maynard and Margaret Syverson for this suggestion.

10. Students often articulate criteria for evaluating Web sites in response to problems that they encounter as they begin Web projects. Common concerns include the legibility of type, often against too bold of a background; the appropriateness of backgrounds and images; accurate descriptions of links; images or multimedia files that are small enough so Web browsers can download them expediently; clear information about who is producing Web material, and in what context; the clarity and accuracy of copy on the pages in question; and the accessibility of frames, tables, sound or video files, long pages of copy, Java scripting, and Java applets and otherwise animated images (particularly from sites equipped with slow modems, machines with low memory, or early versions of Web browsers).

11. The Usenet newsgroup comp.infosystems.www.announce, for example, is an appropriate forum for publicizing WWW sites on any topic. Students can browse other newsgroups in determining their appropriateness for publicizing particular sites.

12. Server administrators can often indicate the best way to set up a message forum. Many books on Web construction, common gateway interface (CGI) programming, and Perl also give information on how to set up interactive forms and message forums. On the World Wide Web, some informative resources include the University of Florida Perl archive (http://www.cis.ufl.edu/perl/), and sections on programming and the common gateway interface from the Web Developer's Virtual Library (http://www.stars.com). Downloadable, freely available WWW message board scripts such as WWWBoard are also available at http://www.worldwidemart.com/scripts/www.board.shtml as part of Matt's Script Archive (http://www. worldwide mart.com/scripts/). Message forums can be programmed to automate functions such as link-making and annotation of literary texts; for some excellent examples of such functions for message forums, see the Literary Contexts and Contests site at the University of Texas at Austin at http://www.cwrl.utexas.edu/~contests. Commercial message forum applications such as NetForum additionally automate some text formatting in message forum postings, such as the paragraph space command. Classroom course management packages such as WebCT, Blackboard, and Lotus LearningSpace also often include Web forum programs.

Works Cited

Anderson, D., B. Benjamin, and B. Paredes-Holt. 1998. *Connections: A Guide to On-Line Writing*. Boston: Allyn and Bacon.

Anderson, D., B. Benjamin, C. Busiel, and B. Paredes-Holt. 1996. *Teaching On-Line: Internet Research, Conversation, and Composition*. New York: HarperCollins.

Birkerts, S. 1994. *The Gutenberg Elegies: The Fate of Reading in an Electronic Age*. Boston: Faber & Faber.

Bump, J. 1996. "Collaborative Learning in the Postmodern Classroom." In *Situating College English: Lessons from an American University*, ed. E. Carton and A. Friedman. Westport, CT: Bergin & Garvey.

Butler, W., and W. Condon. 1997. *Writing for the Information Superhighway*. Boston: Allyn and Bacon.

Faigley, L. 1992. *Fragments of Rationality: Postmodernity and the Subject of Composition*. Pittsburgh: University of Pittsburgh Press.

Postman, N. 1995. "Virtual Students, Digital Classroom." *The Nation* (October 9): 377–82.

Powell, C. Clark. 1997. *Working the Web: A Student's Guide*. Austin, TX: Harcourt Brace.

Vitanza, V. 1996. *CyberReader*. Boston: Allyn and Bacon.

Wann, J. 1996. Personal e-mail, April 17.

Appendix A

Getting Started on Netscape

Using Netscape to explore the World Wide Web is an activity that will help you with your researched papers for this and other classes, that can provide you with a topic for your next paper, and that can put a world of information at your fingertips, from top news stories and e-mail directories to the latest trivia about the *X-Files* (or whatever your interest).

About the World Wide Web

The World Wide Web is a system of structuring information on the Internet that resembles a giant hypertext document. What this means is that it's full of "links"—sound, image, text, and even video files linked to one another—that you can use to get from one document—generally, a "Web page"—to another. (Note: "Web site" is a slightly broader term than "Web page." A Web page is a Web site; a Web site, however, may consist of a homepage and several related pages linked to it. The UT homepage, for example, is basically the cover page for the UT Web site; the Computer Writing and Research Lab homepage is also the cover page for the CWRL's larger Web site.)

There are four basic ways to get around on the World Wide Web:

1. Links. Through the World Wide Web, you can simply click on a link to connect to something else (text links appear in a different color type than the rest of the print on the page; other types of links—image, sound, whatever—generally offer some direction or visual symbol, for example an arrow or a text link, that instructs you to click on it).

2. Buttons (such as "forward," "back," or "home" at the top of your screen, once you're in Netscape).

3. Searches. UT's homepage links to several keyword search programs that will search the World Wide Web for you. Experiment with various keyword searchers (sometimes called "Web browsers") to see what works best for you.

4. Addresses, or "Universal Resource Locators" (URLs). If there's a specific Web page you're looking for, you can type in the address (what generally begins with "http://www") by selecting "open link" from the file menu. Think of URLs as something like e-mail addresses or telephone numbers.

To open Netscape from a CWRL classroom: simply double-click on Netscape from the Internet folder. Netscape should open automatically to the Computer Writing and Research Lab homepage. Move on to the Netscape Scavenger Hunt; you're ready to begin.

Appendix B

Netscape Scavenger Hunt
To do in groups of 3–4 (move through each part sequentially).

PART ONE: COMPUTER WRITING AND RESEARCH LAB

1. What is the URL for the Computer Writing and Research Lab homepage?

2. From the "Online Courses" link on the CWRL homepage, click to another class's InterChange transcript. List the name of the instructor and the basic topic of the InterChange.

3. From the "Student Resources and Handouts" link on the CWRL homepage, click to the "UT e-mailsetup for Macs" directions. Give the directions' URL.

4. From the "Personal Home Pages" link on the CWRL homepage, browse CWRL staff pages, and list the name of one CWRL staff person who features a photo of him- or herself.

5. From the "Research Starting Points" link on the CWRL homepage, click to a "CWRL-recommended Web site" and describe it in a sentence or two.

6. From the "Division of Rhetoric and Composition" link on the CWRL homepage, click to the Undergraduate Writing Center homepage and answer the following questions:
* How late is the Undergraduate Writing Center open today?
* What could you talk about with an Undergraduate Writing Center Consultant, if you so chose?

PART TWO: UNIVERSITY OF TEXAS AT AUSTIN

1. What is the URL for the University of Texas at Austin homepage?

2. What is the title of one of the front-page stories from today's *Daily Texan*?

3. What is the office phone number of UT's president?

4. From the "Registered Student Organizations" link from UT's "e-mail and phone directory":
* when and where do UT's College Republicans meet?
* name two of the officers of UT's University Democrats.

5. From the "Student Affairs" link on the UT homepage, link your way to what's for supper today in UT's residence halls. What is tonight's entree?

6. From the "UT Library Online" link on the UT homepage, go into UTCAT. What is the call number for Ed Krol's book *The Whole Internet: User's Guide and Catalog*?

7. From the "UT Library Online" link on the UT homepage, link to "Quick Reference." From *Bartlett's Familiar Quotations*, copy one quote from Shakespeare's *Hamlet.*

PART THREE: OUT INTO CYBERSPACE

1. Using the "search" link on the UT homepage, and then linking to "keyword search" and an appropriate keyword searcher (I recommend "Aliweb," "Web

Crawler," or "Yahoo Search"), find one interesting fact about Shakespeare—where a given play is being performed, the opening line of a play or a sonnet that you can access online, the answer to a frequently asked question (FAQ) about Shakespeare—or whatever. Give the URL for where you found the information.

2. Using any of the keyword searchers listed above, list another book, besides those in the Vampire Chronicles, that Anne Rice has written. Under what pseudonyms did Anne Rice write?

3. Using any of the keyword searchers listed above, list who or what is on the cover of this week's *Time* magazine—both the U.S. edition and the international edition.

4. Using any of the keyword searchers listed above, find your way to the Manga Publishing homepage. List one interesting fact about the *X-Files, Mortal Kombat,* or whatever else you find in the Manga Publishing Web site.

5. Using any of the keyword searchers listed above, find a political or advocacy group's homepage (e.g., the NAACP, Christian Coalition, National Organization for Women, American Indian Movement (AIM), Amnesty International, People for the American Way—or whatever). Name it, and list an interesting fact, an urgent issue, or an address, phone number, or e-mail address for the organization. Give that organization's URL.

6. Using the World Wide Web Yellow Pages directory, find a listing for an Austin business. List its phone number—and its e-mail address, too, if it has one.

PART FOUR: YOUR FAVORITES

1. Browse in any remaining time that you have left, and list the URL of the top one or two Web sites that you would recommend to your classmates.

IV Publishing on the Web

14 Living Texts on the Web: A Return to the Rhetorical Arts of Annotation and Commonplace

Dean Rehberger
Michigan State University

Exordium

> Hypertext is a kind of weaving—"text" derives ultimately from the Latin texere, and thus shares a common root with "textile"—a structuring with texture—web, warp, and weave, allowing for infinite variation in color, pattern and material; it is the loom that structures the "text-ile."
>
> Kathleen Burnett, "Toward a Theory of Hypertextual Design"

To begin, a word of caution. Too often, the excitement generated by new computer and Internet technologies intimidates many of our fellow faculty members who have found their computers to be nothing more than glorified typewriters and file cabinets. They see the use of the Internet for teaching and publishing as a move toward forcing writing instruction to take a back seat to the teaching of computer skills. For many, the Internet will open information floodgates, drowning our students in trivia and misinformation. Thus, it is best to begin by reminding instructors (and students) that the Internet allows us to take steps both forward and backward. On the one hand, the Internet is creating exciting new spaces that allow for new forms and genres, new ways of processing and thinking about information, knowledge, and creativity. Yet on the other hand, the Internet is simultaneously taking us back to a time before the book became an established object, a cultural "hard fact," and when rhetoric was at the heart of education.

As we know, before the printed book, it was the scholar's job to transcribe manuscripts. In doing so, the scholar would often make changes and annotate to clarify and deepen arguments. Monastic scribes would think little of "individualizing or 'unconsciously modernizing'" a manuscript (Anderson 1983, 47). At the same time, the educated classes would collect poetry and text fragments in commonplace books, intermingling the thoughts of others with their own. Little concern was placed on ownership, and imitation (not the incessant call for originality) was the primary means of learning to compose. The way to the sublime, as Longinus observed, was through "the imitation and emulation of previous great poets and writers" (1967, 80).

In some respects, the texts on the Internet—homepages, Web resources, e-mails, listservs, MOOs, newsgroups, and chats—take us back to the time before the printed book, to a sense of writing as more fluid and malleable. The skills of the Internet harken back to older rhetorical arts of linking, cataloguing, annotating, and collecting, rhetorical arts that remain the primary tropes of academic writing. We do, after all, read texts as hypertexts. Rarely reading a book from cover to cover, we use tables of contents, indexes, footnotes, and endnotes to make links from passage to passage, text to text, idea to idea. We collect and catalogue information—building bibliographies, resources, and libraries—and then turn around and deploy the information—paraphrases, quotations, and imitations—finding "originality" often in synthesis and syncretism. To this end, in my classes I use the Internet to emphasize these older rhetorical arts to create what I have come to call living texts (a term without the "cyber" and "hyper" that, when used, can instantly close the mind of the technophobe).

For Internauts, the living text is simply the familiar forms of homepages and Web resources, but it calls on students to link and network with each other as well as past and future classes. In my courses, students build Web resources as a class, which they add to as a group and individually. Thus, when students have completed the course, their work will remain published for years, a work they can point out to parents, fellow students, and employers as a resource they helped to create. In this paper, I will discuss one example of how students create living texts in a first-year composition course: the structure of the class, the sequence of assignments, and the use of technology. In doing so, I hope to point out that the Internet is not a foreign land or a beautiful paradise but a writing tool that can help our students understand basic academic rhetorical strategies. We must remember, for instance, that the Latin word for introduction, *exordium,* originally "meant 'beginning a web'—by mounting a woof or laying a warp," a wonderful metaphor that calls on writers to weave the multiple strands of their work into a pattern that will entice and entrap the reader (Corbett 1971, 303). That is to say, webs are familiar territories for rhetoricians.

Hyperbole and Litotes

> *And yet to disclose the machinery behind the god is simply to substitute metaphors—indeed, to place the organic in the position of the before, the position of the facade, where it was situated all along. Refusing the face-to-face, we are talking over the shoulder.*
>
> Susan Stewart, *On Longing*

When speaking of the Internet, it is easy to slip into hyperbole. The Internet is compared to the printing press as an agent of social change. Some people believe that it will usher in a brave new world of radical democracy and new forms of information exchange, a means to revive the arts and bolster an ailing culture. It would be easy to make similar hyperbolic claims about how using the Internet for teaching writing can radically improve or destroy student writing, revolutionize or bankrupt the classroom, and save or destroy academic culture. Perhaps it will take one path or the other, but I want to make much more understated claims. In simple terms, the value of using the Web is that it offers a portable class network that is fun, cheap, and easy to use, thus helping instructors employ the current methods of writing pedagogy. In reducing the power of the Internet to a classroom tool, I am not arguing that those who make more grand claims for social change are wrong (nor am I arguing for some mediated position between the overstated and understated), but as Susan Stewart (1993) reminds us, engaging in litotes, to shrink something to the miniature for personal possession, is to expose the "illusion of mastery, of time into space and heterogeneity into order" (172).

Using the Web and computer-assisted instruction not only helps me avoid the presentational mode of teaching while emphasizing a student-centered classroom but also helps me reinforce the theoretical goals of my course. In my teaching, I apply my theoretical interests in critical theory and cultural studies to composition. To help students understand the goals and methods of contemporary cultural studies and writing theory that decenter the subject and destabilize the traditional links among power, mastery, control and knowledge, I avoid traditional teaching methods that often imagine the teacher as the gatekeeper of knowledge and the student as the empty vessel. Students are, after all, much better postmodernists than we are because they are born into a world that constantly bombards them with the fragments and shards of many cultures, an indeterminate world that they must constantly (re)negotiate and (re)construct. Thus learning is not a process of teaching students to "think" (imagining that their minds do not work before they come to the college "fix-it shop") but helping students to articulate their experiences, to understand the experiences of others, and to use different language registers to express their ideas about themselves, others, and their cultures. To accomplish these goals, I have students move out of the classroom, having students read not only written texts but social texts and cultural spaces (from museums and libraries to shopping malls and town halls). One of the best and most efficient ways to do this (avoiding the costs and insurance problems of travel) is to use the Internet to make these visits.

Similarly focusing on portfolios, workshops, group projects, collaboration, revision, and process can help to improve student writing, but these writing strategies can be difficult to negotiate, demanding intricate scheduling, hours of class time, and endless hard copies. By having students post their writings on the Web, these problems can be minimized. It makes workshopping easier, less time-consuming, and more environmentally friendly (no paper). A whole class can read and workshop several student papers without the need for copies. Students can workshop, revise, and workshop again in a single class period. Workshops can extend outside the classroom because students can read several classmates' essays (all if a read-around is called for) before class. Students can thus make better use of class time to discuss comments and revise. Students can also exchange comments using e-mail. Once students start workshopping outside of class, they often continue to do so even when a workshop is not assigned.

While group work can be difficult outside of the class because of busy student schedules, the Internet allows students to meet and work without being present in the same place at the same time. One member of the group can post work, and by using a chat room or e-mail the group can critique, extend, and revise the project. Perhaps most important, the Internet allows for large-scale class publications. While the thought of doing class newspapers, newsletters, magazines, collections, and books has always been enticing, the cost of reproducing even a short publication for a whole class can be prohibitive (especially if a department does not support copying student work). Once images, color, and multiple drafts are added to the mix, doing class publications becomes impossible. On the Internet, however, class publications and resources can be created and revised endlessly. Images, color, sound, and video clips can be added and changed without cost, and the publication can remain alive and useful, long after the class has ended.

One thing I did not expect the Internet to change was the portfolio. I thought that the online portfolio (Webfolio) would differ little from the traditional hard-copy version. Students would simply collect their writings for the term in an electronic folder rather than a pocket folder. Yet here I was wrong. The Webfolios are much more efficient and effective than traditional portfolios. Webfolios allow students to collaborate and share more easily. If a student is having trouble with an assignment, he or she can visit the work of other students in the class to get a sense of how to revise. Students also reported that they returned to projects and reread and revised more because unlike a folder in which they store paper or even a disk on which they store files, the Webfolio kept work continually present and easy to revise. The Webfolios also allowed students to keep their work more organized and available for reflection (a nice break for instructors bombarded by thick portfolios leaking paper).

Similarly, using the Internet makes evaluating student papers much more efficient. Once students have posted their work, the files can be downloaded and called up in a word-processing program. I can then go through and mark surface errors and make comments (using capital letters or a different font) at the site of a problem. I can quickly make revisions as examples to help students without cramming comments in margins and above lines (as a left hander with rather poor penmanship and spelling habits, marking papers has always been a problem). I can then return the paper using e-mail. In doing so, I can give more feedback in less time because I can use computer tools to check my comments for errors in minutes. This method also solves the problem of instructors having to write on students' "master copy." By having students in workshops use the same methods for evaluation, students end up with several evaluated copies of a piece that they can then use to revise the original posted work.

Perhaps most important, the use of word-processing tools has helped me to solve the central problem of marking surface errors. We all know from the work of Mina Shaughnessy and others on evaluating student writing that marking all surface errors does little for students except to discourage them and reinforce the idea that good writing

equals errorless papers. It is much better to give students clues for finding their own errors and to mark only a few chronic errors. While good in theory, to evaluate student papers for chronic surface errors can take a great amount of time. Using computer tools allows me to scan papers rather quickly for the most typical errors (run-ons, fragments, passives, agreement, punctuation) and then mark only some chronic errors for students to edit. I put two asterisks by chronic errors and usually correct a few as examples. I also mark a few of the simple random errors that students can easily correct (typos, spelling, syntax) with one asterisk. Finally, I have found the Internet to be an invaluable tool for handouts and exercises. By posting handouts, I can keep them easily available (and updated) for a whole semester so students have them when needed. Students can also download exercises and work-shop questions into a word-processing program, avoiding the busy work of recopying materials or the waste of reproducing hard copies. In short, while it may take some class time to teach computer skills, in the end, using computers frees up class time for more work on writing skills and revision.

Many of the above practical benefits can be accomplished using pen and paper, a computer and disk, or specialized writing software that turns computer labs into local-area networks (e.g., Norton Connects, Daedulus, Aspects); using the Internet, however, not only saves time and money (Web browser software is free of charge, while obtaining local-area network software can be costly for students or departments to obtain and upgrade) but also helps create a student-centered classroom that leaks beyond borders of class space and time. Hard copy assignments (unless reproduced on a large scale) must be funneled through the instructor and are usually filed after use, while local-area networks confine students to using specific labs at specific times. The Internet allows students to disseminate work to the class (without first going through the instructor) and allows them to respond and comment on writings from any computer linked to the Internet at any time.

However, I will not belabor these points because although it is important to bring diversity into the classroom (as well as redefine the classroom), what is most important is that we teach different ways of reading and writing texts, two processes that are obverse and reverse of the same coin. This is the primary reason for having students create hypertexts. Hypertexts can help students to understand the complex rhetoric and terms of contemporary critical theory and cultural studies. It can do so not by presenting students with texts to be "learned" but by showing students in practice how contemporary theories can help them to understand and negotiate everyday life, or in Kenneth Burke's terms, help them to see how language can be "equipment for living." That is, the Internet and hypertext do not so much introduce them to a new postmodern age but help them to understand their cultures that are already striated and informed by the postmodern.

For example, students can more easily understand an idea like Jacques Derrida's "play of signifying references" with a simple hypertext exercise (Derrida 1974, 7). I have students take an everyday word like *man* or *woman* and define it with a single sentence. The students then define the key terms of the sentence they have created through links. They repeat this process with the definitions of each of the key terms. The small hypertext they create (it gets big fast) becomes a visual representation of how words (signifiers) gain meaning through difference both in space and time, showing the endlessly commutable nature of the signified or, in Roland Barthes's terms, the slipperiness of language. By looking at a few student examples, it is also possible to go on to discuss cultural logic of signs (how, in this example, they often rely on gender stereotypes). With hypertext, it is easy to create exercises that demonstrate Mikhail Bakhtin's "dialogism" or Michel Foucault's "archeology." Exercises like these work both to help define concepts and to teach students in practice how to do hypertext links. In the next section, I will discuss at greater length how I help students to create Web pages and hypertexts.

[handwritten marginalia: excellent assignment! do in a group.]

The Commonplace and Other Annotations

> *1578 Cooper, Thesaurus Introd., A studious young man . . . May gather to himselfe furniture both of words and approved phrases . . . And to make his use at it were a common place booke. 1599 Marston Sco. Villanie xi, 226 Now I haue him, that . . . Hath made a common-place-booke out of playes, And speakes in print.*
>
> Commonplace-book, *Oxford English Dictionary*

At Michigan State University, students are given an e-mail account and four megabytes of space on the main server, called the Andrew File System or AFS. Students can post documents to their AFS space using an FTP program or directly once they have logged on to campus lab computers. I usually schedule two class meetings a week, one of which meets in a computer lab. During a fifteen-week semester, I have students do eleven microprojects. The microprojects differ in length and genre and are sequenced so that students can draw on one to write the next. The microprojects vary from creating a homepage to completing documentation exercises in small groups to working on short summaries to writing longer essays. All student microprojects are posted on the Internet in their Webfolios and may include images, animation, audio files, and video clips. Before submitting the Webfolio for evaluation (which they do twice during the course), students choose any two text-based microprojects for revision. Beyond the microprojects, students also write weekly reading responses using e-mail and complete two group projects using the Web. The group projects draw on materials from the students' Webfolios.

At the beginning of the course, I split the class into small groups of four to five students. The groups work on several projects from workshopping microprojects to completing in-class writings (e.g., text maps, presentations, prewritings, analyses, summaries, discussions, exercises). The groups also create e-mail aliases that allow students to send a message to all members of their group, an alias that includes my e-mail address. The students use the alias to work on group projects and to send out their weekly reading responses. It is important when setting up the groups to find those individuals who have experience with computers and divide them equally among the groups. Often I have the "computer experts" act as captains who draw names from hats (one for women and one for men to ensure gender balance) to form groups. After midterm evaluations, I break up one group and allow students to change groups. I do this because after working in groups for eight weeks, students can handle larger groups and sometimes want to change groups for the sake of variety or because of personality conflicts. The second project also works better if groups are larger, and I find that breaking up one group allows me the chance to get rid of a group that is not working well (one in each class always seems to have problems).

To help students create Web documents, I have created several Internet e-sources: one, an online syllabus (syllaweb) that gives the standard information of all syllabi but has links to additional materials (writing resources) and to student e-mail addresses and homepages; two, a page of links to help students post documents on the Internet, including information about network services at Michigan State University, software download sites, and HTML tutorials; and three, a set of templates for creating homepages, Webfolios, and hypertexts (and syllawebs for instructors). Unlike templates that ask users to fill in the blanks, these templates offer choices and explain the meaning of the different HTML codes used. Students download the templates and open them using a word-processing program. To view their work, students save the file as "text only" and open it using a Web browser. Many new versions of word-processing programs do this automatically. The above materials as well as other handouts can be found at http://writing.msu.edu/rehberger/web.html.

Beyond the Web resources, I prepare three handouts for students: a simple list of HTML commands, an explanation of how to use the word-processing program, and a list of procedures for posting documents on the Web. In preparing the handouts, it is best to keep them brief, minimize written instructions, and maximize visual images. It is better to have a picture of the "tool bar" or "window" the student will encounter than an explanation of it.

During the first class meeting in the computer lab, students are introduced to the word-processing program and the Web browser used by the class; using a template, they also create a homepage. Although this seems like a lot to do in two hours, it works best to do several things and stress only a few skills. It is often good to pair new users with experienced people and to encourage play, hands-on work, and collaboration. For example, I will have students open the word-processing program and play with fonts, challenging them to make the largest possible point size. I will also challenge them to see who can write the most in a five-minute freewrite with the least number of spelling errors (forcing them to use the "word count" and "spell check" tools) or who can find the most interesting color for their homepage. The only skills that need to be stressed are how to open files and save them in the correct format and place. At our second lab meeting, students work in groups to post their homepages and Webfolios on the Internet. We also work on doing Internet searches and downloading images. Using the templates and discussing the HTML handout is all the teaching about creating Web pages that I will do (and it is all students seem to need). I do incorporate new word-processing and hypertext skills into lab exercises, and each week students will write on the chalkboard new techniques, resources, and codes they have found for enhancing Web pages, but after the first two weeks the focus turns from computer skills to writing skills.

The following schedule and assignments are typical for my first-year writing classes (although the explanations of assignments have been truncated for the purposes of space). During the first half of the course, we read several essays about multiculturalism in the United States and the issues surrounding race, ethnicity, and immigration. The second half of the course focuses on contemporary culture and the influences of popular media. For this section of the course, we read about movies, TV, music, style, advertising, museums, and architecture. Students are encouraged to find and write about examples of these that go beyond the readings; group members are encouraged to focus on the same medium so that they can share research materials and focus their projects.

1. Microproject #1: Homepage—Using the template, students create a homepage in class. They can do anything to their homepage, but for the duration of the course they must keep links to the writing center, the class syllabus, and their Webfolio.

2. Microproject #2: Webfolio—The Webfolio is where students store their writings for the course. They create a folder in their AFS space and a page of links that lists the contents of the folder. The Webfolio includes all microprojects and other samples of student writing (i.e., poetry, short stories, essays, personal writings).

3. Microproject #3: Commonplace Site—This is a place to collect ideas from our readings. Students may quote or paraphrase passages and are encouraged to collect those things that strike them as important, interesting, or well said. Students are directed to be sure to introduce the text fragment so a student who has not done the reading could understand what it is about. They should add at least two passages a week to their commonplace site for the remainder of the course.

4. Microproject #4: Summary—Students summarize one essay from the week's reading. The summary is written for a fellow student who has been ill and unable to do the reading.

5. Microproject #5: Imitation—Students do two imitations of one passage selected from the readings. The first imitation keeps the same topic but is rewritten as if it were written by a student in class talking while eating at Taco Bell. The second imitation keeps the same level of formality and structure but focuses on a different topic. Beginning with an introductory page, students create links between the different imitations to form one hypertext.

6. Microproject #6: Editorial—Based on class readings, students write an editorial in response to the question, "Because of the many cultures in the United States, how is the 'American' identity being redefined?" Students use materials from their readings and microprojects to complete the editorial.

7. Revision Week: Midterm Webfolio—Focusing on microprojects #4, #5, and #6, students revise any two for the first Webfolio evaluation; they also complete a reflection.

8. Project Week: What Is an "American"?—Pulling together the different viewpoints in their groups and from the readings,

students define what it means to be an "American." They *Canadian*
write for other first-year students who are not in this class.
They use writings directly from group members' Webfolios
(although they often revise material to fit the new rhetorical
situation). Creative responses to the assignment are encouraged. Although the project may be a traditional linear text,
the final project may present a unique organization and form,
and it may include text fragments, links, images, definitions,
sound, video clips, and much more. The only limits are virtual.

9. Microproject #7: Summary—Students write a summary of a
   particular cultural artifact (a movie, a TV show, a fad, a shopping center, an album, a performance, and so on). The summary is written for a colleague in the field of cultural studies
   who has not seen the artifact.

10. Microproject #8: Review—Get together with another mem-
    ber of your group and do a Siskel-and-Ebert-style review of
    your cultural artifacts. In creating your hypertext, you can
    write it as a dialogue.

11. Microproject #9: Rhetorical Analysis—Working in groups of
    three, students choose one of several cultural critiques found
    on the Internet to analyze. Using hypertext links, they anno-
    tate the essay, explaining its rhetorical situation (PRESS): pur-
    pose, audience, evidence, structure, and style. They also de-
    fine any difficult or key terms.

12. Microproject #10: Prewriting Cultural Critique—Working in
    pairs, students complete a prewriting exercise for microproject
    #11.

13. Microproject #11: Cultural Critique—Based on class readings
    and their microprojects, students write a cultural critique.
    They are encouraged to visit the prewriting microprojects
    (#10) of other students to get more ideas. This project is a
    longer essay and is discussed extensively in class.

14. Revision Week: Final Webfolio—All students are required to
    revise microproject #11 as well as one other from the second
    half of the course (#7, #8, #9); they also complete a reflection.

15. Project Week: Analyzing U.S. Media Culture—Using the
    course anthology as a model, the class constructs a cultural
    studies reader with their cultural critiques. The groups are
    each responsible for writing one chapter. Each chapter has an
    introduction, and each critique has a headnote and study ques-
    tions. Creative responses are again encouraged.

For the two group projects, students are expected to write some new
text but can rely on materials from their Webfolios to build the group
project. It works best if group members are assigned specific roles as

specialists: Web builder (who codes and posts projects), library researcher (who collects library materials), Internaut researcher (who
collects Internet resources), media specialist (who collects images,
icons, and media files), and Webitor (who edits the final project). While
all members of the group are responsible for all areas of the project, the
student with an assigned role will collect and redistribute materials
from the group members, will ensure that his or her area is completed,
and will meet with the instructor as a specialist group. For example, all
of the Webmasters will meet with the instructor to discuss problems and
exchange ideas. Meeting with individual groups and specialists is an
effective way to do Web projects in large classes of fifty or more
students.

Ambiguity and Other Conclusions

> *For one may know what has been put into the pot, and recognize the objects
> of the stew, but the juice in which they are sustained must be regarded with
> a peculiar respect because they are all in there too, somehow, and one does
> not know how they are combined or held in suspension.*

> William Empson, *Seven Types of Ambiguity*

As I reflect on the problems created by a Webbed writing environment,
I find myself listing those things that all writing instructors should be
prepared for in any writing class whether computer technology is used
or not. To make the Web projects work, an instructor needs to emphasize
group work, to allow room for failure, and to expect the unexpected. As
it is with writing itself, group work is the best means for learning to use
computers. When students help other students, they not only feel a
sense of accomplishment but they reinforce their own skills. The
presentation mode is a sure way to failure because students need hands-
on work with computers. It is best to mix the learning of computer skills
with the learning of writing skills: working on freewrites, prewritings,
exercises, revisions, workshops, and editings in the computer lab is a
nice way to blend the two skills.

Instructors will find that students have problems the first few
weeks coding and posting their work and thus should build in extra
time during lab periods and into the syllabus for students to finish their
work in class and not be penalized for projects posted a few days late. In
other words, it is not a good idea to schedule student workshops or
peer-editing groups during the first three lab periods that demand all
students have completed drafts. It is better during this time to have class

workshops that evaluate sample projects or a few of the student projects. As always, students will have surprising interpretations of assignments; thus, modeling workshops as a class will help students to understand the expectations of both class writing assignments and student workshops (peer-editing groups).

Strangely, publishing on the Internet presents only a few problems for students and instructors that go beyond the normal problems of the writing class, yet even these are not common concerns for all writing instructors. Students should make back-up copies on disk of all Web materials and turn in the disks at the end of the term, and instructors should be prepared to answer questions about the problems of using different operating systems. Internet servers are generally safe places to store materials (often safer than disks and hard drives), but they can have problems. The problems of using different operating systems and getting connected at home or in the dormitory are best handled in two ways. One, the instructor should find the links and numbers of campus computer consultants and incorporate them into the syllaweb. And two, the instructor should take ten minutes every few weeks to have students discuss problems of doing class work on their personal computers and in other campus computer labs. Often, the answers are simple and can be supplied by the students in the class. These two steps help keep the class "student centered" and reinforce the idea that students must take the initiative (especially at a large university) to seek out those resources designed to help them during their college careers.

NB Backups

Although I have been using the Internet for only a few years, I have had great success. As one student (a senior and the best writer in the class) reported, "This is the first time I have ever asked others to read what I wrote for a class." The students have enjoyed the experience because they have found Web publishing to be fun and exciting. Much of the fun comes from playing with a new medium, adding color, links, images, sound, animation, and video to their writing experience. As the Internet becomes more ordinary, part of the everyday lives of students, using the Web in writing classes may lose its power to generate interest in the writing process and excite students' imaginations. We are thus living in one of those rare historical moments when older forms of language are struggling with new forms. While the question of how much the Internet is responsible for this clash is open to debate, it does make the cultural struggle visible, and it may be worth our while to take advantage of the Web while the moment lasts.

Works Cited

Anderson, Benedict. 1983. *Imagined Communities: Reflections on the Origin and Spread of Nationalism.* London: Verso.

Burnett, Kathleen. 1993. "Toward a Theory of Hypertextual Design." *Postmodern Culture* 3(2) (January). http://muse.jhu.edu/journals/postmodern_culture/v003/3.2burnett.html.

Corbett, Edward P. J. 1971. *Classical Rhetoric for the Modern Student.* 2nd ed. New York: Oxford University Press.

Derrida, Jacques. 1974. *Of Grammatology.* Trans. Gayatri Chakravorty Spivak. Baltimore: Johns Hopkins.

Longinus. 1967. "On the Sublime." In *The Great Critics: An Anthology of Literary Criticism,* trans. W. Rhys Roberts and ed. James Harry Smith and Edd Winfield Parks, 65–111. 3rd ed. New York: Norton.

Stewart, Susan. 1993. *On Longing: Narratives of the Miniature, the Gigantic, the Souvenir, the Collection.* Durham: Duke University Press.

15 Students as Builders of Virtual Worlds: Creating a Classroom Intranet

Douglas Eyman
Cape Fear Community College, Wilmington, North Carolina

As composition pedagogy has moved from the current-traditional model toward a collaborative process-oriented model which focuses on an epistemology of socially constructed knowledge, the concurrent advent of computer-mediated communication technologies now affords the classroom instructor the medium through which a social-epistemic rhetoric can be enacted, serving as both a focal point for the building of community and a method of collaboration. I see the use of World Wide Web (WWW) software as a method to build a collaboratively created community space within a composition classroom; however, the predominant style of most WWW-based hypertext pages (i.e., emphasizing graphics and lists of links), does not lend itself to the kind of academically oriented expression we are expected to teach our students in first-year composition classes. To mitigate the possibility of the current style of Web document design undermining the purpose of the composition class, I propose that instructors create distinct and separate Web spaces for their classrooms—thus making these technologies useful for instructors who do not have Internet access, and also creating a less public (and therefore more "safe") writing space for students to collaboratively create and explore.

Creating what Michael Joyce (1988) terms a "constructive" hypertext—one which can be built upon by readers who write themselves into the text—is difficult to accomplish using the World Wide Web as the hypertext medium. While the WWW can be useful for composition instruction in a variety of ways (as evidenced elsewhere in this volume), it does have its downside. Not only is it difficult to support constructive hypertext on the WWW, the Web is a very public space, and a paradigm of Web publishing has evolved which is contradictory to the kinds of composition we teach in our classes. Despite these drawbacks, I hear ever more writing teachers confessing their excitement that their classes have access to the Web or proclaiming their disappointment that their classes do not have access; if our focus becomes so narrow as to see the WWW as a necessary tool for writing pedagogy, we may lose sight of the other opportunities available to us.

When I was teaching composition in a networked classroom, I tried unsuccessfully to convince my department that having access to the WWW would be useful for my classes, and I too was initially disappointed that my students were being prevented from using what I perceived as an excellent resource. However, since I wanted my students to explore hypertext composition (and move from creating individual texts to creating interlinked collaborative metatexts), I decided to build my own Web—a Classroom Wide Web (CWW) rather than a World Wide Web. In so doing, I discovered that there are several benefits to building such a web (and I seem to have anticipated the popularity of "intranets" by about a year):

- The intranet provides a safe learning environment for initial writing projects.
- Using an intranet requires fewer technology skills than using the Internet.
- Intranets also provide reliable access and high connection speeds.

A networked classroom can easily be configured as an "intranet" or internal web accessible only to those with access to that particular network, so the first benefit I noticed was that the students felt comfortable working within a known and supportive social atmosphere—unlike the WWW, the CWW did not present student work to the relatively scary real audience that resided on the Internet (some members of whom can be harsh or unjust critics). I did want my students to experience the sense of having a real audience, however, so I gradually guided them from writing for each other to writing for other composition classes which met in the networked classroom (a benefit of teaching more than one computer-assisted composition class in a given semester). Using an intranet in this way also removed a layer of bureaucracy associated with using the Internet in the same way— student work was not "published" as such, and I therefore did not have to worry about the administrative aspect of a variety of issues ranging from student permission for publication to copyright infringement and plagiarism.

Another benefit of building an intranet is that I could make it very easy for students to work with each other's texts, enabling the establishment of constructive hypertexts; the intranet required only that students learn to use a browser and a word processor (or an integrated browser/editor such as Netscape Communicator), eliminating the need to learn telnet, FTP, and other programs that would be necessary to accomplish the same goal via the WWW (allowing me to maintain a focus on communicating in writing, rather than on the use of particular applications of technology). A final benefit of using an intranet is that one need not worry about lost connections or unknown hosts, and the speed of access and interaction (for both reading and writing) is greatly increased.

The decision to utilize technology as a communication medium in my composition classes was an easy one for me because I believe that computer-mediated communication can help students learn to communicate in writing; however, my first attempts at incorporating technology into my classes were not resounding successes. I had been taught to teach writing in non-technology-enhanced classes and classes where computers were present, but were not utilized for communication, only serving as word processors for students to use in class. I discovered that using computer-mediated communication technologies in my classes required me to rethink my whole pedagogy. It is not sufficient to transfer traditional composition pedagogies (in this case, traditional refers not to theory, but to practice—non-computer-facilitated classrooms) to the computer-assisted composition class; in order to be successful, students have to see the use of technology as an integral part of the structure of the course. It is not enough to explain the technology and provide tip sheets and then expect students to use the technology for the assignments which are designed for completion in a computer-facilitated medium. Students must learn to use the technology in the context of the writing assignments; there must be a convergence of the learning of computer-mediated communication and the practice of writing. Thus, over the course of several semesters, I began to devise a curriculum that placed computer-facilitated writing assignments at the core of the course.

A critical factor in the successful incorporation of computer-mediated communication technology in the classroom is the presentation of the technology itself. I found that teaching students how to create hypertext (using hypertext markup language—HTML) as a unit in and of itself was counterproductive; my students did not see the connection between learning the technology and learning how to write, and they ended up resisting the technology because they saw it as a superfluous assignment being forced upon them by an overzealous technophile. I made this mistake during my earlier attempts to incorporate hypertext in my composition classes—I was still teaching from a "traditional" mode of operation and had not yet fully grasped the need to completely revise my pedagogy. On successive attempts to incorporate the technology into my classes, I found that teaching HTML in the context of the writing assignments was far more readily accepted by the students as a legitimate endeavor, particularly when creating hypertext documents was made an integral component of the course (as opposed to one unit out of several). For this same reason, I had difficulty transferring my hypertext-based course to a traditional classroom: requiring students to make extensive use of technology without providing a convenient means of demonstrating or facilitating its use led once more to student resistance. It is important to present the technology in the context of the practice of communication and composition, and it is important to fully support the incorporation of the technology by providing students with regular, facilitated access to a networked computer environment. I found that it was also helpful to move students from less complex, more nearly linear uses of hypertext to more complex, more nearly nonlinear uses; I was also able to nicely integrate this approach to teaching the technology into my pedagogical goal of moving students from expressive to transactional epistemologies. The general theme of my course became a movement from lesser to greater connectivity (both in terms of the act of composition as a social connection and in terms of technological connections).

The main projects of my hypertext-intensive course consist of four computer-facilitated writing assignments, supplemented by the use of electronic journals, participation in a class newsgroup, reading assignments (from both printed texts and digital texts) and group discussion. The four primary assignments in this first-year composition course are: an autobiographical description intended for a small, known audience (the class itself); the writing of an individual hypertext essay, organized as linked lexia; the linking of the previous essays to other students' essays, with the creation of "bridge" pages which explore the process of collaborative intertextuality; and the creation of a hypertext journal (based on the collaborative peer-review process employed by *Kairos: A Journal for Teachers of Writing in Webbed Environments*).

The structure of my hypertext-based class moves students from creating public personal narratives (acting as individual writers, but writers with a real audience) to working in collaborative teams to produce knowledge bases which can be linked to and explored by other students—the students are thus engaged in a continuing process of learning to write both individually and collaboratively. The progression of the course is intended to bring students through the goals of an expressivist pedagogy into a social constructivist pedagogy; from a subjective to a transactional epistemology (Berlin 1987).

As students in my courses move from personal narrative (expressivist epistemology) to the collaboratively produced journal assignment, they can see how their writing changes as they move from individually authored singular texts to individually authored lexia which take their shape and context from interactions with other individually authored lexia. The form of collaboration in the final assignment includes texts which are written by several students working together to form a single lexia (or set of lexia—a hypertext node) and the weaving of individual lexia into a larger metatext created by the interaction of the individual voices speaking to, at, and with each other.

Because hypertexts are constructed of autonomous lexia which are then linked together, collaborative writing can be conducted in several ways: for instance, students can individually create lexia and then together decide upon links, students can work together on both lexia and links, or students can create larger hypertext documents (both links and lexia) and then weave *them* into larger hypertext documents. Because hypertext authorship can focus upon either individual-centered writing or collaborative, group-centered writing, it has the versatility to guard against the resistance to collaboration that frequently occurs when students are asked to write together. Hum Sue Yin (1992) argues that "when we, as teachers, create artificial environments and mandate that our students work in groups, we do our students a disservice. These students are used to depending on themselves; they are uneasy about depending on others for their grade. Hence, group work for them is often threatening and uncomfortable" (31). Multiply-authored hypertexts allow the student to write individually and then link his or her individual writing to a larger text; therefore, the student can be evaluated as an individual and as part of a larger group without necessarily having to depend on others. Simultaneously, the dialogue-oriented nature of hypertext can encourage students to participate in the authorship of the hypertext document by providing multiple points of intersection for the individual discourses.

Because students can more readily view and share their hypertext lexia, it is easier for them to visualize extended pathways of links which move between and among multiple texts. One of the benefits of *not* having Internet access is that students' visions of what hypertext is and what it can be are not contaminated by the all-too-prevalent "list of links" style of writing for the Web; rather, they are free to create the World Wide Web for themselves, if in miniature. In this scenario, students can build their own comprehensive web using the classroom as a world in itself. I like to work in this type of environment before introducing my students to the Web at large because I can make them think of hypertext in terms of composition and communication; that is, they have the opportunity to define hypertext for themselves as a medium with far more depth than its current incarnation on the WWW actually has. And the more we teach our students to take their writing seriously, and to see their work as a contribution to the larger activity of social meaning-making, then there will be a better chance that the Web itself will reflect this activity, rather than becoming a series of "homepages" which, although often at least entertaining, rarely contribute much original thought or argument.

If we encourage our students to see that they can create their own WWW right in the classroom, a wealth of possibilities for writing assignments presents itself; moreover, these assignments focus not only on the process of composing, but also on the goal of communicating. Each student, for instance, could be asked to build a node on this web about a particular facet of a common topic which the class is exploring as a whole, or small groups of students could create sites which relate to their particular disciplines. For the first assignment, students could be able to link their work together by seeing where the facets of the common topic align themselves to form a recognizable subject; for the second, the students' projects could be linked to a central, class-designed index page from which a reader can go to any project. Additionally, these assignments can be continued with new classes over the course of several terms, constantly expanding and growing until the web does become a world of socially constructed knowledge in its own right. Aside from creating sites, students can also analyze and critique the sites of their classmates (and of those who contributed before them) and in turn make their critiques part of the growing web.

The First Homepage: Autobiography of the Student-as-Writer

For the first essay, I usually ask students to see themselves as writers and create an autobiography which focuses upon their history and experience of writing; this assignment stresses internal dialogue—the goal of expressivist epistemology. During the course of this assignment, I introduce basic HTML and teach the students to post their "final" (or "more nearly finished") drafts to the CWW (the intranet). Students end up creating a "homepage" which is accessible from the initial course syllaweb (also located on the intranet, although I make a version without links to student works available on the WWW as well, so students can access it outside of class). This homepage will be subject to revision throughout the course, and a space is reserved on the initial lexia for links to the other assignments in the course. Because these homepages are not connected to the Internet, I feel comfortable teaching my students to add images of themselves to their pages; I find that students who are unfamiliar with the WWW (or are only passingly familiar with it) become very excited when they see themselves (both visually and textually) on the screen. A variant of the writer's autobiography is an assignment in which the student creates an image of him- or herself as an iconographic representation, along with a critical examination of the reasons and implications behind the choice of icon. There are, in fact, many possible approaches to the first assignment, but in order to follow the progression from self-investigation to other-investigation, I do not encourage hypertext linking or collaboration for this initial text.

The Hypertext Essay

The second essay introduces the students to the writing of hypertext lexia and hypertext linking. Students spend a good deal of time in class discussion (both in class and on the newsgroup) exploring issues of hypertext organization and navigation. I generally ask the students to create a hypertext essay that examines their current choice of a major (often based on Kiniry and Rose's [1993] "Exploring the Discourse of One's Major" from *Critical Strategies for Academic Thinking and Writing*, 2nd ed., pp. 775–806). The final part of this assignment requires the student to create a lexia about the organization of the hypertext, encouraging a critical examination of the hypertext style employed; this final lexia is linked from the student's homepage and includes within it links to the assignment. This assignment, too, draws more from expressivist epistemology in its emphasis on self-awareness and in the form of the composition; however, the content encourages students to see themselves as members of distinct discourse communities whose bases of knowledge have been socially constructed.

Building Collaborative Web Sites from Individually Authored Nodes

The third assignment asks students to read each other's hypertexts and create links between them based on content and on the final lexia about organization and navigation of hypertext. Each student must link his or her work to the work of at least two other students; after determining where the links would occur, students create links to intermediate "bridge pages" (rather than linking directly to each other's work). These bridge pages are collaborations between two or more students wherein the students describe their reasons for linking to particular texts from their own and/or argue against particular links. This is a particularly difficult assignment in terms of logistics, and it sometimes becomes necessary to mediate the formation of the collaborative groups (e.g., if one student's work has eight links to it, only three of those other students should work on the collaborative bridge page).

I find that some students have difficulty critiquing other students' work—they simply acknowledge the work without offering any constructive criticism. With this assignment, though, the collaborative bridge pages serve to draw students into a more critically oriented frame of reference, and I have noticed that I needed to provide active mediation in order to make sure that the students did not feel that their work was being attacked or invaded—and this is also one of the reasons that I do not encourage the interlinking of personal narratives.

The Hypertext Journal Project

Finally, for the Hypertext Journal project, students are divided into small groups which work together to determine topics of mutual interest to the group which are relative to the course (or in the case of a journalism class, "beats"), and asked to report upon or address those topics. Ideally, the focus of the journal and the topics themselves will be generated by the class, but if the current incarnation of a given course is focusing upon a particular theme or discipline, the topics may be assigned.

The students are asked to consider their hypertext journal as an online publishing venue for the class; in order to be successful, the students will have to consider their intended audience, the larger context of publishing venues in which their journal will appear, and questions of copyright and acknowledgment (the legal aspects of publishing). For this assignment, I ask students to combine traditional library-oriented research on their topics with primary-source gathering activities such as interviews and attendance of public lectures, city council meetings, poetry readings, etc. Each group must work as a team in order to produce an essay for inclusion in the journal—but the essay (a hypertext essay) must be constructed of individually crafted lexia. In addition to writing individual parts of the essay, each student is assigned an additional role within the group—one person works with the "editorial staff" and one with the "editorial board" (acting as a representative of their group), one person is responsible for copyediting the entire essay, one person works with the graphic-arts design team.

The editorial staff (made up of one representative from each team) is charged with developing the organization of the journal and making sure submissions are appropriate and completed on time. When the journal is complete, the editorial staff will write a collaborative "From the Editor" lexia for inclusion in the issue. Each member of the editorial board chooses two essays to work with (excluding their own groups') and are charged with providing constructive criticism and feedback. The editorial staff and editorial board will work together at the initial stage of development, the topic proposal period, wherein each group submits a proposal outlining their topic, approach, and initial thesis. The instructor acts as an ex officio member of both editorial board and editorial staff.

The copyeditor must follow the journal's style guidelines (I usually use a combination of MLA and ACW) and make sure that his or her group's essay is free from surface error. The copyeditor also serves as a "links editor," assisting in the organization and navigation of the hypertext essay during its production and making sure there are no broken links during the final copyedit.

The graphic-arts design team works on the visual appearance of the journal and designs the interface which will hold all of the essays in one issue of the journal. This team is encouraged to research the design of existing online journals and is required to provide a lexia describing their research and choices (similar to the editors' lexia).

I allow each team to work independently, providing some time in class for students to work on the journal and some class discussion time devoted to journal issues; however, other reading and discussion assignments continue during this time, so students are also expected to work outside of class. In order to make sure that the students are completing their tasks in a timely fashion, each student is required to make a weekly report to the class newsgroup. Requests for help and conflict mediation, on the other hand, are sent directly to the instructor.

Although this assignment is designed for implementation upon an intranet, it could easily be replicated on a server with WWW access: once completed, the journal (which may be modeled after existing online journals, such as *Kairos*) can be advertised on the WWW and responses (letters to the editor, or submissions for a "feedback" column) can be included in the journal as well. Additionally, each term a new class can add an "issue" to the continuing run of the journal (or new classes could create new journals altogether).

As a final note about the hypertext journal project, Keith Dorwick (1996) has collected a list of classes writing publications on the World Wide Web entitled "Writing for the World: Student Writing For and On the Internet"; his pages point to a wealth of resources and examples for any teachers contemplating this assignment.

Placing the computer-facilitated medium at the core of my composition course has helped me to realize a student-centered pedagogy—as the students work, individually and collaboratively, they become engaged in the assignments and begin to see me less as an authority figure and more as a facilitator. The students begin to ask each other questions about both what they are writing and how to achieve a particular technological effect, rather than always seeking my approval. The class itself is energizing to me—unlike some noncomputer assisted classes I have taught, the students do not seem to dread coming to class; instead, they are working together, moving around and collaborating in what appears to an outsider to be a completely chaotic fashion. Once I learned to let go of the control that seemed expected of me in the traditional class, I learned to thrive on the living chaos of engaged and excited learners around me.

Of course, there are caveats. In any computer-facilitated class, it's imperative to make sure that the students themselves don't get lost in the matrix of technology within which they must write. After a few initial disasters, I found that the students were more comfortable, at least initially, if they had a set of codified rules (particularly important for naming documents) and had some handouts explaining the performance of basic tasks. As they learned more about the programs they were using (by using them for their assignments), they often taught themselves more advanced techniques (which they excitedly shared with their peers). Many of my students have begun the class terrified of computers. It's important to give them permission to make mistakes and to provide a supportive learning environment for the technologically hesitant. It is also extremely important to teach all students to back up their work in at least three different places.

As students began building their virtual webs, I saw many of them gain confidence in their abilities, and because the technology was placed at the core of the course—was in fact an intrinsic element for the completion of the assignments—many of my students learned to perceive the technology as transparent, enabling them to focus more completely on the tasks of communication and composition. Until I focused my courses on the creation of hypertexts for each assignment, I had generally incorporated only one or two hypertexts into my class; since hypertext became only one element of the course, the students did not have time to learn how to use it effectively, and they often were unable to see beyond themselves, that is, they could not break out of a subjective epistemology. When I made my courses hypertext-intensive, the students were far more open to collaboration and began to make the transition to transactional epistemology. My students became not only builders of knowledge, but builders of their own virtual world.

Postscript: Implementing an Intranet

An intranet can be created in any networked computer classroom with a minimum of effort—only a copy of any Web browser and a shared directory on the network are required for a minimal implementation. The simplest method of creating an intranet requires each computer to have a browser (I use Netscape Navigator) for each student to use to view hypertext documents. The network must also have a public directory to which everyone has read/write access (the existence of such a directory is fairly standard for Novell and NT networks—if one doesn't exist on your network, have your network administrator create one for you). When a student wishes her hypertext to be placed on the Classroom Wide Web (CWW), she simply copies it to the shared directory (or saves it to that directory directly from a word processor), being very careful to follow the naming convention established for the class (so as to not overwrite someone else's page). Once the page is there, a link can be placed to it using the following HTML syntax:
<a href="file:///F|/shared/angief1a.htm">.
In this example, *F* is the letter of the network drive, *shared* is the shared directory name, and the filename represents Angie Flower's essay 1, lexia a. The .htm extension indicates that the document is a hypertext markup language document (I use Windows 3.1, so can only have .htm; Windows 95 and most other platforms except DOS will allow .html). In order to prevent naming problems, each student could have his or her own subdirectory of the shared directory—the address would then add the subdirectory name after /shared/.

The browsers could be set to open to the class's syllaweb or a homepage for the classroom, providing links to the pages of each class which utilizes that network. If students using the network are prone to mischief or the classroom is also an open lab, it may be advisable to assign usernames and passwords to your students and have your network administrator restrict access to the shared directory to only the students in your class.

If you want to incorporate CGI scripts, Javascript, Java, or plan to set up programs which require a server (such as HyperNews), then you will need to set up a server. Servers are available for most platforms; setting it up on an isolated network is a bit trickier, and I recommend that instructors who desire the use of a server for their intranets engage the services of their academic computer support personnel.

Works Cited

Berlin, J. 1987. *Rhetoric and Reality: Writing Instruction in American Colleges: 1900–1985.* Carbondale: Southern Illinois University Press.

Doherty, M., ed. 1996. *Kairos: A Journal for Teachers of Writing in Webbed Environments.* http://english.ttu.edu/kairos/

Dorwick, K. 1996. "Writing for the World: Student Writing for and on the Internet." http://icarus.uic.edu/~kdorwick/world.html

Joyce, M. 1988. "Siren Shapes: Exploratory and Constructive Hypertexts." *Academic Computing* 3(4): 10–42.

Kiniry, M., and M. Rose. 1993. *Critical Strategies for Academic Thinking and Writing.* 2nd ed. New York: St. Martin's Press.

Yin, H. 1992. "Collaboration: Proceed with Caution." *Writing Instructor* 12(1): 27–37.

16 Using the Web for High School Student Writers

Ted Nellen
Murry Bergtraum High School, New York, New York

By today's pedagogical standards, I am a Constructivist. I have been one since my first days as a teacher of writing in 1974. I have always believed the Deweyan idea that we learn by doing, and having my students do is the best way to have my students learn how to learn. My classroom is student-centered, not teacher-centered. Watching students work out problems in groups or in isolation is education at its best. Constructivists use this term because students construct a solution on their own or in collaboration with others. To best illustrate my constructivist point of view, I direct you to my students' homepages at http://199.233.193.1/work.html. Their work is organized by student and by assignment.

high school students on the web

The World Wide Web provides the perfect environment for the writing process. I believe this because the Web transcends desktop publishing and presentation programs. The Web provides a student writer with complete control over the creation, from inspiration to publication. Student writers have a wider audience, a more democratic audience, and a venue for peer review when they use the Internet. However, once access is achieved, the next question is what do I do? I will attempt to provide the reader with some insights about how I have transformed a traditional writing class into a Webbed writing class. I will provide a glimpse of our students and the electrified environment, the Web tools we use and how we use them, the Webfolio (or wired portfolio), and student Web writing results and teacher resources.

Electrifying the Environment

The 3,200 students in our school (http://199.233.193.1/) are a heterogeneous group picked from the population of every district in New York City. The age range is from 13 to 18. A third are Asian, a third are African American, and a third are Hispanic/Latino. The hallways are alive with the non-English languages which many call their mother tongues. The

Internet is ideal for these students. My classroom (http://199.233.193.1/comprms.html#439) has thirty-four computers connected to the Internet. In the classic Lancasterian mode, I have interns and colleagues-in-training who help manage the room. The interns are students from the previous year who assist the new students and teachers in some of the technical aspects of the class. This is my teacher-training model. Colleagues who wish to use the Internet in their classes also assist during my classes. By working in an active class rather than in the sterile workshop, the teacher-in-training will learn more effectively and quickly. My English class has become a real and virtual community.

I teach Cyber English (http://199.233.193.1/cybereng/), a junior-year course. The students are from special education, deaf and hard of hearing, bilingual, and mainstream populations. The only students I do not have are the honor students. The syllaweb (http://199.233.193.1/cybereng/log.html) is Internet-based. We include all of the elements of any other junior-level English class, except we work exclusively on the Internet. The students work with all genres: poetry, fiction, nonfiction, and drama. Each student contructs a Web page which becomes his or her Web portfolio, or Webfolio. The Webfolio is the key to the success of the class. The Webfolio is the homepage, each student's own page. It empowers each student, and each student has a stake in his or her own education.

I use the Internet in my classroom because it solves so many problems, bridges so many gulfs, inspires so many fertile minds, provides so much information, introduces such a large audience. The Internet is the ultimate presentation format for our students because each student becomes a publisher. The Internet provides the teacher of writing with access to the students' work right from the start and throughout the writing process. I or anyone else can access the student's work through the Web page from anywhere at any time. Since I have more access to my young student writers' work, I can be more effective as a writing teacher. There are drawbacks, however, to creating a Webbed environment. I have worked hard to connect the classroom and its thirty-four computers to the Internet. I needed lots of help from technicians who created a LINUX/UNIX server for me. It took me an entire summer to set all of this up with the IP address for the school, setting up the computers, and preparing the class. In addition, I spend a lot of time maintaining the Internet connection, preparing classes, and grading papers. I would say I spend twice as much time at my craft now than I did before I had all of this "power." So please be warned.

The Web Process

Each student creates a Web page, which is a table of contents for his or her projects. The homepage is such a powerful motivator; the students take great pride in their homepages and in their written work. Like a garden, the homepage demands constant care. By the end of the year, each student has an outstanding Webfolio which reflects his or her work for the year. Webfolios take the writing process to another level: publishing. The publishing process incorporates the writing process and considers the elements of layout: graphics, designs, color, font, presentation, hypertext. Publishing is the ultimate goal for any writer.

The Syllaweb and the Webfolio

The students follow a syllaweb (http://199.233.193.1/cybereng/log.html), an online syllabus accessed through an Internet browser, which explains and serves projects. The Webfolio is the final Web created by each student that introduces the year's work to the reading public.

The students start with three projects that help identify the writer: a short autobiography, a poem about the Internet, and a book report about their favorite book. Much of the students' personalities pour out in a short time in this new medium. After they become comfortable with Web writing, I request that they do three or four of the projects at the same time while maintaining their homepages. These projects include their own poetry, short stories, and hypertext essays. The syllaweb reflects the wide range of choices from the classic literature found in most anthologies, classic literature not found in anthologies, and literature not yet canonized. Using relevant material makes for more receptive students who in turn enjoy and retain what they have learned. I am concerned with creating students who learn how to learn, who learn to enjoy reading and writing, and my approach appears to work well: my students actually do *learn*, and they perform admirably on state standardized tests.

Specific Web Projects

Hypertext essays make every assignment a research paper. The value of using the Internet to publish student work is that the research done to create the essay was done on the Internet, hence hypertext links to the research source can more readily be made by the reader. Each Web project entails Internet research, Internet hypertext links to sources, and publishing. One such assignment used an editorial written in an online college student magazine (http://www.trincoll.edu/tj/tj9.25.95/articles/violence.html) which addressed violence in America. After the students read the editorial, they immediately went on a hunt for more information on violence. They used popular Web search engines (http://199.233.193.1/find.html) like Yahoo, WebCrawler, Lycos, Excite, and others to find articles on violence. The students used the editorial as the basis for their own essays and then used the Internet resources to augment the editorial. In their research they went beyond U.S. borders as they sought information on African female genitalia mutilation, Bosnia, China, South America, and other areas of violence around the world. Their essays (http://199.233.193.1/ce-violence.html) were well done because of their ability to follow relevant links. The essays they eventually wrote had hypertext links back to the articles they had read which had given them the ideas they used in their papers. Hypertext adds so much to writing because the reader can immediately access the resource the writer used to verify or to learn more about the topic; sources are just a click away. It is far superior to the traditional research paper which merely refers to an article the reader then has to seek out in a library. The publishing of the essays brought in a great deal of mail praising and supporting the students' efforts. These kudos served as fuel for my students to continue.

Another successful assignment dealt with the December holidays (http://199.233.193.1/cybereng/09.html). The students researched Christmas, Hanukkah, and Kwanzaa. Again the students sought out the information on the Internet. This multicultural essay could never have been done successfully in a traditional classroom. Hypertext essays give the reader access to the writer's sources, which makes for more authentic writing and reading. These essays became part of the database for other students trying to find out information on the three holidays. It came as quite a shock when my students received letters from other students who asked them about the holidays. My students had suddenly become experts and were being asked questions as they had asked others.

Perhaps one of the most exciting projects for the students was the Cyber Biographies (http://199.233.193.1/cybereng/05.html). This project had them research the people responsible for our cyber community. Since most of these people are both alive and Internet-active, the students were able to visit these folks' homepages. Some bold students even wrote e-mail to some of these cyber pioneers. When mail came back, the students were ecstatic. Publishing on the Web made this interaction possible. As the students were able to access homepages of their subjects, the subjects in turn were able to view the students' Web pages. In addition, these cyber biographies become resource material for future student researchers.

The project which draws the most moans and complaints is the short story project (http://199.233.193.1/cybereng/13.html). The students have to read a classic short story online and then write an essay. They then have to compare and contrast a classic short story with a contemporary short story. Finally, they have to write their own short story. When I introduce them to this project, I am met with a great deal of resistance. However, I let them know that they may write any short story they wish, as long as the stories are not obscene. Living in New York City gives my students plenty of fodder for their own short stories, which are fantastic and great reads. It has become their favorite project of the year. The response to their creations draws the greatest amount of mail. Publishing on the Web gives the students access to a great deal of information and it provides the world access to the students' work. This two-way information flow is a powerful motivator.

A financial by-product of their Web presence is job offers. Publishing Web pages introduces them to potential employers. This necessitates creating an online resume (http://199.233.193.1/cybereng/17.html). Since this is a Web resume rather than a traditional resume, many considerations have to be made. This project is a real problem-solving type of situation because it involves more advanced HTML writing, like tables, and it requires students to transfer their previous knowledge of paper format to Web format. This is the first step in converting from traditional format to Web format on such a serious and important level. Students accept this transfer more easily than adults do. For the students, publishing their resumes has brought job interviews and jobs.

The students were hooked after the first day when we started their homepages. They became addicts when they started receiving mail about their homepages. Introducing the students to the Web was never difficult, and getting them to do the work is no challenge. The biggest problem is getting them to leave when the bell rings so the next class can begin work. Attendance is always close to 100 percent, and we never have an empty computer seat, because students without a class come to work. When school starts the next year, one of the students' first stops is to log on, check mail, and to fix some of their work on their Web pages. Many former students spend a great deal of time rewriting essays, adjusting their resumes, adding new papers to their Web pages. They do this knowing the new work will not affect a grade; they do it because they recognize the power of a published Web page. Some may call it pride.

Publishing Produces Better Writers

The Internet enhances the writing process because the Internet provides the writer, for the first time in the history of education, the power to publish his or her work. Publishing is the power; history tells us this. As the teacher, I can access students' work in progress from any computer connected to the Internet. The teacher is no longer the sole audience: by publishing on the Internet, my students benefit from "telementors," people from all walks of life who discover the students' work, comment on it, and offer them advice. My constructivist pedagogy is satisfied on the Internet.

One of the purposes of writing is to verify what the writer knows. When we write something down, we sort out our knowledge and then we present it. Writing is thinking before speaking and ultimately publishing. An example of this epiphany for the young writer is when he or she sits with a writing teacher and tries to explain what was meant in a recent essay. At some point the teacher asks, "What exactly are you trying to say here?" The student immediately breaks into a long discourse on what was meant by that vague sentence. When the teacher can get a word in, the advice is to put this rambling on paper. The writing process is that activity which reveals to the writer his or her knowledge on a topic culminating in publishing.

Student publishing is successful because the teacher, peers, and mentors can monitor the young writer's progress at any point. This constant access allows the teacher to intervene earlier and more often in the writing process. Mistakes are not repeated incessantly because they are caught early. Good habits are instilled early in the writing process, eliminating the "red-ink shock syndrome." Previously, a student might have invested a lot of time in a paper, only to be disappointed when I returned it with a low grade. Now, I begin looking at work in progress from the time it comes into being. I follow its growth from beginning to publication and beyond. Students have become very good editors of their own work because they accept peer review willingly and spend much time reviewing their work and others. Oftentimes I see students revise work months after publication.

The Internet provides an audience for my students: peers and mentors. Our students communicate with peers in Sweden, Japan, China, and Spain (http://199.233.193.1/ip.html), as well as with students around the United States. Our mentoring program (http://199.233.193.1/mentor/mentor.html) includes an Internet community which chooses to assist me in my classroom. We have had people from the business world, retirees, college students, and peers view our students' work and then comment on it. Essentially, people who choose to be mentors do it because they have decided to interact with students. Internet mentors do not come into the classroom, but instead visit virtually. They use e-mail to communicate and provide guidance, writing help, and an audience for my young writers.

I have always been a person who learned things by doing. I was told by sages that homework was practice, and everyone practiced. If I practiced throwing a ball, riding a bike, or playing the piano, then I should do my homework, they told me. When I became a sage, I dispensed the same axioms I had heard. My students practiced writing by writing. Now my students create, design, and publish their work on the Internet. They are learning about writing by writing and publishing. Publishing one's writing, after all, is one of the goals of writing, though it is often a forgotten part of the writing process. The World Wide Web changes all of that as young writers learn how to write by including publishing. Today learning by doing is called constructivism. Looking for a better way to teach writing has been a professional goal of mine since before I became a teacher. It has taken me over twenty years to realize a better way on the Internet, but I have realized a few things:

- Make sure each student has access to his or her own computer.
- Have each student create a homepage which provides immediate involvement and a sense of belonging.
- Provide multiple projects so the student can move from one project to another at will.
- Don't worry about providing all resources; leave some discoveries for the students.
- Work with the students, discover alongside them, show them how to follow hunches and clues to discovery.
- Keep it simple. Avoid glitzy, gourmet-type software.
- Use real-time applications as opposed to hypothetical situations.
- Look at what other teachers have done by examining their syllabi (http://199.233.193.1/resource.html#syl) and borrow ideas.
- Be willing to share ideas with others. Do not go it alone.

I began using computers in my writing classroom in 1983. Now with the Internet, I believe I have come to as perfect an environment for the student writer as possible. The Internet has eliminated many of the negative aspects of writing while providing many positive aspects. Write on!

Good essay - practical (building web sites for businesses)

17 Systems Analysis and Design Projects: Integrating Communities and Skills through the Web

Joy L. Egbert
Indiana University

Leonard M. Jessup
Indiana University

Educators all over the world are using computers in various ways in their classrooms, and more classrooms come online every day. As the growth in educational computing spreads quickly, the problems and possibilities of computer use in education are widely discussed in both paper and electronic forums. In some cases technology use has been shown to be a negative contributor to learning in that it can isolate learners, provide them with insufficient time and feedback to complete their tasks, and disallow creative response. (McGrath 1992; Klobusicky-Mailander 1990; Salomon 1990). Although guidelines for and instances of "good" educational computing are hotly debated, it is clear that the use of technology in classrooms does not eliminate the basic need to create optimal learning environments, including among other conditions an authentic audience, an authentic task, learner control, and social interaction (Egbert 1993; Egbert and Jessup 1996). In addition, the integration of comprehension and production skills with computer-based tasks is critical to producing successful learners.

Educators can relate many anecdotes about the suboptimal implementation of classroom technologies, and arguments against using the World Wide Web have many supporters. One trend that is being contested is to have learners construct their own homepages. Although making Web pages can be fun for learners, it is hard to disagree that page development is often structured in such ways that it

ESL students

requires little social interaction, the only authentic audience for the page is the learner, and there is no authentic purpose for page development other than perhaps for learners to say that they did it and to show it to their friends. Depending on how they are done and used, these kinds of tasks can take away from the worth of the Web as an instructional tool. However, there are many ways to use the Web that can enhance the development of optimal classroom learning environments. Systems analysis and design (SAD) projects are one example.

The SAD project described in this essay draws on instructional methods from two academic disciplines, Management Information Systems (MIS) and English as a Second Language (ESL). It was developed as a use of the Web that is driven by real-world needs and issues; organizations around the world employ the SAD process for systems development. This project, in which learners participate in a process to develop Web pages for a client in the community, supports conditions for optimal learning in many ways. First, these projects provide community members and teammates as authentic audiences with whom learners interact socially and professionally. In addition, building Web pages which clients can choose to use as their official Web pages is an authentic task (someone has to do it!). Equally important, in SAD projects learners have control over much of the decision making, from choosing their work teams to deciding on the layout and background color for their Web pages. These projects also involve critical skills such as problem solving, decision making, synthesizing, summarizing, and working cooperatively.

assignment Creating web page for business

The Project Plan

This project was initially applied in a seven-week advanced English as a Second Language (ESL) classroom with academically oriented international students, although the six-part plan for the SAD project described here can be adapted easily for different learner populations. The goals of the elective course, "Computers for Business and Academics: Systems Analysis and Design," were for learners to learn and practice English language skills, to learn about advertising and local businesses, to improve on and acquire computer skills, and to use critical thinking skills such as synthesizing, summarizing, and planning. Learners met in a computer lab for four hours per week; additional instruction took place via e-mail interaction. The course plan is structured enough to guide learners but also flexible enough to encourage learner interests and creativity. Below is a general overview of the project, followed by specific examples from the ESL class.

Preparation

Before the course begins, a small group of community businesses and organizations are asked to participate in the projects. In a course of short duration, managers are visited by the instructor and given a letter outlining the project and the responsibilities of the participants. In longer courses, learners themselves might target specific businesses and solicit their participation. Also in preparation for the activity the syllabus for the course and related handouts can be posted to the local Web server. Activities should be developed that assist learners in becoming acquainted with important aspects of the Web, including searching, printing, and navigating.

Step 1: Forming Teams and Choosing Clients

At the beginning of the course, learners participate in a variety of activities focused on learning about the Web, their classmates, and making good decisions about choosing teammates. Learners can introduce themselves face to face and through e-mail, interview other learners, prepare a resume or other materials to assist them in "applying" for a team position, and so on. The instructor can use learner rankings to make groups or encourage the learners to choose their own teams. After the teams are chosen, learners meet with their three-person teams and choose among the potential "clients" who have agreed to participate in the project. These clients include local businesses, academic units, and nonprofit organizations.

Step 2: Competition Analysis

Using a form like the one in Figure 17.1, learner teams search the Web to find and analyze pages of their clients' competitors. Depending on time limits, learners can complete anywhere from three to ten or more analyses. Learners note the features of the pages and comment briefly on highlights and possible improvements. When they have completed this task, learners summarize their findings and add a written summary to their documents.

Step 3: Client Interview

Using information gathered through the competition analysis, learners formulate specific questions to ask during their interviews, aimed at determining the client's requirements for the Web page(s). Learners can use the guidelines in Figure 17.2 to assist them in focusing their questions.

Web Search Form

Competition Analysis

The purpose of this form is to help you to analyze Web advertisements from your client's competitors. Print as many forms as you need (you are required to complete at least three) and attach copies of the competition's pages to the form.

What is the name of the competitor?

What's the location of the page?

What features does the page have? In other words, what do you see?

What functions does the page include? In other words, what can you do on this page (Can you order something? Send for information? Comment?)?

What do you like about the page (be specific)?

What do you not like/think can be done better (be specific)?

Other comments:

Figure 17.1. Competition Analysis

After learners have practiced their interviews and feel that they are ready, they arrange and conduct the interview with their client. During the interview, they present to their client relevant information that they collected as a part of the competition analysis. They also collect artifacts from the client, including logos, photos, and other materials. After the interview, a written interview summary is turned in by each team.

Step 4: Page Development

Armed with their competition analysis and interview responses, teams use a graphics program such as MacPaint (Macintosh) or Corel Draw (Windows) to develop a preliminary Web page design. After a basic introduction to HTML, the teams divide up the formatting task and create the actual Web pages for the client. During the creative process, learners communicate with their clients by phone, e-mail, or face-to-face meetings.

Client Interview

Your interview task is to determine your client's requirements for the home page that you will be developing. Using the general guidelines below, please formulate specific questions that you will ask during your interview.

Type of organization

Product or service it offers

Customer base (who it serves/wants to serve)

Current needs/wants

Successes/failures in advertising

Trademarks relating to your client's organization (graphics/logo/slogan)

Future plans

Other

Figure 17.2. Client Interview

Step 5: Presentation/Report

Upon completion of the initial draft of the pages, learners present their pages to the class. They use their classmates' comments to edit their pages, and then compile reports for their clients. The report includes all of the project work that has been completed, along with a hard copy of their Web page(s) and a summary for the client that describes the ways in which their page meets the client's needs.

Step 6: Client Evaluation

Learners meet with their clients to present the report. The clients discuss the report with the teams and complete the client evaluation form, shown in Figure 17.3.

After this meeting, teams edit their pages as necessary and add the revised pages to their report to form a final project report. This report includes a final evaluation and reflection on the project, noting

---

Client Evaluation

Please answer the following questions about the Web page(s) developed for your organization.

In what ways is the appearance of the page appropriate to your organization (is it attractive to your customer base, etc.)?

In what ways is the appearance inappropriate?

Which features of the page (graphics, sound, text, other) do you particularly like?

What features could be added/improved?

Which functions of the page do you particularly like?

Which functions are unnecessary or need improvement?

What functions should be added to the page (ordering forms, commenting capability, e-mail contact with the organization, other)?

In what ways does the page meet or not meet your expectations?

Other:

Figure 17.3. Client Evaluation Form

what was done and how the project met the course objectives. Finally, the pages are uploaded and the clients view the electronic copy of the document to decide whether they want to use the pages as their "official" homepages.

Evaluation

Evaluation of this project can take many forms. Individual tasks can be assigned a point value based on how well they were completed. The overall task can be evaluated based on the final report and its presentation. Evaluation can also be based on the client's final evaluation and on the learners' reflections or on evaluations by other learners in the class. A form such as that in Figure 17.4 can be used by the instructor, other learners, or external judges to evaluate the project outcomes.

A Sample Project

Six local businesses and organizations agreed to participate in the project with the ESL class; the four chosen by learners included a local retail shop, a statewide nonprofit organization, a nationwide minimarket, and a worldwide restaurant chain. In the ESL class, two out of four

---

Systems Analysis and Design Final Project Evaluation
CONSULTANTS_____
CLIENT _____

Use Of WEB PAGES: Functional, includes functions requested by clients
1..................... 2 .... 3 .... 4 5
Poor   Adequate   Superior

Appearance OF WEB PAGES: Simple, clear, focused, attractive
1..................... 2 .... 3 .... 4 5
Poor   Adequate   Superior

Content: Complete, relevant
1..................... 2 .... 3 .... 4 5
Poor   Adequate   Superior

Knowledge of audience: Tailored to client's/customers' needs and wants
1..................... 2 .... 3 .... 4 5
Poor   Adequate   Superior

Structure: Logical navigation, clear organization
1..................... 2 .... 3 .... 4 5
Poor   Adequate   Superior

Creativity: Material presented in an innovative, interesting manner
1..................... 2 .... 3 .... 4 5
Poor   Adequate   Superior

OVERALL Evaluation:

Figure 17.4. Project Evaluation Form

clients (the nonprofit and worldwide restaurant chain) adopted pages completed during the course as their "official" Web pages.

Following is a sample of how one learner team completed each project step. The project team consisted of a woman from Venezuela and a man from Japan. The group's client was a local trendy clothing store that the team chose because of the members' interest in retail sales.

Competition Analysis

Each member of the team completed three competition analysis forms. Because no other local clothing stores had Web pages that they could locate, the team analyzed competitors from the region. Figure 17.5a provides an example of one competitor's Web page and Figure 17.5b shows the analysis that this team completed.

The analysis of this page is at a very simplistic level. As the learners analyzed a variety of other pages, their analyses became more critical and sophisticated.

Figure 17.5a. Competitor's Web Page

In the case of this ESL team, the summary of the competition analyses turned out to be a critical component in supporting interaction; although collaboration during the analyses was our initial expectation, the team had divided the work, each member taking responsibility for a set number of analyses. They did not actually work together much until they had to synthesize their findings into a single summary. As they used listening and speaking skills to write the summary collaboratively, they also negotiated about grammar, content, and format. The result was a finished product in which the strengths of both team members were clearly evident.

Interview Summary

This team gathered quite a lot of information from their client over two initial interviews. Excerpts from this team's interview summary show that they used the interview information and information from other advertisements for ChaCha to compose their summary:

> ChaCha is not a chain store, which means it is unique. They serve 75% for women, 25% for men and it is based in contemporary clothing. Thus, they basically serve women from 17–45 and men from 17–35.

Competition Analysis

The purpose of this form is to help you to analyze Web advertisements from your client's competitors. Print as many forms as you need (you are required to complete at least three) and attach copies of the competition's pages to the form.

What is the name of the competitor?
Stone and Thomas Web Site! The Store for Today's Shopper!

What's the location of the page?
http://www.rgn.it/BCC/home.html

What features does the page have? In other words, what do you see?
It has models showing their clothes and all the stuff that they sell

What functions does the page include? In other words, what can you do on this page (Can you order something? Send for information? Comment?)?
They don't have any information about it

What do you like about the page (be specific)?
They show different designs with models, so that I can have an idea about their clothing

What do you not like/think can be done better (be specific)?
They should give information about their phone, address on the first page

Other comments:
I think it is pretty good, but they should give more information about the store because we know looking at the picture that they have different kinds of clothing and different Information, bet we have to get into Netscape to know more about them. It's not very practical for people who don't know very well how to get into the system.

Figure 17.5b. Competition Analysis

> They have had success in advertising, such as radio (WTTS, WBWB), newsprint (IDS, Bloomington Voice). Moreover, they have a logo based on the name of the store, which takes people's attention at first sight.
> Among its features ChaCha is a denim friendly contemporary clothing store located one block from the university. ChaCha sells Lucky Brand, Silver, Acquaverde, and Buffalo denim collections as well as vintage Levi 501's.

As the team worked to solve the problems that they saw in competing Web pages and to meet the client's needs, much of the phrasing and information in this summary made its way into the pages that this group designed.

Although one of the team members admitted to speaking more during the interview, in terms of language learning this step was a success. Both students took notes in English while listening to a native speaker, and they again worked collaboratively to negotiate about and produce the summary. Not that it all went perfectly smoothly; the instructor was asked for help in settling a variety of questions (cultural, linguistic, and content-based) that came up during the process. From the instructor's point of view, however, disagreements between team members served as an impetus for the students to learn more about the language, culture, and content.

Page Design

In addition to gathering information and collecting artifacts such as the store's logo and informational flyers, this group took many photos around the store and used them as the basis for their design. They used MacPaint on the Macintosh platform and then drafted Web pages following the initial design plan. Figure 17.6 shows details of the Web pages.

At the top of the homepage the learners placed a scanned version of the store's logo; the background is an embossed version of the logo's graphic, created easily in Adobe Photoshop. The photos that the learners took are placed strategically throughout the linked pages. The learners expressed an interest in placing the photos randomly, but were discouraged that this could not be done easily in the time allotted. Much of the text is from information the team received from the client. This team, along with the other learners in the class, willingly spent long

Figure 17.6. ChaCha Clothing Store

hours outside of class to develop their projects in order to avoid, as one learner put it, "being embarrassed" when they showed their projects to their clients. The final results were impressive (The Web page can be viewed at http://php.indiana.edu/~hiwata/ChaCha.html; or http://ezinfo.ucs.indiana.edu/~hiwata/ChaCha.html.)

During this step, the team members discovered cultural and personal differences in definitions of "aesthetically pleasing." They used other Web pages to search for design possibilities and for the underlying hypertext markup language (HTML) code. This was a great exercise in scanning, searching, deriving patterns, and making connections between forms; all of these are critical skills for language learners.

Evaluation

This team, rather than having the client complete the evaluation form, used the questions on the form to interview the client about their project. The team wrote the following in partial evaluation of their project:

> Mr. G. likes the graphics, especially the pictures. They are useful to advertise because they strongly appeal to customers. As ChaCha always changes its [stock], it is necessary to change in a short time. As they serve only one shop and it is a small business, they do not need particular functions. However, if they can use html and computers and have enough time to change the home page periodically, they are interested in keeping the home page and keeping in touch with customers on e-mail.

The team used comments from their client about content, spelling, and grammar to revise and edit their pages. This client did not immediately adopt the Web pages for use, but noted that it was due to the client's current lack of Internet access rather than the format or design of the pages. The team reflected:

> We have realized that working with the computer helps us to get familiar with it, which is very interesting and exciting. On the other hand, working for somebody else is a difficult job because one does not know what that person really wants, as a result, it gets very confusing sometimes. Having had the opportunity to work with somebody else gives us an idea about how important it is.

All class members expressed satisfaction with the project plan and with their final project as this team did, regardless of whether or not their client had adopted their pages. They gained much from participating in this project: skills for working in teams, practice with and new information in all of the language skill areas, practice with critical thinking skills such as synthesizing, summarizing, and deducing, and computer skills and knowledge that they will use in their university and/or work lives.

Caveats and Options

One problem with the projects was time, particularly in the seven-week course; learners became so involved that they did not want to stop improving their pages and learning all of the possibilities of HTML. In addition, although the clients were very cooperative, it is critical to ensure that they know what their responsibilities are and that they will have the time to meet with their student "systems designers"; one client was out of town regularly during the project, making it difficult for his team to confer with him.

There are several ways in which SAD projects could be enhanced and improved. In future iterations, a more stringent timeline for each phase of the project could be introduced so that time management plays a more prominent role. Time allowing, learners could solicit their own clients after practice and discussion in class. In addition, a readings packet or text could also add information and instructions to supplement HTML guides and examples from the Web. Finally, in more advanced courses or in courses in which learners have a background in business processes, handouts and other project structures could be eliminated or pared down to encourage learners to develop these on their own.

Conclusions

SAD projects such as the one described above are empowering for learners; these projects involve learners in an authentic task with resources in the community. They also address a variety of skills and content. Learners focus on team work, the use of integrated language skills, and contemporary technologies and issues. SAD projects are successful in bridging the gap between learners and the broader community, supporting their ability to create and encouraging them to think critically. In these ways and others, SAD projects support the development of optimal classroom learning environments.

Note

The authors would like to thank the owners of ChaCha for their participation in this project and the students in the SAD course for their permission to use their work here.

Works Cited

Cha-Cha clothing company. http://php.indiana.edu/~hiwata/ChaCha.html; or http://ezinfo.ucs.indiana.edu/~hiwata/ChaCha.html.

Egbert, J. 1993. *Learner Perceptions of Computer-Supported Language Learning Environments: Analytic and Systemic Analyses.* Unpublished doctoral dissertation. University of Arizona-Tucson.

Egbert, J. and L. Jessup. 1996. "Analytic and Systemic Analyses of Computer-supported Language Learning Environments." *TESL-EJ* 2(1): http://violet.berkeley.edu/~cwp/TESL-EJ/ej06/a1.html

George, J., G. Easton, J. Nunamaker, and G. Northcraft. 1990. "A Study of Collaborative Work with and without Computer-Based Support." *Information Systems Research* 1(4): 394–415.

Klobusicky-Mailander, E. 1990. "Putting the Computer to Work in Your Class." *English Teaching Forum* 28(2): 2–7.

McGrath, D. 1992. "Hypertext, CAI, Paper, or Program Control: Do Learners Benefit from Choices?" *Journal of Research on Computing in Education* 24(4): 513–31.

Salomon, G. 1990. "Cognitive Effects with and of Technology." *Communications Research* 17(1): 26–44.

Other examples of learner projects can be found at:
http://www.indiana.edu/~celtiep/intesolhomeple.html or
http://www.indiana.edu/~imupromo (click on "Tudor Room")

Similar to 17
Students should read
one or the other

239

18 Nobody, Which Means Anybody: Audience on the World Wide Web

Catherine F. Smith
Syracuse University

Here's a practical problem for World Wide Web writers: Web readership is amorphous. Audiences can be intended but not predicted. Authors may address particular readers, but any reader (or search engine) may visit a web. Moreover, readings are idiosyncratic. Readers traverse a web according to individual interests. Finally, readers can relate a current web to other webs in patterns such as hotlists or web rings created by the reader. Thus, a web's meanings and contexts are always more controlled by readers than by writers.

Historicizing the problem: The Internet is now privately owned and supported by telecommunication industry consortia rather than by the publicly funded United States National Science Foundation that initiated the network. Partly due to this change in ownership, the network's purposes are changing rapidly.

The World Wide Web has become the primary interface for the Internet. The Web itself has quickly evolved from its origins as a particular research community's communication tool to become a public marketplace. Commercial entities are now the largest group in the Web's population, on evidence that more "com" addresses (for businesses) are annually assigned by network administrators than are "edu" (for schools), "org" (for noncommercial organizations), and "gov" (for governmental agencies) combined. The Web's current marketplace character conditions any individual web's potential for meaning.

An ethical dimension of the practical problem: while the Internet continues to be an online society of eclectic communication subcultures, and while Internet administration is still largely hands-off, local controls are increasingly being applied to network content and use. In China and the United States, for example, national governments are making new laws or applying (often inappropriate) existing laws to regulate Internet access. Cultural institutions (libraries, schools, colleges, universities, corporations) are creating policies to control or to limit use, sometimes in conjunction with new "filtering" software that censors Internet content. Social and cultural values, now codified in rules and tools, constrain any web's potential for meaning.

Therefore, due to the World Wide Web's hypertextual capability and the Internet's cultural reception, Web audience is a significantly different problem for Web authors than for other kinds of writers. To explore effects of this difference, in this essay I describe teaching experiences showing me that we need to develop accountable, Web-sensitive pedagogy for "audience." I refer to my experience with a successful Web authoring assignment that, as a by-product, exposed new potential for conflict between educational goals and social policies. Reflection on this experience leads me to argue that when we teach writing on the Web we are teaching public discourse. Because this is so, Web-cognizant pedagogy for "audience" is tied to understanding "public(s)."

Background: Why and How I Teach Writing on the Web

I teach on the Web, partly and simply, because multimedia Web authoring is fun. But there are other reasons, too.

I use hypertext and telecommunication technologies to facilitate two kinds of cognition: associative thinking, on which conceptualization relies, and relational thinking, on which analysis and synthesis rely. Hypertext materially supports such cognition, I believe, through capabilities for linking, traversing, and reconfiguring information.

World Wide Web communication makes these processes public. The public aspect is becoming, for me, the most important reason for teaching digital composition. The Web opens the classroom by letting academic work out and the wider world in. Students writing on the Web are participating in public discourse.

Logistics of Web-Mediated Teaching

In my university's writing curriculum, I teach junior-senior level organizational and professional communication in a classroom equipped with twenty computers (five each on four circular tables around the room). When students or I want to make a presentation to the whole group, we access presentation files from an additional computer (with projection) at the room's front, where a pull-down movie screen is available.

I compose all instructional materials for the Web and archive them in a course Web site. Students work on the Web; we are paperless, so all products are presented in Web form. Each student builds a portfolio of products, which is accessed by selecting the student's name in an active list of participants in the course Web site. Portfolios include transcriptions ("papers" coded for Web display) and original webs (digital compositions comprised of written text, graphics, possibly motion or sound).

To develop skills necessary for Web authoring, I introduce students to basic HTML (hypertext markup language), then students self-teach advanced HTML, image processing, sound processing, animation, or other applications according to interest. I introduce UNIX directory management and file transfer operations. Students store and manage files in their individual university computing accounts. Each has the university-standard allotment of five megabytes of storage.

How do students react to Web-based instruction? Usually, they are enthusiastic. They take real-world writing more seriously when it is done on the Web, where it might actually be seen and used. Already advanced in their major specialties when they take my writing course, they say Web writing gives them critical perspective on traditional knowledge construction and communication in their fields. Controversies regarding Web use in their discipline or future workplaces take on personal relevance as they become accustomed to communicating professionally via the Web. Some seniors say the course enhances their credentials and expands their job opportunities (yes, their portfolios include online resumes).

An Assignment: Client Web

Web site design and development introduce students to workplace writing practices including team writing, structured project planning, document design for multiple media, consideration of legal and proprietary limits on information use, and anticipation of situated text reception by complex audiences.

All these practices are taken up in the assignment to do a client web. In that exercise, students design and develop webs for client organizations inside and outside the university. A communication objective of the assignment is to represent a collective. A cultural goal is to diversify the Web's population.

Students freely choose their clients. The only constraint is that clients must not already be on the Web. Beyond diversifying the Web's population, this constraint ensures that students will build from scratch rather than rebuilding an existing site. Students are encouraged, but not required, to seek clients lacking resources to develop a web themselves.

Students usually find clients in their jobs, internships, memberships, personal relationships, involvement in public affairs, or community service. In two recent offerings of the course, clients included student-owned businesses in music, fashion design, house painting, and lawn care; family-owned businesses in agriculture, real estate, construction, engineering, and manufacturing; campus chapters of Amnesty International and Habitat for Humanity; university centers for career development and academic learning support; campus chapters of national political parties and national sororities or fraternities; international student associations; student chapters of professional associations; and hometown clubs.

In the best instances, students defamiliarize a culture of which they are a member in order to see it freshly and to conceive ways of presenting it to the outside world. They do detailed observation, interviews, and interpretation in the research phase of design. Most clients cooperate well with the research. Because clients are not Web-experienced, students get design review and technical help from peers and the instructor.

Some client webs are designed to function as a service, putting the client's functions online. More often, webs are designed to advertise the client. Students choose clients whom they want to promote. Looking at client webs from a writing instructor's perspective, I characterize their genre as entrepreneurial ethnography. Perhaps it is an academic Web genre for our time.

Problematics of the Assignment

If writing instructors want to use the client web assignment, I can confidently predict good and interesting results for both students and teacher. However, along with my enthusiasm for the assignment comes new caution to consider contexts of instruction that might affect course planning. I can pivot both my enthusiasm and my concern on discussion of "audience" next.

In a recent client web exercise, we used a structured design approach including tried-and-true techniques of rhetorically analyzing audience and purpose. These techniques are familiar to teachers of technical, professional, and organizational writing. Analysis emphasizes purposefully tailoring information to targeted audiences. As our textbook's authors remark, "Creating effective communication, particularly mediated communication, requires that you plan what you want to communicate to whom. Information about the target audience for your information is crucial for creating successful communication" (December and Randall 1996, 826).

However, students found that clients wanted open-ended audiences, not targeted ones. Clients perceived the Web as providing greater interaction or expanded markets. But they did not have a clear idea of who uses the Web and thus whom they might reach. Student developers knew that Web audiences would be broad, but they could set no reasonable boundaries on expectations. Targeting, and a loss of opportunity to do something different, seemed inescapable. Most clients and students resolved the dilemma by aiming to communicate with "the public," which included but was not limited to the client's usual audience. Tailoring was rejected in favor of inviting. The aim was to attract outsiders while speaking to insiders.

According to the client's purpose, target groups included customers, citizens, humane people, or members. Illustrations: "Soft as a Grape" advertised student-designed-and-made clothing to potential buyers (Maurer 1997). "Office of Residence Life at Syracuse University" communicated university information to enrolled students (Ierardi 1997). "Amnesty International at Syracuse University" enabled letter-writing campaigns to protest treatment of individual political prisoners (Vogel 1997). "Dark Side of the Sun" announced weekly screening schedules and previewed video clips for the Japanese Animation Club, a registered campus activity (Horne 1997). "Union of Writers of the African Peoples" provided chat opportunities for academic scholars of African literatures to talk with African writers, as well as bibliographies linked to publishers' sites (Allenbaugh 1997).

All client webs met course criteria and functioned as intended for clients. However, a change in the institutional environment had, unbeknownst to us, created a new potential for problems. I turn next, in this discussion, to that environmental change and its implications.

The potential—and I emphasize potential—for a new kind of problem arises from web content. Because students' coursework is produced using university facilities and communicated via university-provided access to the Internet, it comes under the following clauses of new university computer use policy (announced as the coursework I am describing here was under way): *AUP*

- Do not use any of Syracuse University-owned computers, workstations, or networks for other than a University course, research project, departmental activity, or personal communications. In particular, Syracuse University computing resources are not to be used for commercial purposes.

- Do not place any of the following type of information or software on any University-owned computer system or print on any University-owned printer: anything that infringes upon the rights of another person, that is abusive, profane, or sexually offensive to the average person, that consists of any advertisements for commercial enterprises, or that consists of information which may injure someone else and/or lead to a lawsuit or criminal charges. (Examples of these are: pirated software, destructive software, pornographic materials, or libelous statements.) (Syracuse University, 1997)

Four of the illustrative client webs—"Soft as a Grape," "Dark Side of the Sun," "Amnesty International at Syracuse University," and "Union of Writers of the African Peoples"— *might* have violated these restrictions. Those webs advertised commercial products (t-shirts, videos, books), or they included material possibly considered offensive. Only "Office of Residence Life at Syracuse University" did neither. That is the normal ratio of safe to risky client webs, I would predict: for every safe web there will be three or four risky ones. However, all webs appropriately fulfilled the assignment.

In practice, neither I nor my students experienced any difficulties due to this assignment. Nobody got into trouble. In fact, we could not have violated the no-commerce prohibition, as I later learned. Online commerce (e.g., ordering with a credit card) requires secure communication, and the university has always provided only nonsecure protocols on its computer system. Thus, in addition to codifying policy, the university blocked commerce technologically.

I bring this case to our attention not because of outcomes (nothing out of the ordinary happened), but rather because it points up a condition of teaching with technology that deserves renewed attention: effects of institutional network use policies. Because there are new policy restrictions, assignments have taken on added implications of possible legal prosecution. Teachers now need to be aware of policies against commerce, for example, as they have long been aware of policies against copyright infringement. The new potential is, of course, not unique to Internet use, but the policies seem directed at the Internet, particularly the Web. Consequently, Web-based coursework exposes an academic context in which education commingles ambiguously with institutional nonprofit status and legal liability. What's exposed is a knot of tangled rights and responsibilities.

As teacher, I cannot untangle the knot. My task is to teach in the current environment. In this chapter, I wish to alert Web-writing teachers and students to the growing potential for conflict between teaching and learning objectives and institutional policy. Next, I suggest practical strategies for preventing conflicts. Finally, in conclusion, I want to move beyond damage control to suggest accountable pedagogy that is cognizant of an evolving Internet and its variable receptions.

Practical Strategies

Check Institutional Policies

Before assigning exercises such as client web authorship, check institutional policies on Internet use. There may be no codified policy. If policy exists and appears to preclude assignments you wish to make, inquiry may prove that it does not preclude them. Even better, policy might be changed through dialogue. Start a conversation with campus network administrators.

Develop Policy in the Classroom

In your course, add a policy component to the Web design process. In the course described here, I developed a policy in discussion with students regarding ownership and maintenance of client webs, as follows: a client web is a student-created educational product residing on university servers during development. After it is developed, the web remains stored on university servers and accessible through the course Web site until the student developer's graduation (when files are routinely purged). If the client wants actually to use the web, the student grants the right and the files move to a server provided and maintained by the client. (We asked some clients to provide a link back to the course Web site so that educational uses of the client web might continue).

The policy was not defensive. We did not develop it to protect ourselves from prosecution. Rather, it derived from confronting the resource demands of graphic images, an issue that we addressed in terms of utility and ethics. The Web is a visual medium. Recognizing that communicating graphically is good, we also acknowledged that the time required to download images is a significant factor in a web's usability and, for some clients, affordability. We therefore specified standards for image size conscious of usability and needs for low-cost access. That kind of deliberation carried over into other decisions balancing clients' interests against academic interests. The policy tying rights to use webs to responsibility for storing files, summarized above, was a result. We negotiated policy in the classroom; clients were informed about the policy but not involved in negotiating it. (They might be in future assignments, if practical.)

Our policy motivations were keyed to serving academic needs (supporting creative work), campus community well-being (avoiding overloaded networks), and clients' interests (functional webs). Thus, independent of (actually, unaware of) university policy, we self-regulated as part of normal coursework. I recommend similar proactive policymaking as democratic practice in Web-related classrooms (C. Smith 1996). Start a conversation with students early, before the client web assignment, about resources and conditions of Internet use, in order to recognize needs for policy and to begin articulating policy.

Seek Out Different Textbooks

For the client web assignment, composition or technical writing textbooks might suffice. Or, you might supplement them with communication textbooks or handbooks, especially those that discuss communication law. Start a conversation with teachers or practitioners in speech communication, journalism, communication design, library and information studies, and public administration.

Reflective Pedagogy

For the remainder of this essay, I will outline a conceptual framework for accountably interpreting "audience" to mean "public(s)." The framework echoes intuitive moves I observed my students and their clients making to figure out their audiences. I relate their moves to perspectives from rhetoric, ethics, and human-computer interaction that view the writer-reader relationship as interaction or transaction.

I present the framework abstractly, as a set of claims adding up to an orientation. I intend the orientation generatively, to stimulate pedagogical imagination. I offer it conversationally, as if thinking aloud among teachers.

Claim #1: WWW authors are not writers. They are rhetors.

Elsewhere in this collection, Dean Rehberger remarks that webs take us back to a time before books "when rhetoric was at the heart of education." To familiarize the Internet in terms other than "cyber" and "hyper," he characterizes webs as "living texts" or inter-texts made on an inter-net as writers have traditionally made texts, by linking, cataloging, annotating, and collecting (Rehberger 1999, 193).

I see webs as rhetorical, also, but I characterize their rhetoric differently. Looking at web production, Rehberger sees inter-text. Looking at web reception and use, I see social inter-action.

Claim #2: WWW rhetors interact publicly, in the presence of others.

For ethicist Hannah Arendt, "public" signifies two things: "can be seen and heard by all (each differently)," and "occurs in common space constituted by interest . . . something which inter-est, literally 'is between' . . ." (Arendt 1989/1958, 182). For Arendt, the human inter-est is the condition of being human. Human action inevitably causes human reaction, always with unpredictable consequences. That the action and reaction are evident to all makes the condition manageable.

The Web materially manifests Arendt's vision. This is ironic, since Arendt wrote in opposition to technology. Nonetheless, her pluralist vision of sustaining human experience by public disclosure, while not adequate to address all Web-related cultural dissonance, is arguably foundational to an ethic of Web authoring.

Claim #3: The Web rhetor integrates human and computer, with potentially contradictory consequences.

Computer-mediated thinking integrates the human and the computer system (J. Smith 1994). The integration generates powers in tension. An example is the contrary powers of the search process. A single reader using a search engine finds more than the reader could find alone, thus expanding intellectual choice. Contrarily, reader-collectives employ search engines to "filter" or block individuals' access to content, thus limiting intellectual choice.

Conclusion

Traditional audience conceptions do not translate well to Web conditions. We should assume that Web publishing is what the word "publishing" implies, making meaning public(ly). When writing for the Web, we should expect to encounter complexities that public life entails.

Returning to present Internet history, I observe that commercialization increases the medium's attraction for writers. Perhaps we writing teachers should value commerce because it encourages authorship. In literary history, authorship increased and new authoritative cultural voices (e.g., women's) emerged when printing became a business in the late eighteenth century. The reach of these voices grew when new technology lowered costs of print distribution in the late nineteenth century. Now, as the Web commercializes and shrinks the costs of distribution again at the end of the twentieth century, we might expect similar leaps in numbers and diversity of authors. The attraction for writing teachers is the opportunity to transform writers into rhetors.

How might we teach Web "audience"? We begin by construing it as "the general audience." It is time to stop advising student writers that "there is no general audience, only specific audiences." I have so advised, many times. Wrong, or not quite right, for the Web. To get it right for the Web, we start by factoring in some of the medium's technological characteristics. First, the Web medium supports inclusion, not exclusion. Anybody with access may use the Web; the technology makes no social or cultural distinction among users. (I refer here to the medium's capability for use by anyone, not to demographics of actual users who, as we know, are still not diverse enough.) Second, the medium supports communication by one to few that many can overhear, each differently; the technology sets no limits on extent of disclosure. With these material features and with characteristics formed in receptions of the medium, a general audience enters our classrooms with the Web.

Maybe analogy can highlight the human-computer hybridity of Web audience and illuminate its peculiar demands. In the UNIX operating system, there is a permission setting for files designated as "nobody," which allows "anybody" (any user, server, or process) to access a file. By analogy, the Web rhetor addresses somebody in the presence of any reader, server, or process.

Acknowledgments

This chapter is motivated by creative Web design and development by my students at Syracuse University, of whom Chad Allenbaugh, Kobie Horne, Dean Ierardi, Ian Maurer, and Tracy Vogel are recognized here. John Smith's reference to UNIX's "nobody, which means anybody" snapped this chapter's idea into focus. Reviews of drafts by Sibylle Gruber, by SU colleagues Marjorie Ledden and Paul Bender, and by NCTE's anonymous reader, helped me say everything here better.

Works Cited

Allenbaugh, C. 1997. "Union of Writers of the African Peoples." Web site for the African Studies Association. Web site no longer available.

Arendt, H. 1989/1958. *The Human Condition.* Chicago: University of Chicago Press.

December, J. and N. Randall. 1996. *The World Wide Web Unleashed 1996.* 2nd ed. Indianapolis, IN: SamsNet Publishers.

Horne, K. 1997. "Dark Side of the Sun: S.U. Japanese Animation Club." http://web.syr.edu/~kjhorne/JAC/

Ierardi, D. 1997. "Office of Residence Life at Syracuse University." Web site no longer available.

Maurer, I. 1997. "Soft as a Grape." Web site no longer available.

Rehberger, D. 1999. "Living Texts on the Web: A Return to the Rhetorical Arts of Annotation and Commonplace." In *Weaving a Virtual Web: Practical Approaches to New Information Technologies,* edited by Sibylle Gruber. Urbana, IL: National Council of Teachers of English.

Smith, C. 1996. "Thomas Jefferson's Computer." *Computers and Composition* 13: 5–21.

Smith, J. 1994. *Collective Intelligence in Computer-Based Collaboration.* Hillsdale, NJ: Erlbaum.

"Syracuse University Computing and Electronic Communications Policy." http://cms.syr.edu/about/about_computepolicy.html

Vogel, T. 1997. "Amnesty International at Syracuse University." Web site no longer available.

19 Donut Shoppes and Tea Rooms: Getting in the MOO(d) for Hypertext

Mick Doherty
Dallas Convention and Visitors Bureau, Dallas, Texas

Sandye Thompson
Texas Woman's University

Part One: The Introductory

Cross-media publication always stretches the boundaries of credulity—or perhaps it simply extends the definition of "the possible." We found writing about MOOspace and hypertext in an environment constrained to the linearity of paper text to be an exercise in frustration—the kind matched by students told to constrain their own ideas within a particular written format. If there is one thing that MOOspace and writing to the WWW share in common, it is the chance for the author to experiment with "writing outside the lines," abandoning what Baldwin (1996) called "the Essay-a-sauras" for less structured, or "nimbler," forms of writing.

Indeed, Rickly and Crump (1995) tell us we must "Be prepared to be nimble" in order to "Save the Academy." The very purpose of including this chapter is to remind us that in order to be nimble we must stretch ourselves to keep in shape. MOOing is one way of stretching our electronic communication skills; it is a face-paced sprint toward knowledge that can be frustrating, challenging, and invigorating all at once. A MOO is a place where, as you will see one student phrased it, a book chapter can "be happening," and a place where the boundary between student and teacher is blurred, and the definition of "author" is . . . well, "stretched." What happens (happened) in this chapter is a stretching exercise for writers, and it is one way to take all the "stuff" you gathered earlier in this book and "try it out." There are other ways.

Muds /Murs

So we invite you to momentarily step outside the print paradigm—in high school we learned to call stepping out of "rational" linearity the "willing suspension of disbelief"—to "@join" us (and, more important, our students) to eavesdrop on a discussion about MOOing, hypertext, Web text, and how it all ties together. Or doesn't.

```
telnet purple-crayon.media.mit.edu 8888
<connect>
**********************************

** Welcome to MediaMOO! **
**********************************
```

PLEASE NOTE:

MediaMOO is a professional community, where people come to explore the future of media technology. The operators of MediaMOO have provided the materials for the buildings of this community, but are not responsible for what is said or done in them. In particular, you must assume responsibility if you permit minors or others to access MediaMOO through your facilities. The statements and viewpoints expressed here are not necessarily those of the janitors, Amy Bruckman, or the Massachusetts Institute of Technology, and those parties disclaim any responsibility for them. A note to guests: guests' connection site information is publicly readable, and included on all mail messages posted.

Type:

'connect <character-name> <password>' to connect to your character,	
'connect Guest'	to connect to a guest character,
'help @request'	for information on how to get your own character,
'@who'	just to see who's logged in right now,
'@quit'	to disconnect, either now or later.

connect Guest
@join Mick

Shamrock's Donut Shoppe

Welcome to Shamrock's Donut Shoppe, where it's truly the Luck of the Irish if you actually get served a donut! Shamrock's is currently under construction; however, there are several places to make yourself comfortable and enjoy conversation while waiting for

Godot-nuts. Take a seat at the counter (sit stool1, etc.); sit in the Big Fluffy Chair (sit fluffy) or Little Comfy Chair (sit comfy); or on a reg'lar chair or sofa (sit chair, sit sofa). Thanks!

Obvious exits: south to Sandye's TeaRoom
Mick is standing here.
You see Memex Board and trialtape here.
You join Mick.

Mick waves and welcomes you.
Mick says, "Just type an "s" and we'll move out the south exit to Sandye's place. She's already there, waiting for us."
Mick heads south.

Sandye's TeaRoom
You see Sandye's sanctuary, the place where she can unwind from the stresses of the day (or night) amidst the joys of gracious living. Please sit down (there's a chair, a sofa, and lots of floor space), relax, and partake in the pleasures of tea.

Obvious exits: north to Shamrock's Donut Shoppe
sandyet and Mick are standing here.
You see Sandye's Message Board, Dessert Platter, Sandye's Teapot, and Tray of Sandwiches here.

sandyet waves and welcomes you.
Mick sits down on the sofa.
sandyet sits down on the sofa.
You sit down on the chair.

sandyet says, "anyway, we were discussing how to turn our ideas into a book chapter . . ."
Mick says, "since we're more used to writing in electronic environments."
sandyet says, "we've both been lucky enough to teach in places that encourage technology in the classroom, and to help our colleagues who are working elsewhere by "guest-hosting" their classes remotely in MOOspace occasionally."
Mick says, "that's how we've found that it's our students who've shown us not only what is possible, but what *they* believe is *necessary* for webbed writing."

Chartreuse_Guest barges in.

Chartreuse_Guest says, "Mick, it's Shawn Connolly, from your Tech/Pro class. This where the book chapter is happening?"

Chartreuse_Guest bows to you and says "I'm a junior at Rensselaer Polytechnic Institute in upstate New York."

Mick [to sandyet] "case in point . . . !"

Mick [to Chartreuse_Guest] "sort of, Shawn. This is where we're starting, anyway. I guess this is sort of our "home node," if you know what I mean."

sandyet says "Shawn, we were just discussing our reasons for using this format . . . and why we asked you and the other RPI students to discuss your experiences with us."

Chartreuse_Guest laughs.

Chartreuse_Guest says, "Sure, it's like I said in class the other day. I honestly think that the BEST resources are not journal entries or research foundations, but rather US—that is, the people who go out and USE the damn things. You can find them on newsgroups, in MOOs, on listservs, and generally in many places you don't expect to. I'll take the opinion of an Internet user over the opinion of some J. Random Doctorate Candidate any day."

Mick sighs.

sandyet giggles.

sandyet says "we really want to forefront the kinds of writing-through-thinking that students can do in MOOspace, and how that affects—and is affected by—webbed writing . . . oh, please help yourselves to tea and snacks."

Chartreuse_Guest inhales at least twenty cinnamon & raisin scones.

Mick swallows a few cucumber & dill hearts. You enjoy a cuppa Earl Greyer.

Mick says "really, as I've read postings and MOOlogs from my students, they've struck me as being as . . . well . . ."

Chartreuse_Guest says, "brilliant? witty? publishable?" sandyet laughs. exactly!

Mick says "We made a conscious decision in writing this text to only use resources that were published electronically, in e-journals or elsewhere on the WWW."

sandyet "and we decided to *forefront* student comments. Shawn may have been going for a laugh, but what makes anything Michael Joyce or Stuart Moulthrop has to say about electronic writing more valuable than what Shawn or Jenn Bowie or any other student in that kind of environment has to say?"

Mick says, "we like talk about de-centering the classroom and publishing student writing, and then we point them to a canon, of all things! So we thought we would present "our" ideas primarily through the words of our students—and compare their conclusions with the "canon," by putting the "published" stuff in footnotes.

sandyet sighs and says, "but that didn't work, really . . ."

Chartreuse_Guest says, "wouldn't that more or less mean you had to validate our ideas by pointing to the "canon," by "linking" to the footnotes? That's a little . . . offensive."

sandyet nods emphatically.

Mick says, "I guess I thought it was cute, or cutting-edge—like David Porush says, footnotes are the poor scholar's nod to hypertext. So this could be showing off hypertext in print format. Only, like Shawn said—it actually ended up doing the opposite of what we hoped."

sandyet says, "Instead of forefronting the student ideas it made them look as if they had to be *completed* by the published work. So we dropped the footnotes entirely."

Chartreuse_Guest phews.

Mick says, "In the end, we decided to box the "published" comments near to the appropriate area of the text."

Chartreuse_Guest says, "So you don't *have* to read the boxed stuff."

sandyet says, "no, you don't have to read it. Putting the "scholarly" information in the boxes sort of marginalizes the "published" texts and, hopefully, makes it clear that we *value* our students' words the most."

Mick says, "I guess we could talk more about it . . . but that's hardly the point. Part of writing in the WWW is all about multi-tasking, so I think we should just dive into it."

sandyet says, "we can always come back in here to talk if we need to."

Chartreuse_Guest will keep a MOO window open as he reads.

<disconnect MediaMOO>

How can using MOOspace in the writing classroom help our students think about developing text on the WWW? Or about writing hypertext? We turned that question over to the source . . . the students themselves. To be precise, a dozen students from three separate classes which used MOOspace as part of the curriculum gathered and discussed—entirely online—some of the key definitional problems surrounding the use of MOO technology in a Webbed writing class-room, and argued the pros and cons of that use. Although the following could probably be read in any order, the linearity of print technology inherent to "the book chapter" demands a certain hierarchy of ideas.

Part Two: The Definitional

What Is "MOOspace"?

It's easy to find definitions of MOOspace in FAQs and Web sites of various natures. But if we are suggesting to our students that they can create reality through text (as discussed in another section of this chapter) then we must allow the students themselves to define the space-experience-reality of MOOs.

Dustin Crewell begins by deconstructing the acronym: "MOOspace = MUD Object Oriented (MUD = Multi-User Dimension/Dungeon)." He then explains that a MOO offers "an online virtual space (often accessed by telnet) designed for interaction between people . . . based heavily on social interaction." Crewell's frequent collaborator Colin Mitchell—they have co-authored innovative hypertext fiction without ever reading Michael Joyce's *afternoon, a story*—offers a more experience-oriented definition: "MOO-space is a virtual gathering that you connect with over the Internet. It allows for movement, emotions, conversation, etc., as well as the power to design the environment around you." And "designing your environment," to use Mitchell's phrase, is a concrete beginning to "creating your own reality."

Shawn Connolly adds detail to Mitchell's base

> **"Interactive Novel"?**
> Don Langham (1994), like Connelly, uses a text-based virtual reality metaphor to capture the essence of the technology: "MOO uses written descriptions to create a virtual environment somewhat analogous to the kind of virtual world produced in the imagination when we read novels . . . MOOs create their virtual reality out of textual descriptions similar to those used in novels to create in the reader's mind the world in which characters interact." Similarly, Jeff Galin (1996ff.) provides information on MOOspace's origins, indicating the importance of user creativity as well as the presence of virtual reality in this online environment: "[MUDs and MOOs] started as interactive adventure games similar to Dungeons and Dragons for the computer—but a version that participants could play over the Internet . . . these text-based virtual realities are like real-time conferencing programs that offer a pseudo-physical dimension: Players talk in rooms, can move between rooms, interact with objects ranging from chairs (they return a pre-set message like "You sit down in the chair and relax. Ahhh!"), to bartenders (you can order drinks from them, they answer you, and they hand you drink-objects that you can drink virtually), to games like Scrabble."

write a story based on the print out

definition by stressing the users' ability to create this textual reality, suggesting that MOOspace is "like an 'interactive novel' where all the characters are controlled by people. MOOspace is just like normal space, except that it exists only in the screen in front of you AND (and this is important) in the mind of the users. It's part computer code, part imagination." And lest we lose the metaphoric value of building a reality, Bill Bell reminds us that above all, MOOspace can be fun: "I think it has the feel of a virtual costume party. People can be themselves or they can dress up and hide behind masks!"

The concept of "text-based virtual reality," then, is key to understanding MOOspace—and so is the importance of *play*. These two concepts are brought up frequently by students and scholars exploring the dimensions and definitions of this environment.

What Is "Hypertext"?

Interestingly, defining hypertext seemed somewhat harder for our students than defining MOOspace. Allan Kotmel takes a somewhat light-hearted approach to answering the question: "Hypertext is any document written after drinking five or more cups of coffee within a two-hour period." Melissa Draper offers, "Hypertext is a type of nonlinear communication in which the reader chooses his/her own path," while Bell adds, "Hypertext allows a reader to 'jump' around a page or an entire book (using hypertext links), giving him or her the capability to read the same document (or book) in a different sequence each time. Anyway, hypertext is NOT the ploddingly methodical conquering of page after linear page of text!" And while Anson Tripp recognizes the futility of predefining a developing genre by insisting that hypertext is "any form of text that is not meant to be read linearly. (yes, I realize that that's broad, sweeping, and kind of vague, but that's my intent)," Connolly takes it a step further still: "Hypertext is the next step in

> **The Unknown of Deep Hypertext**
> Nancy Kaplan (1995) defines the (non)genre of hypertext as an area for "multiple structurations." Each time a reader approaches hypertext, it changes: "Such documents consist of chunks of textual material (words, video clips, sound segments or the like), and sets of connections leading from one chunk or node to other chunks. The resulting structures offer readers multiple trajectories through the textual domain." As a result, each time a reader approaches and interacts with the hypertext, making new selections and following new links, a new text emerges. Kaplan asserts that if the hypertext is deeply linked (thus offering an amazing number of options) the "'authors' cannot know in advance or control with any degree of certainty what 'version' of the story a reader will construct as she proceeds."

the evolutionary ladder of textual communication; if you'll excuse the *Nice* cliche, hypertext is to text as humans are to apes." Finally, Nathan Lavertue comments, "hypertext is writing which is not constrained to be linear . . . and also writing which is not constrained to be text."

The key distinction for Nancy Kaplan (1995), as well as for the students above, is the changing nature of the text instantiated by the reader-controlled paths and links. Whether this is the "next step in the evolutionary ladder of text," or "broad, sweeping, and kind of vague," the shift is real—"text" is no longer simply "text"—at least as we have been defining it since Gutenburg started making Bibles.

Part Three: The Comparative

Is There a Difference between "Hypertext" and "Web Text"?

Among the student MOOers, the resounding answer was "yes, there is a difference." The only disagreement came in how the two kinds of text differed. For instance, Jenn Bowie claims, "Web space can be hypertextual, but something being hypertextual does not have to be web space. And web space is not always hypertextual." And yet, Kotmel seems to take an opposing view: "Web space is only one instance of hypertext. Web space is to hypertext as an MS-DOS PC is to a computer, or as a Ford is to a car. There are many other implementations of hypertext. Take the Windows help system, or Hypercard for the Mac for example." Is hypertext a type of Web space? Is Web space a type of hypertext? Both arguments are defensible, apparently. Or, as Draper puts it, "Web space can be hypertextual and hypertext can be represented in web space, but both of these terms can come in different varieties. For example, hypertext can also be in the form of MOOspace and web space can come in a very linear ('non-hypertextual') papertext form."

According to Draper, "In web space you are writing to a general audience and reading material written for a general audience. In MOOspace you are discussing particular topics brought about by the participants and answering specific questions." Connolly equates this general/specific split with the idea of immediacy of interaction: "If I want to respond to a comment that a person makes on his Web page, my options are pretty much limited to sending him an Email and waiting for his reply. On the other hand, to respond to a person's comments in MOOspace, I can quite literally interrupt her in the middle of a sentence!" This last statement may not be entirely accurate.

Umber_Guest says, "Webspace IS less interactive . . . nothing you do gets immediate feedback."

Mick [to Umber_Guest]: so is immediacy what defines interactivity???

Umber_Guest says, "Sure, more interactive. What you say is right there, you can even interrupt in mid-sentence, as someone pointed out."

Green_Guest says, "isn't it more interactive because we are all here at the same time. typing at the same time. But with a website, you don't know when or whether the person has looked at it"

Mick says, "okay umber . . ."

Chartreuse_Guest resumes hanging from the ceiling like a bat

Mick says, "interrupt me in mid sentence"

Mick says, "go ahead"

Teal_Guest's face turns red, so he flips back around to sit in a 'normal' position

Mick says, "i'm waiting"

sandyet grins

Umber_Guest says, "Chart—does that mean upside down?"

Mick says, "c'mon, umber, interrupt me in mid-sentence!"

Chartreuse_Guest says, "Yep."

sandyet says, "are you guys using raw telnet?"

Mick continues typing uninterrupted

Chartreuse_Guest says, "Call it a hunch, but I think Mick is trying to make a point."

<disconnect MediaMOO>

Regardless, Connolly's earlier point(s) remains; and he, Bell, Crewell, Draper, and Bowie all individually insisted that Web text and hypertext, terms which are often used interchangeably, probably should not be used in such a way.

Is MOOing a Hypertextual Experience?

Kotmel claims that the major differences between writing hypertext and writing in MOOspace are "permanence and accessibility." He explains that writing can be placed on the Web until the author is ready to take it down, but during the time it is online the text is available to anyone who wishes to access it. In MOOspace, however, if the reader is not in the room at the time of an "utterance," the text will never be seen.

Bengi Selcukoglu argues that the two forms of writing have at least one similar trait: they are both native to electronic environments. As she writes, "Both are . . . in what I call a virtual environment; that is, there is a 'location' on the computer, whether a room or on a page, where the interaction takes place." And while Mitchell claims, "I don't think MOOing is anywhere close to hypertext . . . hypertext is a document with links or some special form of annotation," Bell argues, "There are no hypertext links to anything in MOOspace, but the idea of hypertext is more than just links."

Crewell sums it up this way: "MOOs could be classified as hypertextual, but it's a bit of a fuzzy issue. By giving different MOO commands, you can 'change rooms,' akin to changing pages in hypertext. It is a different presentation than what we are used to, but it can be considered hypertext (not all MOO sessions are hypertextual, however—it is more like the possibility exists for it to be hypertextual, just like in web space.)" Crewell introduces an important point—the increasingly popular idea that writing (especially in an electronic environment) is a mapping skill. Using the notion of mapping, Steve Wade claims that MOOspace is, indeed, hypertextual:

> The MOO answer to links is the ability to hop from room to room, effectively from node to node, depending on how you look at the situation. Each room contains its own "information," objects, and exits to other rooms (links). And just because the analogy is to rooms in real space, does not mean that the MOO space rooms need to obey any of the laws of physics. The basement can connect to the 42nd floor and the front door can lead to a closet (dead link?). Sounds a lot like hypertext to me.

Or, as Connolly described it in another context, "MOOspace introduces environments and objects using text; it uses text to do more than simply get an idea across. In many ways, MOOspace is the very definition of hypertext." As Crewell and Wade both concluded, the key skill common to both electronic realms—MOO and WWW—is mapping. Moving from room to room via text; is it more than just a metaphor?

<reconnect @MediaMOO>

Teal_Guest says, "So if hypertext implies jumping around between different areas in a document (at least at some level), does that make multi-tasking (like reading the web page and paying attention to the MOO at the same time) also hypertextual?"
Hazel_Guest has left.
Hazel_Guest has arrived.
Hazel_Guest says, "there i just jumped around from here to the donut shoppe and back. i am a hypertext. wheee."

Chartreuse_Guest says, "I think DESIGNING a room or environment in
    MOOspace would be a LOT of help in designing a Web page . . ."
sandyet says, "why chartreuse?"
Blue_Guest agrees w/ ChartGuest says, "Char - especially if you were
    trying to create a virtual room(s) on the page"
Chartreuse_Guest says, "Also, I think MOO interaction gives you a good
    sense for a non-linear flow of information, which is what a Web
    page is . . . or can be . . ."

<disconnect MediaMOO>

So MOOing and hypertext, if not perfectly analogous, do share at least
the inherent spatiality that demands the shift in a writer's responsibility
that Johnson-Eilola (1996) suggests—an author must respect a reader.
Connolly puts it this way:

> If you view Hypertext mainly
> as the substance of the stuff put
> on the Web—i.e., the stuff that
> arises from Hypertext Markup
> Language—Then of course
> MOOing won't be hypertex-
> tual. But I look at it in a broader
> sense. See, "hyper" as it modi-
> fies "text" means taking text to
> a new level . . . if Hypertext is
> more than just "normal text"—
> that is, text in a linear sense, text

The Hypertextual Quality of MOOs
"In many ways, MUDs deliver the
same kind of textual experience that
hypertexts do. Any engagement . . .
involves some level of interactive
writing, as the user describes actions
and receives passages of prose from
the program in reply. In addition, the
MOOs, MUSEs, and MUSHs allow
users to create new spaces, objects,
and even simulated persons."—Stuart
Moulthrop (1989)

as presented on paper—then a MOO must, by definition, be
hypertextual. In Hypertext—MOOs, specifically—the reader IS
the author, along with all the other reader/authors. TEXT is used
to INTERACT rather than just present words and ideas, and THAT
is why I call a MOO a Hypertextual environment.

Map-Making
"Communication used to be about telling stories . . . Relatively recently, though,
the map has started to replace the story as our fundamental way of knowing. . . .
We must reposition ourselves as mapmakers rather than authors . . . Maps, in
fact, provide some of the most powerful ways of understanding communication
as the selective arrangement of heterogeneous fragments and aspects . . . we
might instead begin to value the idea that technical communicators' talents lie
not in their skills at taking (and simplifying) dictation but in constructing novel
and useful (if contingent) structures in fields of information. In other words,
business and technical communicators do not write documentation or author
reports, but make maps."—Johnson-Eilola (1996)

It is this concept of reader-as-author, the nebulous "reading and writing as one act," and the "collaboration of author and audience" which most electronic rhetors will point to as the key benefit of hypertextuality.

So where MOOers are necessarily writing and reading simultaneously ("skimming and diving"), as the text scrolls by in a dazzling display of multivocality, the same kind of interaction is theoretically possible while working in Web space. Unlike the immediacy in MOOspace, however, the turnaround time in rethinking ideas and group collaboration in Web space may be somewhat slower. One of the student MOOers compared working in MOOspace to sprinting, and writing in Web space to running long distances; the same muscles are exercised, but in different ways. And just as marathon runners will occasionally in their training run windsprints, perhaps hypertext authors might occasionally MOO—to stretch muscles in a different way.

Part Four: The Problematic

Working in MOOspace isn't necessarily easy—it does demand a certain amount of time to learn and teach the technology, and to allow for "newbies" to overcome both the "Gee whiz, this is cool" response and the "I don't know enough about computers to keep up with everyone" jitters. As Victor Almeida wrote about his first experience, "For most of us starting out, the MOO was also confusing and frustrating. I had to type quickly and read comments at the same time. . . . In MOOspace

Problems with MOOspace

Reader/Writer Collaborative
Douglas Eyman (1996) examines the reading-as-writing argument, and concludes that a collaborative relationship between reader and writer may be constructed: "the writer provides the lexia and the original set of multiple links which the reader may follow—by choosing certain links and not others, the reader constructs a meaning which is different from the meaning that any other reader will construct, and which may be different from any meaning the writer intended."

And while Eyman feels that hypertext may not be inherently collaborative for the writer/reader, Day et al. (1996) have argued that MOOspace is inherently collaborative: The exploratory nature of the medium makes it ideal for collaboration and invention, for testing new ideas, for capturing thought as it comes into being—before the critical consciousness has a chance to kick in and censor the statement that might, with further consideration, have seemed too odd to utter . . . . Participants must think on the fly, inventing at the edge of consciousness and possibility. In so doing they may stumble upon truths and ideas they might have cast off . . . if they permit these utterances to fly out, others may see in them ideas the original writer had not foreseen, and build upon them. In so doing, the participants collaborate to bring thought-structures into being through writing. As such, the natural heuristic effect of rapid oral interaction can influence the invention process of a conversation that is also a written document.

there was a lot of traffic." Almeida's classmate Dale Older said of the same session, "Being a MOO 'virgin,' I had an idea that people would communicate more freely, but not to the extent that I witnessed. It's funny how comfortable people are expressing themselves when there are no repercussions."

This feeling of freedom can be a problem; even though Older claims "people weren't offended by comments that you would normally see start an argument . . . It was much easier to stay rational, even when touchy subjects were brought up," there can be administrative rules and classroom netiquette concerns to address.

The dozen students involved in this chapter's creation all were assigned to read from one of several netiquette guides, and to respond to Julian Dibbell's notorious essay, "A Rape in Cyberspace; or How an Evil Clown, a Haitian Trickster Spirit, Two Wizards, and a Cast of Dozens Turned a Database into a Society," in partial preparation for the experience so they would be aware of acceptable and expected behavior in MOOspace.

In addition, students needed to learn appropriate "skim and dive" skills. As Michael Day (1996, "Fear and Loathing") suggests, these skills are essential for any research work. The idea that skimming is a useful skill brings us full-circle back to the earlier discussion of immediacy of interaction, and the comparison of Web space with MOOspace; as Selcukoglu writes:

> **Some "Problems" of MOOspace**
> Traci Gardner (1995ff.) points out that the managerial details of bringing students into a real-time interactive writing environment are far more complicated than those that can be solved with the right reading assignment and some class discussion. And Day (1996, "Fear and Loathing") claims that even the apparent problems of working in MOOspace can be turned into positive aspects of the writing environment: Let's start with the problem of students becoming frustrated and disoriented with the quick flow and fast-scrolling screen of the MOO. . . . [The needed] skimming skills are applicable to other contexts besides the Internet. Indeed, how often do we have to skim sources, bibliographies, indexes, tables of contents, papers, and abstracts, in order to find useful information? Do we have time to read every single word? . . . MOO exercises could lead into productive discussion of skimming as a survival research skill . . . if we . . . transfer some of those skimming skills to the general project of developing research skills we often find in writing classes, we might just manage to create a richer environment in our classes because of the wealth of media from which we draw our examples.

> I see MOOspace as an environment where you are able to obtain direct, current, and immediate feedback. Conversations are held, interactions made as if a f2f confrontation was being made. Writ-

ing to the web is not that interactive. Although you are able to browse at your leisure to wherever you'd like to go, you are still on your own—more like you're reading papertext with a few more options, easier access. It is also less spontaneous on the web. Information is handed to you, instead of you being part of the information generated as in MOOspace.

Although text itself, as an alphabetic entity, may always be to some extent "linear," the direction of the reading is no longer solely the responsibility of the author. As Kotmel has suggested, the reader must be an active one and the author must prepare the text to accept and encourage the reader's interaction with the text:

<reconnect @MediaMOO>

Chartreuse_Guest says, "See, by linear I talk less about the reading of the words but the progression of the topics."

Umber_Guest says, "That's the same with the MOO, then. You can choose what you read. Skim and dive."

Teal_Guest says, "But how can you choose what you want to read on a MOO? Everything moves so fast and usually comes in small bursts. You need to read most of it in order to decide where to 'dive'"

Chartreuse_Guest says, "Teal, remember that really long rant I just committed? You could've ignored it, right?"

Teal_Guest says, "I think my CSA professor lectures very hypertextually, and he never seems to use the back button on his browser. :)"

Chartreuse_Guest says, "Skim and dive, like Bengi said. If you do it in a book, you can miss stuff. If you do it in a MOO, anything you miss you can just ask someone to repeat it."

Hazel_Guest [to Chartreuse_Guest]: dah! if you do it in a book you can go back and look at it!

Chartreuse_Guest says, "Yeah, but Hazel, in a MOO there's no need to go back—you go FORWARD to get the repetition. The READER determines the sequence of the text, that's my whole point!!"

<disconnect MediaMOO>

The Associations in Hypertext
"The main objective in building non-linear documents is to look for the associations. You need to find both the obvious and non-obvious ones and take the opportunity to build a link to satisfy those connections. This helps you find and see the connections in your own document, as well as lets the user truly browse your document, letting his mind follow where it wants to go."—Allan Kotmel (1996, "Paperboy")

Whether a reader is "more active" in MOOspace as opposed to Web space led to a lively discussion in the student MOO session—is "interactivity" a matter of speed? Of response? What kinds of reactions matter? These are all questions that face any writer confronting a real/imagined/addressed/invoked audience.

<reconnect @MediaMOO>

Guest says, "You guys are looking at the RATE of interaction. But that's worthless. If I sit here and babble out a sentence every 10 seconds, but don't affect anyone, INTERACTION=NONE!"
Umber_Guest says, "But what about asking someone to repeat?"
Green_Guest says, "but I've been scrolling back a lot just now"
Teal_Guest says, "Good call, Guest"
Chartreuse_Guest says, "They're equally interactive, I think—but in different WAYS. I mean, in a MOO, no one's gonna read my 3-page-long rant about why work sucks."
sandyet nods guest
Guest says, "But if I email someone once a week and get responses to every comment, INTERACTION=100%"
Blue_Guest says, "this interaction is among other ppl, Web interaction is one person w/ written text, like a book and a phone call, just very different"
Mick [to Blue_Guest]: but the text represents the author, right?
Umber_Guest says, "REPRESENTS the author, but isn't the author in person . . ."
Mick [to Umber_Guest]: and your text here IS you in person?
Mick thinks Bengi is treading into some interesting philosophical implications
sandyet says, "my text here represents me . . . and a web site represents the person who created it"

Guest says, "text represents the "narrator" - I can write something that doesn't represent "me" at all"
Umber_Guest says, "I think it is . . ."

<disconnect MediaMOO>

> **Active Readers and Interface**
> "Hypertext and hypermedia provide the thinking reader with the opportunity to interact both intellectually and physically with the text, images, icons, and buttons on the screen. The active reader's decisions are translated into physical actions, like selecting from options, pointing at links, and clicking to confirm choices. The web is more than simply an electronic display of information. It is an interface."—Karen Chauss (1996)

Part Five: The Playful

Perhaps the most enjoyable aspect of bringing MOO technology to your writing classroom is the inherent "play" which drives the textual community. Here, "play" is used in both senses of the word: MOOspace allows for play-acting and for playing around. Kotmel, who compares both MOOing and reading hypertext to "Choose-Your-Own-Adventure and Which-Way books," puts it this way: "I thought it was a great and fun concept when I was ten. Now I see what a useful and academic concept it can be too." Fun, useful, and academic—all at the same time!

Rickly and Crump (1995), in their widely cited Web text "It's Fun to Have Fun but You Have to Know How! or, How Cavorting on the Net Will Save the Academy," discuss the very idea Kotmel's attitude reflects. They advocate breaking away from the notion that seriousness equals success. And, part of what makes a successful MOO session is the "reality" of the environment in which the play occurs. Notice how easily the student MOOers manipulate their "environment" while never losing the thread of conversation; in many places, the emoting and "movement" of the "characters" may even be read as a conscious example of the argument being made:

<reconnect @MediaMOO>
Chartreuse_Guest creates a double cappuccino out of thin air and sips it between drags from his clove cigarette
sandyet says, "but even if we create a friendly atmosphere here . . . what about where you are physically? You might be on stiff chairs and such."
Mick hmms textual reality. Creating reality through writing . . . through words. Anyone? Anyone?
Blue_Guest says, "ever read a book in a bad chair and such and got so lost the RL dissapears? (or "become" the book)"
Guest is sitting in a comfortable chair . . . but wishes his computer hadn't bombed on him.
Chartreuse_Guest says, "If you're in a MOO, the "real world," believe it or not, matters less. Right now I'm in an uncomfortable chair, but I've got Joe Satriani playing in my Walkman and a fun environment to interact with. Thus, it's more fun."
Mick dumps donut batter on claudine
Chartreuse_Guest sits happily onto the Little Comfy Chair.
Teal_Guest says, "True, sandyet. You may not be physically comfortable, but you may be mentally comfortable, which could make you forget your physical condition."

Blue_Guest nodes to Teal
Teal_Guest sips his mochaccino
Chartreuse_Guest says, "It happens all the time, to lots of people."
Guest says, "Mick - perception shapes reality. Words shape perception."
sandyet nods blue and teal
Mick munches chocolate cookies in real life and does not forget that rl experience while mooing
Teal_Guest says, "But, Guest. Reality also shapes perception."
Mick oohs the tautological disagreement
Green_Guest says, "I have gotten lost in a book. So if I was in class and it was boring but we got on a moo then it wouldn't be so bad"
sandyet frowns at mick's munching
Guest says, "Teal - true - It's a feedback loop."
Blue_Guest is just drinking water in real life (where are you mick? maybe I'll come over and steal the cookies)

<disconnect MediaMOO>

It's Fun to Have Fun But . . .
"Go forth with eyes and hearts open. Be prepared to be nimble. Be prepared to be disappointed and surprised. Joy and anguish await you . . . the gliding over the surface of a new topic at thrilling speeds and plunging in occasionally, connecting with others in a frenzied shouting match in a virtual room to the point of exhaustion, then getting up from my chair, looking around, and realizing that I'm the only one home. That's the future. But so is publishing on-line. And hypermedia. And exploring. And punning. And building. And learning. And having fun."—Becky Rickly and Eric Crump (1995)

It is no accident that MOOs, like those we tend to use in our classrooms, are often conflated with MUDs, which are more self-consciously game-playing environs, and often advertise themselves as "alternate worlds." Greg Siering (1995) suggests that these "alternate worlds" should be considered "communicative environments" as he stresses the imaginative component inherent in creating a persona for a character in a MOO. This "imaginative interplay"—perhaps more correctly "Internet-play!"—allows for precisely the kind of "continual re-definition" which Crump and Rickly allude to, and which is the hallmark of the postmodern writing classroom. What is being "continually re-defined"? Reality. How is it being re-defined? Textually. How are the MOOers (re)creating this "textual reality"? They are play-acting.

MUDS as Communicative Environments

"[W]e can begin promoting MUDs as 'communicative environments' rather than alternate worlds . . . [Computer-mediated communication] tends to construct a psychological filter of sorts that allows individuals to separate their real selves from the characters they portray on-line, encouraging the view of the online persona as separate from the 'real life' individual."—Greg Siering (1995)

<reconnect @MediaMOO>

Mick says, "Does the specific environment—like the MOO room we're in—help alter the reality? or does the text of the participants create it entirely?"

Umber_Guest says, "It doesn't for me, I'm too caught up in the subject matter."

Guest says, "Mick - but the "environment" here IS text"

sandyet oooohs Guest

Blue_Guest says, "Now I'm in the tea room . . . so I'm in the mood for tea :)""

Chartreuse_Guest says, "I think the environment CAN alter the conversation . . . but it can't control it."

Teal_Guest thinks that the textual environment provides a starting point, but that the conversation and interaction soon take over.

Mick [to dustin]: the environment is the text? or the text is the environment? are those the same statement?

Blue_Guest says, "If you control the conversation wouldn't that make it more like Web space, w/ an author and readers?"

Chartreuse_Guest says, "Only a little. There's no physical motion, so the effect is less immediate. On the other hand, look at how many people drank tea when we came in here."

Mick says, "ooh, Shawn. nice point. and really, what's the point of drinking tea here? other than to play with new commands?"

sandyet wonders about "physical motion" in MOOspace.

Guest says, "Mick - it's part of the mood, the persona. Role-playing."

Chartreuse_Guest says, "Exactly—you play with the new stuff 'cause you CAN, which is part of what makes MOOs fun . . . A MOO is kinda like a REALLY GOOD game master."

sandyet says, "so in these games you create your own persona. In all writing don't we create a persona?"

Guest says, "That's a point of the internet in general - to explore. Role-playing allowing you to break outside the boundaries of who you are, become something/someone else."

Teal_Guest says, "I think in any acting or writing, there is always some piece of you in what you act or write. The key to good acting/

writing is how closely you come in touch with the related part of your persona."

Mick says, "you just completely conflated acting and writing. you really wanna do that?"

Guest says, "Teal - heading towards postmodern! :)"

<disconnect MediaMOO>

@hug me
"Because I am not nor ever will become a skilled MOO programmer, my ability to manipulate a large but limited set of feature objects created by others shapes my online persona. And that should make for a compelling game of self-construction. I can watch as I create and manipulate my selves within the confines of the virtual world I've entered. But I must always remember that there are several levels of abstraction between the selves I construct offline and those I construct online. The person typing these words may not be a hugger but [my character] self is."— Stephen Doheny-Farina (1995)

So the textual reality is a recursive agency; the players' self-perception is informed by the "surroundings," which they can manipulate and sometimes alter. The surroundings affect the conversation and vice versa; the process itself affects the self-perception and actions of the participants, and the loop starts anew.

Textual construction of the Self (significantly, Doheny-Farina refers to it as a "game") mirrors much of what the process-oriented writing classroom has trumpeted as its goal for two decades—that the ability to learn to socially construct an argument supercedes the many possible "products" our writings may deliver. Haynes and Holmevik (1996) refer to "the radical potential of the MOO as a new and dynamic pedagogical reality," and Day (1996, "Pedagogies") also addresses this concept, emphasizing that MOOs allow both teachers and students to focus on the power of words. If working—no, *playing*—

The Textuality of MOOs
Day (1996, "Pedagogies") also addresses this concept: "Because they are generally a completely textual communication medium, MOOs and MUDS allow classes that use them to focus rather narrowly on writing. Everything that is uttered, created, or described in a MUD or MOO must be uttered, created, or described in text, forcing us to recognize the power of the written word to persuade another, evoke meaning, or spur the imagination into new worlds." Harris (1996) agrees: "Since writing becomes the primary means of communicating with a synchronously present audience, students learn that writing is an important, powerful act—a way to influence one's peers and to convince them of the validity of one's views."

in MOOspace allows our writing students to grasp the potential for electronic text to collaboratively and interactively reshape reality, that may be reason enough to include it in our ("radical") pedagogy.

Part Six: The (In)conclusive

Whither Writing?

As teachers of writing, we've all heard the question, in some form, probably every term, every class we've ever taught. You know—the "why" question.

"Why do we have to take this class, anyway?"

"Why is this important to me? I'm a [fill in the blank] major."

"Why do we have to be in the computer lab? Isn't this a writing class?"

Those of us who call ourselves "teachers of writing" are suddenly faced with an onerous task—redefining our pedagogies and reconceptualizing our theoretical backgroundings in terms of a much wider epistemological approach than Alexander Bain ever imagined. It's just as hard as it sounds; in fact, given the immense force of popular culture and advertising, given President Clinton's threat—er, promise—to have the Internet available to every American classroom by the year 2000, we actually must stop asking the question, "Can using the technology help people teach writing better?" and begin asking, "How can we use technology to help our students survive in a post-Gutenburg communications infrastructure?"

Note the shift—from "writing" to "communication." As Hart-Davidson (1995) has suggested, we might start considering that the teaching we are doing in electronic environments moves us still further away from the traditional writing classroom. Though we cannot teach a kind of discursive competency that "transcends" technologies, we can—as in the case of using MOO technology in the Webbed writing classroom—try teaching from and within multiple technologies to provide students with alternative perspectives on "the possible."

Of course, what Hart-Davidson is advocating implies not only a changed view of "writing" but of the classroom. When we bring MOO technology into our class—wait, stop, reverse that: when we bring our classes into MOOs—we are ourselves actively advocating the decentralization of the classroom power structure and redefining our role(s) as "instructor." We don't have a comfortable fallback position—as Fanderclai (1995) writes, "the novelty of being in a virtual classroom

---

"Do you want to teach writing?"
"The ways we teach writing attempt to get at a sort of pure layer of writing ability—a basic discursive competency—that transcends writing situations and writing technologies . . . our motivations for teaching writing may be naive; though we may act out of a commitment to ensure literacy for all, our pedagogy, our technologies, and our definitions of writing may be working against this goal. . . . And this leaves me with yet another version of the question I seem to keep asking my fellow writing teachers: 'Do you want to teach a class called "print conventions and culture?" Or do you want to teach writing?'"
—Bill Hart-Davidson (1995)

---

will not last through an on-line lecture; MUDs are designed for interaction, and students will soon want to DO something." Ideally, that "something" they will want to DO—is write. To each other, with each other, at each other.

It may be an uncomfortable place for many teachers—suddenly no longer at the "front" of the classroom, perhaps even ignored onscreen if the students are enamored enough of their own writing! But the students are writing actively, rather than dutifully. As MediaMOO Wizard Amy Bruckman claims, "I think people should be active participants in culture, not passive recipients of commercially produced content . . . We're increasingly surrounded by technology . . . It's still up in the air: will people have meaningful control over that technology? . . . I think people can and should have that control" (qtd. in Wick and Siering). Allowing our students to "MOO what they can" with their writing allows them precisely that kind of control. In fact, Lasarenko (1996) argues that in taking this kind of control of the electronic rhetorical ("netorical") situation, students are best served in self-determining the content of their writing.

Should you use MOOspace in teaching writing to the WWW? The decision is one that may be getting easier, as creative technowonks like Cross and Fulgevik (DaMOO) and Haynes and Holmevik (LinguaMOO)

Fighting the Shoebox Structure
Texas Tech University technology support specialist Joseph Unger says, "Instructors who come into the computer-based classroom have to fight the network itself if they want to try to force traditional pedagogies onto the classroom, in a similar way that non-traditional instructors have to fight the shoe-box structure of the traditional classroom . . . The instructor's role is one of constructor of an environment (with a little help from me) and coach rather than lecturing professor. The student, on the other hand, is much more self-guided and must work with other students in collaboration" (qtd. in Wick and Eyman).

---

are creating "WOOs"—a new hybrid technology which the SenseMedia Surfer describes as "the result of the collision between two well known internet services: The World Wide Web and Multi User Object Oriented Domains."

Should you use MOOspace in teaching writing to the WWW? The only viable answer, really, is "maybe." Better yet, the answer might be "let your students decide." It makes a rhetor think about reading and writing and the roles of the author and audience; it is a textual environment, a reality created through writing, that can help students (re)consider the power of words to shape meaning and of meaning to shape "textual reality." If you're teaching hypertextual approaches to writing, MOOspace can "exercise the muscles" necessary to approach writing as a mapping skill.

And it's fun. If anything, writing should be that.

Ethos in Action
"Research skills, critical thinking skills, literature, and writing can all be taught in unique and exciting ways in MOOspace . . . [S]tudents can discuss and analyze MOO transcripts so that their own linguistic behaviors become the object of their study. Moreover, students can create their own 'characters' on a MOO, the quintessential embodiment of ethos in action. Students can create web pages, share essays, and write stories in MOOspace as well. In all content areas, the students' own behaviors, interactions, text, and experience become the subject matter to investigate, thereby increasing metacognitive skills."
—Jane Lasarenko (1996)

A Final Word

The greatest of all life's puzzles, to the student, is "what does the teacher want?" Using MOOspace—decentering the classroom, instantiating the multivocality of the collaborative, interactive, realtime written text—just might help us move away from having to answer that question, even if it still (inevitably) gets asked.

<reconnect @MediaMOO>
Umber_Guest says, "Did we do what you wanted here, Mick and sandyet? We didn't seem to stick to the topic very much."
Mick [to Umber_Guest]: did you think we didn't do our job in enforcing the conversation, Bengi?
Umber_Guest says, "Not the way I thought you would have, trying to stick to the topic you emailed us about. But then again, I didn't know the intent of this session . . ."

Chartreuse_Guest says, "I think this is an excellent example of a typical MOO dynamic, actually . . . we were kinda a control group, in that sense."

Guest says, "Mick - plus the personality shift . . . I'm rarely this talkative IRL class."

Umber_Guest says, "Me, too!"

Chartreuse_Guest grins. "I'm usually MORE talkative in class. 'Course, in class I can't smoke."

Chartreuse_Guest lights up still another clove cigarette.

Umber_Guest says, "Well, in discussions, anyway."

Teal_Guest says, "Actually, I think this is one of the most interesting MOO sessions I've ever been in."

Mick says, "Maybe that's because you were controlling the conversation instead of us?"

Blue_Guest says, "I think the only reason I was talkative in Mick's class was we started out mooing and emailing. I got more comfortable and . . ."

Umber_Guest says, "I have to admit, I was a little nervous about this meeting. But it's a lot less intimidating via the computer than IRL"

Chartreuse_Guest says, "See, Bengi, that's almost what I mean. It's EASIER to interact in a MOO—you don't have to see someone try not to laugh at you if you screw up. You don't get embarrassed. You LET GO."

Blue_Guest says, "In a moo you can become what you may consider your "real self" one that is not clouded by any outside perception, like how you look"

Umber_Guest eats another donut

Blue_Guest says, "Its because you can bee who you wnat and say what you want"

Mick [to Jenn]: so how we look has nothing to do with our real self?

Guest agrees with Blue A LOT!!!

Umber_Guest says, "You can also become someone completely different . . . ?"

Guest says, "In a MOO, you can become who you want to be"

Umber_Guest says, "I think mooing can affect who you are IRL . . ."

Blue_Guest agrees with Umber

Umber_Guest says, "It gives you greater confidence in what you say . . . makes you think you might actually be able to say them . . ."

Chartreuse_Guest says, "Mick, I'd love to do this again! Watching academic discussions turn to mush is fun!"

Blue_Guest laughs out loud.

Chartreuse_Guest says, "Oh, wait . . . this can't be MUSH. This is MOO.
sandyet smiles and kills the log.
@quit

disconnected

Not Exactly a Bibliography

As noted in the early part of the MOO log(s), "We made a conscious
decision . . . to only use resources that were published electronically, in
e-journals or elsewhere on the WWW." As such, you will notice a dearth
of "page numbers" attached to these citations, and in the internal
citations previously listed throughout the chapter. All URLs listed were
functional as of May 1, 1998.

    Additional cited material in this chapter is excerpted, with
written individual permissions, from classroom electronic mail discussions and informally logged MOO sessions with students.

    Primary credit for the development of this chapter, then, belongs
to:

Dustin Crewell, Allan Kotmel, Melissa Draper, Nathan Lavertue, Collin
    Mitchell: Spring 1996 "Writing to the WWW," Rensselaer Polytechnic
    Institute. http://www.rpi.edu/dept/llc/webclass/web/

Bill Bell, Jennifer Bowie, Dale Older, Anson Tripp: Summer 1996 "Writing to
    the WWW," Rensselaer Polytechnic Institute.
    http://www.rpi.edu/dept/llc/webclass/summer96/

Victor Almeida, Shawn Connolly, Bengi Selcukoglu: Fall 1996 "Technical &
    Professional Communication," Rensselaer Polytechnic Institute.
    http://www.rpi.edu/dept/llc/techpro/doherty/

Note: In the MOO sessions cited in this chapter, the following students
    participated: Connolly (Chartreuse_Guest), Selcukoglu
    (Umber_Guest), Kotmel (Teal_Guest), Bowie (Blue_Guest), Crewell
    (Guest). The authors of this chapter also "Multi-Tasked" as
    Hazel_Guest (Doherty) and Green_Guest (Thompson).

EXTERNAL LINKS

Baldwin, Beth. "Evolving Past the Essay-a-saurus: Introducing Nimbler
    Forms into Writing Classes." http://www.missouri.edu/~rhetnet/
    baldwin_snap.html

Chauss, Karen. 1996. "Reader as User: Applying Interface Design Techniques
    to the Web." *Kairos* 1.2 [Summer]. http://english.ttu.edu/kairos/1.2/
    features/chauss/bridge.html

Day, Michael. 1996. "Fear and Loathing in Paradise: Making Use of
    Dissensus, Disorientation, and Discouragement on the MOO." Sidebar

to *Kairos* [Summer]. Coverweb "Pedagogies in Virtual Spaces: Writing Classes in the MOO." http://english.ttu.edu/kairos/1.2/coverweb/dis.html

———. 1996. Introduction to *Kairos* [Summer]. Coverweb "Pedagogies in Virtual Spaces: Writing Classes in the MOO." http://english.ttu.edu/kairos/1.2/coverweb/coverweb.html

Dibbell, Julian. 1993. "A Rape in Cyberspace, or How an Evil Clown, a Haitian Trickster Spirit, Two Wizards, and a Cast of Dozens Turned a Database into a Society." *Village Voice*, 23 December. http://www.levity.com/julian/bungle.html

Doheny-Farina, Stephen. 1995. "Representation(s) and a Sense of Self: The Subtle Abstractions of MOO Talk." *Computer-Mediated Communication Magazine* 2(5). http://www.december.com/cmc/mag/1995/may/last.html

Eyman, Douglas. 1996. "Hypertext in the Computer-Facilitated Writing Class." *Kairos* 1(2) [Summer]. http://english.ttu.edu/kairos/1.2/features/eyman/

Fanderclai, Tari. 1995. "MUDs in Education: New Environments, New Pedagogies." *Computer-Mediated Communication Magazine* 2(1) [January]. http://www.december.com/cmc/mag/1995/jan/fanderclai.html

Galin, Jeff. "MOO Central." Now available off the LinguaMOO main page: http://lingua.utdallas.edu/

Gardner, Traci. 1995. "MOO Teacher's Tip Sheet." http://www.daedalus.com/net/MOOTIPS.html

Harris, Leslie. 1996. "Writing Spaces: Using MOOs to Teach Composition and Literature." *Kairos* 1(2) [Summer]. http://english.ttu.edu/kairos/1.2/coverweb/Harris/contents.htm

Hart-Davidson, Bill. 1995. "What's Dis'course About? Arguing CMC into the Curriculum." *Computer-Mediated Communication Magazine* 2(1) [January]. http://www.december.com/cmc/mag/1995/jan/hart.html

Haynes, Cynthia, and Jan Rune Holmevik. 1996. "Lingua Unlimited: Enhancing Pedagogical Reality with MOOs." Available in *Kairos* [Summer] Coverweb "Pedagogies in Virtual Spaces: Writing Classes in the MOO." http://english.ttu.edu/kairos/1.2/coverweb/bridge.html

Johnson-Eilola, Johndan. 1996. "Stories and Maps: Postmodernism and Professional Communication." *Kairos* 1(1) [Winter]. http://english.ttu.edu/kairos/1.1/features/johndan.html

Kaplan, Nancy. 1995. "Politexts, Hypertexts, and Other Cultural Formations in the Late Age of Print." *Computer-Mediated Communication Magazine* 2(3) [March]. http://www.december.com/cmc/mag/1995/mar/kaplan.html

Kotmel, Allan. 1996. "Hypertext vs. Papertext: Don't Fire the Paperboy Yet!" http://www.rpi.edu/dept/llc/webclass/web/filigree/kotmel/

Langham, Don. 1995. "The Common Place MOO: Orality and Literacy in Virtual Reality." *Computer-Mediated Communication Magazine* 1(3) [March]. http://www.december.com/cmc/mag/1994/jul/moo.html

Lasarenko, Jane. 1996. "So You Wanna MOO?" Available in *Kairos* [Summer] Coverweb "Pedagogies in Virtual Spaces: Writing Classes in the MOO." http://english.ttu.edu/kairos/1.2/coverweb/bridge.html

MediaMOO: A Professional Community. telnet purple-crayon.media.mit.edu 8888

Moulthrop, Stuart. 1998. "Traveling in the Breakdown Lane: A Principle of Resistance for Hypertext." http://www.ubalt.edu/www/ygcla/sam/essays/breakdown.html

Rickly, Becky, and Eric Crump. 1995. "It's Fun to Have Fun but You Have to Know How! or, How Cavorting on the Net Will Save the Academy." *Computer-Mediated Communication Magazine* 2(1) [January]. http://www.december.com/cmc/mag/1995/jan/rickly_crump.html

Siering, Greg. 1995. "Reconceptualizing the Virtual: Bringing CMC Back into This Reality." *Computer-Mediated Communication Magazine* 2(1) [January]. http://www.december.com/cmc/mag/1995/jan/siering.html

Wick, Corey, and Douglas Eyman. 1996. "Another Perspective: *Kairos* Talks with Technology Support Specialist Joseph Unger." *Kairos* 1.3 [Fall]. http://english.ttu.edu/kairos/1.3/news/intermoo.html

Additional Recommended Reading (this book was released after the text for this chapter was complete and revised):

Haynes, Cynthia, and Jan Rune Holmevik, eds. 1998. *High Wired: On the Design, Use, and Theory of Educational MOOs*. Foreword by Sherry Turkle. Ann Arbor: University of Michigan Press.

V Resource Appendix

20 The Craft of Teaching and the World Wide Web: A Reference Essay for Educators

Kevin M. Leander
Vanderbilt University

Like others represented in this volume, I believe that particular educational practices with the Web have tremendous potential to shape how we engage in the processes of learning. At the same time, we often describe the Web with metaphors of the "sea," or as a vast outer "space," and many teachers who set out to work on the Web describe their experiences in terms of being adrift or disoriented. Other educators, through initial experiences with the Web, separate "real work" from the relatively purposeless wandering or "surfing" that the Web appears to encourage. It is my hope that this essay will help narrow the distance between the educator who is a novice Web-user and the loosely structured, ever-becoming nature of the Web—that it can be a mediating tool to scaffold and inspire further discovery.

Overview of Goals

Teaching is a type of craftwork, in which one has a range of tools with which to work, a particular vision of this work, and a set of dispositions and goals. The advent of the Web marks a significant historical shift in the availability of teaching and learning tools. Yet, as noted above, because of the dramatic growth of the Web, as well as its loose, nonhierarchical structure, sifting through and accessing relevant tools is a major problem for novice and experienced educators alike. Thus, the first goal of this chapter is to serve as an introductory reference to the Web, pointing educators in the direction of useful Web resources, as well as building productive relations between them. For instance, the first three parts of the essay refer to exemplary Web sites that offer perspectives from the classroom, from large-scale projects, and from student work, portraying teaching craftwork-in-action on different scales. In sum, my first goal is that this essay would serve as a manageable starting point—a home base for educators who are seeking to explore the Web as a teaching and learning resource.

Of course, in any process of selection a particular vision and set of values becomes evident, a critical purpose comes into play. In the following I have foregrounded this critical purpose by reviewing select Web sites. In these reviews I hope to venture beyond the generalized critical frames currently popularized by programs ("engines") that search the Web, which award Web sites four stars or three mice for vague categories such as "presentation" and "content." Rather, in the literal sense of "re-viewing," or seeing again, I deliberately examine a group of Web sites not merely as technological constructions, but as noteworthy sites of teaching and learning. In these reviews, my goal is to discuss educational practices that are enhanced or made possible through the World Wide Web, as well as to indicate emerging and largely unrealized potentials. Together, the reviews function as an illustrative essay, building a multistrand argument through repeated examples. As such, I have termed this chapter a "reference essay," in order to highlight both its practical, reference-based function and its critical, value-based function.

Pedagogical Values That Inform My Selections and Reviews

Despite the "Education" subject groupings necessary for search engines, it becomes rapidly clear that on the Web there is not A World of Education, but many such worlds, with radically different conceptions of teaching and learning. In producing this guide, I have become more aware of the lenses through which I am selecting and reviewing, values which are more or less implicit in my work. These values, which I share with many other educators, frame the essay's vision of the Web as an educational medium:

- student and teacher inquiry and constructivist practices
- student and teacher production and publication through diverse media
- communication and interaction with diverse communities located outside of schools and universities
- the use of multimedia to assist different types of learners, better represent experience with the world, and motivate learners
- a belief that virtual communities, resources, and activities can and should enhance their off-line counterparts, and develop complex relations with them
- the Web not as a stable tool or resource to be "mined," but as a medium for which a new range of tools and practices can and should be developed

My hope is that this reference essay will promote dialogue on pedagogical values and the World Wide Web, and that such dialogue will promote greater self-reflexivity within and around the medium of the Web. Reflective engagement is already latent within the everyday functioning of technological tools. These moments find us when technology calls us up short, when computers and networks crash, when demos dissolve—in general when we are urged by our tools to reconsider why we picked them up in the first place. In addition to these spontaneous moments, with respect to the Web in particular there is an increasing need for deliberate, reflective critique as the medium expands and develops a history and identity as a particular set of educational tools. In turn, such reflections on technologies can provide a mirror to our larger practices and beliefs, making more explicit, and sometimes more troublesome, our educational purposes and ideologies, and the histories to which they belong.

Additionally, I hope that the following reviews and references assist you in imagining and planning for your own craftwork. Because this guide may be read hypertextually or linearly, I have listed the sections below. Within each section, you will find Web addresses ("links" or "URLs") to exemplary educational Web sites—some reviewed, others briefly described—as well as links to "Jump Stations," or Web sites that index many other valuable links. In all cases, I have avoided simply presenting long lists of links.

I. Classrooms Using the Web
II. Large-Scale Educational Projects
III. Student Work on the Web
IV. Discipline-Specific Sites
V. Journals and Magazines
VI. Digital Museums and Libraries
VII. Professional Development and Organizations
VIII. Tools and Strategies for Searching the Web
IX. Technical Help for Web Projects
X. Final Reflections

I. Classrooms Using the Web

Currently, to speak of putting courses on the Web—especially courses that are not structured primarily for distance learning—means generally giving access to course descriptions and syllabi, and less often making lecture notes and assignments available online. This present state of affairs is understandable for a number of reasons: first, these Web texts represent paper documents traditionally handed out to students; second, these ready-to-hand documents are easily transferred to a digital medium; and finally, indexed by these documents is a style of teacher-centered learning that is prevalent at the secondary and university levels. In sum, a predominant "vision" is to use Web technology to make public or broadly accessible the practices we have always performed. The course development work of Jane Leuthold and Michael Hinton are refreshing examples of challenging such norms.

Dr. Jane Leuthold
University of Illinois at Urbana-Champaign
    Microeconomic Principles
    http://www.cba.uiuc.edu/college/econ/econ102/Webproj.html

    Introduction to Public Finance
    http://www.cba.uiuc.edu/college/econ/econ214/e214hmpg.
    html

    Taxation in Developing Economies
    http://www.cba.uiuc.edu/college/econ/econ415/e415hmpg.
    html

Review
    Leuthold's work in various courses pushes in several innovative directions, among them student ownership and publication, ongoing dialogues among all participants, and interactivity. In an introductory course to Microeconomic Principles, Leuthold has developed a traditional assignment—the short term paper—into what she is calling a Web Paper. In this case the assignment is writing a descriptive analysis of a market, which seems ideal for the Web as a medium. Through their links, the students take advantage of the large commercial presence on the Web, and use the market's own tools—images and graphs—to reflect back upon it. The papers represent a high sense of student ownership, audience, and meaning beyond the course that surpasses many writing assignments within general education courses.
    Leuthold gives a good deal of thought to a particular use of the Web with various course goals and student groups. In the site for Introduction to Public Finance, we get a sense of the interactivity and

dialogue that Leuthold is moving toward and shaping for an audience that is much larger than that of the microeconomics course. Here, Leuthold has created Powerpoint slides of lectures, and a "lab" each week consisting of readings, images, links, a computer-checked self-quiz, and student contributions to a class chat line. For still another contrast, consider how Leuthold has used the Web in a graduate-level seminar most often taken by international students: Taxation in Developing Economies. In the context of this course, Leuthold's students have created Web pages concerning taxation in their home countries. Additionally, Leuthold has constructed an "Econ. 415 Alumni Guestbook," where former and current participants can keep in touch with one another, and the international community that the course aims to foster can continue beyond its formal, temporal structure.

Michael Hinton
Urbana High School, Urbana, Illinois
    Advanced Placement Physics
    http://cyber.ccsr.uiuc.edu/cyberprof/ap-physics/Urbana-High

Review
CyberProf (http://cyber.ccsr.uiuc.edu/cyberprof/general/homepage/Newpage/first.html) is a Web-based learning and communication utility that has been developed under the direction of Alfred W. Hubler at the Center for Complex Systems Research at the University of Illinois, Urbana-Champaign. CyberProf is a valuable utility that could potentially motivate and guide students in the solving of complex problems across a range of mathematical and scientific disciplines. The utility has several functions, including the posting of lecture notes, online conferencing, and a grade book. The most developed and unique tools of the suite allow users to construct problems with intelligent feedback—the software permits the problem-writer to build in hints, suggestions, and final feedback; in effect, to construct online tutoring into the problems. These problems follow a number of different formats, and make use of a range of media, including video and graphics.

    Currently, a most exciting pedagogical use of CyberProf is under way in AP Physics at Urbana High School, where Michael Hinton's students actually write Web-based problems for one another in their study of mechanics, electricity, and magnetism. Hinton writes that as authors, students interact with the problems at a higher cognitive level than they would if they were only working textbook or teacher-generated problems. Additionally, Hinton notes that the students are more capable than textbook authors in developing motivating problems. Clearly, a student's sense of identifying with a discipline could be highly enhanced through constructing careful problems, predicting and responding to potential difficulties in solving them, using powerful technological tools for this work, and receiving feedback from a wide audience of peer problem solvers.

Valuable Links and Jump Stations: Classrooms Using the Web

- Large institutional projects often give one a sense of vision for what might be possible with the Web as a medium and resource in K–12 education, but a vision of what the activity looks like at the level of the classroom is often missing. An effective yet time-consuming way to capture such a vision is to visit classroom sites that have a Web presence and are indexed by directories such as Web 66 (http://Web66.coled.umn.edu/schools.html). One institutional project that bridges classroom and broader visions in its Web representation is LDAPS (http://ldaps.ivv.nasa.gov/index.html), a constructivist approach to science and engineering through Lego projects.

- Perhaps the largest single collection of university courses with at least some material on the Web can be found at the World Lecture Hall (http://www.utexas.edu/world/lecture). This is the place to go to find course syllabi, assignments, lecture notes, exams, class calendars, etc. The unfortunate name captures a bit of the spirit of the site, but there are some innovative pedagogical uses of the Web embedded within the hundreds of courses, lectures, and syllabi indexed therein.

II. Large-Scale Educational Projects

There are a number of large-scale research and development projects that have made use of the Web to network students, researchers, scientists, and new technological tools. Such projects are often in the sciences, and are often funded by groups from the government or private industry. However, it is also possible to begin a large-scale project by way of the Web through a single person's efforts to bring widely distributed participants together around common goals, as the first exemplar highlights.

News Web
http://www.nvnet.k12.nj.us/newsWeb/index.html
Created by Brian Hanson-Harding

Review
　　News Web, created by Brian Hanson-Harding, a New Jersey English and journalism teacher, describes itself as "a free, on-line newswire and resource center designed for high school journalists and their advisers." The initiative takes advantage of the nature of the Web to bring multiple functions together in one location: student writers can publish and share stories, graphics, and valuable links; advisors and editors can discuss publishing problems and solutions in a weekly live round-table discussion; and through a clickable map, any user can access current Web-based student newspapers across the country. These features and others hold promise for building community among student journalists and their advisers, who are often isolated, work with few resources, and have limited readerships.

　　This site is clearly based upon principles of dialogue: not only is student writing centrally published and disseminated, but co-developed interviews are produced and made widely available through a feature dubbed "On-Line Press Conferences," where national experts are interviewed by student journalists and advisers. The potential of News Web extends beyond newspaper production and high schools. Rather, the site serves as a model for how we might imagine the Web educationally: a medium that permits us to co-construct widely distributed dialogues, resources, audiences, and communities that were previously thinly formed or altogether absent.

CoVis
http://www.covis.nwu.edu/
Learning through Collaborative Visualization

Review
　　CoVis brings together "thousands of students, hundreds of teachers, and dozens of researchers and scientists" in its efforts to develop inquiry-based learning in the geosciences at the middle and high school levels. The CoVis site gives a rich background of the project's goals, philosophies, and tools (although currently lacking much representation of student work). The key goal behind CoVis is to create "communities of practice": "Hopefully, by supplying students with some of the tools and data used by scientists in the field, engaging them in the practice of scientific inquiry, and facilitating interactions between them and members of the scientific community, they can become 'legitimate peripheral participants' of that community."

There are a number of Web-based student-to-expert communication projects that are built around the format of "Ask Dr. X" which have value in their own right. CoVis, however, is designed to reach beyond such one-shot encounters by developing project-length "telementoring" relationships, where scientists can play a number of roles, such as helping students develop research questions, locate Web-based resources, and analyze data. Mentoring and student research are facilitated by technological tools created by CoVis, such as the Weather Visualizer, which is a graphical interface that represents real-time weather data and allows students to create weather maps customized around their inquiries. Collected data, notes, and dialogues with scientific mentors can then be recorded within the online Collaboratory Notebook, a multimedia and multiuser tool that has been developed to scaffold the inquiry process. Even a quick comparison between the traditional school laboratory notebook and the Collaboratory Notebook suggests the potential richness of this project and its creation of tools for new visions of participatory learning.

Jump Stations: Large-Scale Educational Projects

- In ChickScope (http://vizlab.beckman.uiuc.edu/chickscope/homepage.html), students in grades 2 through high school have been able to operate an MRI (Magnetic Resonance Imaging) microscope over the Web to observe the development of a chick embryo. The site demonstrates how the Web can virtually place advanced scientific instruments into the hands of students.

- Global SchoolNet's Internet Project Registry (http://www.gsn.org/pr/) is a central location where you can find K–12 classroom projects carried out in collaboration with organizations such as GSN, I*EARN, IECC, NASA, GLOBE, Academy One, TIES, Tenet, and TERC. Teacher-initiated projects are indexed as well. Keyword searchable.

- Many large-scale projects are in the sciences, and NASA's Online Educational Resources (http://quest.arc.nasa.gov/OER/edures.html) is a good place to explore some of this work.

III. Student Work on the Web

The relation between new tools and their possible social meanings is uncertain; at times the changes that technologies permit us escape us, or occur years after the creation of the tools themselves. Although there is currently a very large educational presence on the Web, much of this material reproduces our traditions in education to celebrate the educator's or institution's experience over the student's. The examples that follow, however, foreground student experience and knowledge constructions, exemplifying the ways in which the Web can be used not simply to reproduce tradition, but to produce progressive, student-centered pedagogies.

Blackburn High School
http://www.ozemail.com.au/~bhs56/index.html
Blackburn, Australia

Review
        After looking at many school and university homepages, my general sense about them from a pedagogical standpoint is that they are not very interesting. Rather, such pages are often overtaken by marketing and public relations purposes, and as such the sense of the lived experiences of students and teachers gets buried under a clickable map of the campus, a picture of the front statue or main building, a generalized and puzzling mission statement, and a long list of courses or degree programs. The homepage of Blackburn High School in Blackburn, Australia, is a potent and wonderful exception to this trend, demonstrating how the multimedia functionality of the Web is capable of representing a vast range of student work and expanding its everyday audiences. The Web audience can view a photo of the "Year 9 boys" soccer team, read copies of student poems and short stories (and write back to the authors), and review student drawings and paintings.
        But the real feature of this Web site is the music of the students. The site is a virtual concert of student-produced music, including the Symphony Orchestra performing Antonín Dvořák, the Senior Singers performing Cy Coleman, or some of my favorites, the Stage Band playing Matt Harris and George Shering. Midi files of student arrangements and compositions are also available. While the Blackburn High School homepage may not win awards for glitzy design, it places the experiences and accomplishments of the students at its very center, and hence decenters the idea so often conveyed in school and university homepages that educational institutions would keep moving along just fine without students.

Sundial Project, Urbana High School
http://www.cmi.k12.il.us/Urbana/projects/UHSArt/mic3/gallery.html

Review

     An integrated art-science project developed at Urbana High School, in Urbana, Illinois (my former hometown), is a wonderful example of using the Web as an expressive medium. The project involved students researching sundials (which itself made use of the Web and e-mail communication with distant authorities) and then creating their own sundials out of clay, which were glazed and fired. Pictures of these beautiful sundials (one is in the shape of a "sun god," another shaped as a pair of hands) were then imported into the Web page, which also includes student journal entries about their work, a few video clips of the project, and scientific information on the sun's rotation and the functioning of sundials. Thus, this final virtual display integrates not simply science and art, but student sculpture, reflective writing, photography, film, research, layout and design, as well as technical knowledge. Additionally, the project, like Blackburn High School's Web page above, is an excellent example of how Web page design projects can be collaborative efforts by large groups and do not have to follow the one-person, one-computer model of some technology efforts (characteristic of the "create your own homepage" assignment commonly given). For both projects, while many students likely planned and gave feedback, the final Web page itself could have been created with only a computer or two accessible to the classroom.

Job Search and Employment Opportunities: Best Bets from the Net
http://asa.ugl.lib.umich.edu/chdocs/employment/job-guide.toc.html

Review

     Best Bets is a Web site that indexes and reviews job search and career information. The site was created by Phillip Ray and Bradley Taylor while they were graduate students in the University of Michigan's School of Information and Library Studies. The authors state that their intent is to "save you the trouble and frustration of following up on leads that are narrowly focused; are not updated regularly; or are not organized in a way that leads one to use the material easily." Best Bets also practices what it preaches. Its own material is very accessible and is scaffolded with the user in mind, from the most general to more specific searching tools.

     Perhaps most significantly, Best Bets represents an important shift in student work—learning—audience relations. The Web is often and rightly imagined as expanding the audience of student work to include a broad range of public. Through Web publication, student products and performances that were once enclosed in classroom walls can be appreciated, and even responded to, by distant audience members. As rich as this vision of interacting with a public is, it still is a fairly unidirectional exchange, relying upon a public to participate (and respond) out of good will, general interest, or commitment to educational values. Rather than presenting "school work" to a broader audience, Best Bets sheds the nature of work *qua* school work and becomes a resource that carries out a life of its own by providing a service for a highly motivated audience. This is not to suggest that all Web-based educational work ought to be based upon a model of production and consumption; however, such goals of public utility may often, in practice, enhance educational goals. In Best Bets, for instance, there is clearly a sense of technological savvy displayed, but much more so the work represents a vast amount of research, the creation and use of a framework for critical review, and the development of a strategy and forum for meaningful communication.

Jump Stations: Student Work on the Web

- Harnessing the Power of the Web (http://www.gsn.org/Web/index.html) gives links to exemplary student projects on the Web at the elementary, middle school, and high school levels.

- Jim Levin (http://www.ed.uiuc.edu/People/Jim-Levin/), a professor in the educational psychology department of the University of Illinois, has undergraduate and graduate students create major Web-based projects in a number of courses he teaches. Other valuable resources for project development can be accessed through his course pages.

- Kids Did This! (http://www.fi.edu/tfi/hotlists/kids.html) is a subject-based index of links to student projects, part of the Educational Hotlists (http://www.fi.edu/tfi/hotlists/hotlists.html) produced by the Franklin Institute.

IV. Discipline-Specific Sites

While it is beyond the scope and purpose of this chapter to offer a broad range of disciplinary sites, I hope you will find that the sites below, and others reviewed in Craft, will suggest ideas and visions that transcend disciplinary and age-level boundaries. The three reviewed sites represent new forms of disciplinary resources on the Web; respectively, a Web-based filing cabinet, a hyper-textbook, and a multimedia demonstration.

English Composition ("Filing Cabinet")
    On-line Writing Lab (OWL)
    http://owl.english.purdue.edu/
    Purdue University

As teachers it is tempting to think of the Web as a means by which we can access esoteric or difficult-to-find material. However, sites such as the On-line Writing Lab at Purdue demonstrate that the Web is also useful as a means of gathering together materials that have become common tools of a trade, serving as a virtual filing cabinet for needed resources. One of the main features of the OWL is an extensive library of brief guides to common writing problems and issues, covering topics as broad as comma splices and "avoiding wordiness," which are often accompanied by exercises. From my perspective as a writing teacher and former writing lab consultant, the available guides and the problems they address look both very familiar and highly useful. For the student working in an online writing environment, OWL captures the value of many reference guides that one might find in a writing lab, and could readily become an essential part of the "writer's desktop" of resources. Finally, for both student and teacher the site helps to situate writing well beyond issues of technique through its pointers to a wealthy range of locations, including indices, professional journals and associations, and search tools and directories.

History (Textbook)
    Exploring Ancient World Cultures
    http://eawc.evansville.edu/index.htm

Exploring Ancient World Cultures, under the direction of Anthony F. Beavers at the University of Evansville, Indiana, considers itself to be an "introductory, on-line, college-level 'textbook' of ancient world cultures." The project is in its early stages of development, but it already prompts us to imagine the possibilities for the transformation of textbooks within the environment of the World Wide Web. Currently available is a highly accessible Chronology of the Ancient World, based upon a search engine ("Argos") also under development at Evansville. The chronology, as a hypertextual timeline, permits one to consider a point in time within a culture, situate this point within a broader spectrum of history, or cross multiple cultures for any given period. As a Limited Area Search Engine, Argos is also worth further note. While many Web-based resources direct scholars and students off into the sea of resources on the Web through links, Argos is being constructed through selection and quality control. Thus, in reading chapters and essays, or using the array of maps and other resources, students and scholars alike will be able to access a preselected library of materials to pursue their inquiries. Web-based resources such as EAWC locate and construct themselves within a productive tension of resource openness and closure, and as such hold promise to represent scholarly dialogue much more actively than do traditional print textbooks.

Science (Demonstration)
     San Francisco Exploratorium
     http://www.exploratorium.edu
     Cow's Eye Dissection
     http://www.exploratorium.edu/learning_studio/cow_eye/
     index.html

"Yeah, it's a real cow's eye . . . no bull." (Exploratorium "Explainer"/ Dissector)

There are a vast number of resources on the Web for science education, which is not too surprising given the history of the Web and Web authoring as embedded in scientific and technical communities. What I find most impressive about the Cow's Eye Dissection site is its valuing of on- and off-line experience in the learning of science. Rather than pretending to replace hands-on science with Web-based representations, the site celebrates both worlds and their rich intersections. At one level, virtual activity and learning can occur; at another level, learners are motivated and guided to further explore the natural world. Through text and images, and especially sound files, the stepwise group experience of the dissection is brought to life, complete with the "ooh's" and "aah's" of the students, and even the "crunch" of the splitting cornea, which the instructor compares to the sound of Rice Krispies. From a pedagogical perspective, the site provides multiple representations of the material through multimedia, through a linked glossary of technical terms, through "Hints and Tips" from Exploratorium "Explainers," and through links to other sites. Also within the Cow's Eye Dissection site is a small downloadable application, a "Cow's Eye Primer," which is a simple vocabulary-image matching game that could function well to both scaffold the learning, guide the dissection, and review important concepts.

Jump Stations: Discipline-Specific Sites

- For K–12 lesson plans in a variety of subjects, try the AskERIC Virtual Library (http://ericir.syr.edu/About/virtual.html). The library also provides access to ERIC databases of interest to both teachers and researchers in education. Also from the AskERIC homepage, among other resources is a Q & A Service (http://ericir.syr.edu/Qa/), permitting teachers and researchers to e-mail their questions and issues of interest and receive information back from information specialists in the vast ERIC system (http://www.aspensys.com/eric/). The ERIC system also has a trove of resources for higher education (http://www.gwu.edu/~eriche/).

- Educational Hot Lists (http://www.fi.edu/tfi/hotlists/hotlists.html) is a master list of pointers to K–12 education resources that "stimulate creative thinking and learning about science." The resource categories, including "Africa," "Composition & Writing," and "Insects," are eclectic and clearly extend beyond science subjects.

- Education World (http://www.education-world.com/) is a keyword searchable database of links to over 20,000 sites of potential interest to educators of students at all levels. For discipline-based resources, check especially the Subject Index and Teacher's Resources sections.

- The Learning Resource Server (http://www.ed.uiuc.edu/) of the University of Illinois at Urbana-Champaign provides links to resources for K–12 education, teacher education, and other areas of higher education. The site is designed to promote a movement from "accessing knowledge" via the Web to "creating knowledge."

- The Subject Area Reference Pages (http://www.wcsu.ctstateu.edu/sarp/homepage.html) is a list of links to very general and specific resources for K–12 and higher education; there's everything from Kurt Vonnegut to the U. S. Department of Education.

V. Journals and Magazines

If you have never looked at a journal or magazine ("e-zine") on the Web, here are a few education general interest examples to get you started:

- The Chronicle of Higher Education: Academe this Week (http://chronicle.merit.edu/). The best-known weekly in higher education. After you find a job, check out their feature "This Week's Internet Resources."

- CyberSchool Magazine (http://www.cyberschoolmag.com:/ csm/in0.htm). An interesting general interest magazine for students and K–12 educators and much more. Don't miss the Surfin' Librarian, which indexes a tremendous number of useful links to all types of educational resources.

- Education Week on the Web (http://www.edweek.org/). A rich resource. Includes current issues in education with background information, a separate Teachers' Magazine, a job search engine for K–12 and higher education, and a very nice archival database of all of their published articles since 1989.

- Harvard Educational Review (http://hugse1.harvard.edu/ ~hepg/her.html). Predates the Web by over sixty years, but here it is, or at least part of it. Article abstracts only, but full text on book reviews.

Jump Stations: Journals and Magazines

- From the University of Tennessee, the *Daily Beacon* lists campus newspapers accessible by the Web, sorted by circulation schedule (http://beacon-www.asa.utk.edu/resources/ papers.html).

- e-journal (http://www.edoc.com/ejournal/). A major resource for finding online academic journals. Peer-reviewed, student-reviewed, and nonreviewed journals comprise separate categories. Journal preprint services are also indexed. For a well-organized and up-to-date general list of journals and newsletters on the Web, try NewJour (http://gort.ucsd.edu/newjour/).

- John Milam Jr. has created a valuable list of Higher Education Publications available in electronic format (http://apollo. gmu.edu/~jmilam/air95/higherpu.html).

- Education Journal Annotations (http://www.soemadison. wisc.edu/IMC/journals/anno_AB.html). A richly annotated list of both research journals and children's magazines, with a focus on K–12 education. A selective and unusual mix that evidences some good educator souls behind the project.

VI. Digital Museums and Libraries

In his 1996 election night acceptance speech, Vice President Al Gore enthusiastically reminded us that national Internet connections for education are essential to progress, as this would permit all students to "absorb" the vast "world of knowledge" contained in the Web. Through exemplars, I have been arguing that "absorption" is a misdirected way of thinking about the Web. But we also need to give thought to the metaphoric or actual "world of knowledge." Museums and libraries are significant constructions of our knowledge worlds, yet simply translating major museums and libraries into digital form seems only an elementary view of how new technologies might permit us to reshape geographical and social spaces for learning. Among other qualities, the following exemplars demonstrate careful design, selection, and movement between digital "objects" and texts, and the creation of new spaces for dialogue.

WebMuseum
http://sunsite.unc.edu/wm/

WebMuseum was created by Nicolas Pioch, a computer science teacher at Ecole Polytechnique in Paris, France. WebMuseum's popularity (currently over 200,000 visitors a week) and critical acclaim is likely due to a number of factors: high quality images; written documentation of the works, artists, and historical contexts; and a linked glossary of terms to clarify specialized vocabulary. Perhaps the most impressive feature of WebMuseum, however, is that it has digitally created a space to present art treasures unlike any physical space that existed previously; it is a virtual "traveling" exhibit that draws from many permanent collections and is always available. In the Famous Paintings Collection (http://sunsite.unc.edu/wm/paint/), for instance, one can view and read about works ranging from Botticelli's *Madonna of the Pomegranate* to over a dozen impressionist works each by Edouard Manet and Mary Cassatt to David Hockney's pop art rendition of *A Lawn Being Sprinkled*. While students can and should visit the Louvre's collections online (http://mistral.culture.fr/louvre/), WebMuseum's eclectic assemblage of significant works from many collections permits the art novice to cross periods, genres, and geographical locations with relative ease, with no expense, and without sore feet. Be sure and see the site's unique exhibit of *Les Tres Riches Heures* (http://sunsite.unc.edu/wm/rh/), a wonderful series of illuminated manuscripts.

Perseus
http://www.perseus.tufts.edu/

Perseus was developed through the Department of Classics of Tufts University and is under the direction of Gregory Crane. Originally developed (and currently available in most complete form) as a CD-ROM stack, Perseus is described by its creators as an "interactive multimedia digital library of Archaic and Classical Greece." More recently, the project has expanded to include an array of resources for study of the Roman Empire as well. The project is a fine example of how distinctions between libraries and museums tend to break down in Web environments. Like a library, the site features texts in Greek and in translation, secondary sources, and its own searching tools. However, like a museum, Perseus also contains 14,000 images of vases, coins, sculpture, architecture, and archeological sites in the ancient world, and is expanding to include panoramic photos and the rotation of objects in space through Quicktime technologies. As exciting as its vast size and breadth is the kind of interactivity that Perseus permits. All entries are extensively cross-indexed, and a powerful "Perseus Lookup Tool" provides sophisticated interaction between different types of information. One could be reading an English translation of the *Odyssey,* and in becoming interested in Poseidon, follow links not only to other texts, but to representations of Poseidon on ancient vases and in sculpture. Alternatively, one could move from the text or vase to explore temples to Poseidon through an online atlas, and view satellite pictures of the current state of these archeological sites. Significantly, the project is also committed to thinking about how such digital collections and tools might be best used in teaching. Be sure to follow the site links from "Teaching" and browse the syllabi and class notes from diverse subjects, the evaluation materials, teachers' help guides for students, and professors' reflections on their classroom experiences.

Other Valuable Links and Jump Stations

- The Electronic Text Center of the University of Virginia (http://etext.lib.virginia.edu/) is a valuable and easy-to-use repository of a large number of digitized texts in five different languages. Especially valuable is the Modern English Collection (http://etext.lib.virginia.edu/modeng.browse.html).

- Internet Public Library (http://www.ipl.org/) calls itself "the first public library of and for the Internet community" and has its own MOO space (Multi-User Object Oriented Environment) for interactions between people and objects.

- LibWeb's List of Library Webservers (http://sunsite.berkeley.edu/LibWeb/) is an easy way to quickly link to academic, public, regional, and national libraries.

- The Science Learning Network's list of science museums (http://www.sln.org/museums/index.html) is a good jumping-off point for Web-oriented museums.

- The Science Teaching and Learning Project (http://www.si.umich.edu/UMDL/HomePage.html), developed by Eliot

Soloway's research group at the University of Michigan, relates digital library development with a framework for inquiry-based pedagogy.

- The World Wide Web Virtual Library (http://vlib.stanford.edu/overview.html) has a stunning number of links to available libraries and resources by way of a "distributed subject catalogue." It also includes a directory of international digital museums and exhibitions that you can search by topic or browse by geographical location.

VII. Professional Development

"Professional Development" has widely varying meanings among different groups of educators. University educators may not think about their own professional development as an activity apart from the professional organizations, conferences, and networks in which they participate. K–12 educators, in contrast, typically have fewer valuable opportunities and resources for development within their normal work practices, overtaxed teaching schedules, and day-to-day contacts. In this sense, the Web could be a major medium of professional development for K–12 educators. The subsections below reflect a range of audience goals and needs among secondary, junior college, and university educators.

Research and Funding

- Internet Resources for Institutional Research (http://apollo.gmu.edu/~jmilam/air95.html), developed by John H. Milam Jr. of George Mason University, discusses and provides links for Web-based institutional research. The site is also informative for a general orientation to Internet-based research through its review of types of available resources, and through case studies of how the Web has been used for actual work projects.

- For research grants of all kinds, including dissertation research, consult the Illinois Researcher Information Service (IRIS) (http://www.grainger.uiuc.edu/iris). Includes links to international funding sources.

- GrantsWeb, the Research Administrator's Resources site (http://sra.rams.com/cws/sra/resource.htm), contains information on government and private funding in the United States, Canada, and the United Kingdom, as well as a whole host of other resource information of interest to researchers and administrators.

International Scholarship and Study

- The Digital Education Network (http://www.edunet.com/index.html) gives information on international conferences, seminars, distance education, and study abroad, with an emphasis upon Teaching English as a Foreign Language (TEFL).

- NAFSA (http://www.nafsa.org/) provides information on opportunities for international study and scholarship, including an online version of their *International Educator.*

Continuing Education Courses

- In many respects, the boundaries between "distance education" and locally situated education are becoming blurred as resources and practices of both forms are shared. An interesting example of such hybridization, for those interested in graduate study in library and information science, is the LEEP3 program (http://alexia.lis.uiuc.edu/gslis/tmp/leep3/) at the University of Illinois at Urbana-Champaign. The program involves initial face-to-face community construction and the subsequent development of this learning community online.

- The College Guide by Lycos (http://lycos.com/resources/college/index.html) is a well-organized resource for finding out about traditional and distance education programs at the undergraduate and graduate levels.

- Global SchoolNet (http://www.gsn.org/teach/pd/index.html) offers a number of different ways to earn graduate credit through learning about the Web and developing student-centered projects.

- For Web-based continuing education courses on literacy issues, try the Indiana University School of Education Distance Education Program (http://www.indiana.edu/~eric_rec/disted/menu.html).

- For graduate-credit science and mathematics study, NTEN (http://www.montana.edu/~wwwxs/index.html#Topics), the National Teachers' Enhancement Network, offers a highly interesting range of courses taught by university scientists, engineers, and mathematicians.

Other Development Resources: K–12

- Staff Room/Professional Development (http://www.schoolnet.ca/adm/staff/pd.html) is a site of links to professional development resources for K–12 educators maintained by Canada's SchoolNet.

- Teachers Helping Teachers (http://www.pacificnet.net/
  ~mandel/). Created by Scott Mandel, this project exemplifies
  the professional development philosophy held for many years
  by programs such as the National Writing Project; namely, that
  teachers are their own best teachers and have a wealth of expertise and resources to share with one another when given the
  opportunity.

- TEN, the Teacher Educator's Network (http://www.
  exploratorium.edu/isen/ten/index.html), has a host of different development resources for K–12 science teachers and train-
  ers. See especially the "Resources" section for a wealth of links
  to information on inquiry-based learning, including professional
  development materials for workshops.

- TENET (http://www.tenet.edu/professional/profdev.html)
  has a unique annotated list of links, including categories for
  Action Research, Learning Communities, and Staff Development Models.

Professional Organizations

- Scholarly Societies Project (http://www.lib.uwaterloo.ca/soci-
  ety/overview.html). Produced by the University of Waterloo
  in Ontario, Canada. Users can browse forty-four different subject areas or search alphabetically for international organizations. Also includes lists of upcoming meetings, conferences,
  and archives of society serial publications.

- Societies, Associations, and Non-Profit Organizations (http://
  info.lib.uh.edu/societies/orgssocs.htm). Provided by the University of Houston Libraries. Several categories of organizations
  of value to educators, including business, computer science,
  education, humanities, sciences, and social sciences.

- Yahoo!'s searchable database of Education Organizations (http:/
  /www.yahoo.com/Education/Organizations/), divided by
  various categories, is also an excellent place to find a particular
  site or just browse. The Yahoo! section on Education Conferences (http://www.yahoo.com/Education/Conferences/) is
  also a good, general, up-to-date source for international conference information.

- American Council of Learned Societies (http://www.acls.org/
  welcome.htm). Valuable as a source of links to a number of
  prominent (member) scholarly societies in the humanities and
  social sciences, for information on its own programs and grants,
  and for its carefully selected list of links to other fellowship programs, archives, and research libraries.

VIII. Tools and Strategies for Searching the Web

Directories

Directories are Web sites that contain links toward tens, hundreds, or thousands of other Web sites. Directories are put together by humans and thus involve some process of selection. Large directories sometimes contain their own databases, allowing users to enter keywords for searching within them. Directories are the best places for users who are relatively new to the Web and who do not have specific, burning issues and questions to begin searching (see "Search Engines"). Further, an effective way to investigate such a terrain is to "mine" a chosen directory for resources. Return to the directory again and again until you have exhausted its best resources, exhausted yourself, or have been led to a more interesting directory.

- Global SchoolNet Foundation's wealth of resources (http://www.gsn.org/index.html) includes a project registry where educators can find out information about Web-based education projects. For another index of projects, check CNIDR (http://k12.cnidr.org/k12-lists/lists.html).

- Kathy Schrock's guide (http://www.capecod.net/schrock guide/). A great initial one-stop shopping location for K–12 educators interested in using and learning about the Web, including slide shows on searching and creating homepages, as well as directories for a range of subjects from arts to world cultures and regions.

- NASA's On-line Educational Resources (http://quest.arc.nasa.gov/OER/edures.html) is much more than space-shuttle updates. Categories of resources include "Subject Trees on Education," museums, libraries, resources specific to colleges and universities, and others focused on collaborative technologies.

- My Virtual Reference Desk (http://www.refdesk.com/edu srch.html) brings together a number of major directories for education and a range of subjects in one location. The Reference Shelf (http://www.tech.prsa.org/refshelf.html) is another useful collection of desktop resources for educators.

For that classic directory—the phone book—try Four11 (http://WWW.FOUR11.COM/). Also useful for finding the e-mail address of your long-lost friend in Boise.

Directories That Review and Award

Some directories (and search engines) review and rate sites. Such awards and ratings can help you avoid irrelevant, poorly designed, or very thin sites and find some of the best. On the other hand, some sites are awarded again and again simply because they have been made more visible, or have powerful budgets and flashy graphics, and the popularity of these featured sites can help hide some lesser-known treasures. Be sure to read, if you can find it, the information on how the sites were rated and awarded.

- CyberSchool Magazine Editor's Choice Awards (http://www.cyberschoolmag.com:/csm/eca.htm) is an excellent resource for finding a handful of choice sites for general education purposes. Includes brief education-focused reviews.

- Education World Awards (http://www.education-world.com/awards/) lists monthly about twenty sites of choice and gives "grades" for the categories of content, aesthetics, and organization. The reviews give a good deal of useful and well-written content information about the sites.

- For search engines with rating and review capabilities, try the Lycos Top 5% site (http://www.pointcom.com/categories/), with categories in Education and many other fields, or Magellan (http://www.mckinley.com/).

- Most important, to help you teach students how to critically review, try Teaching Critical Evaluation Skills for World Wide Web Resources (http://www.science.widener.edu/%7 Ewithers/Webeval.htm). Another good evaluation tool is at (http://www.mwc.edu/ernie/search/search-Web12.html).

Search Engines

Unlike directories, which are built by hard-slogging individuals, search engines are computer programs whose job is to locate and categorize Web pages, and not make selections. These programs, sometimes called "spiders" or "robots," continually traverse the Web and index pages according to various criteria, such as document titles or even text within document bodies. Search engines are readily accessible through most Web browsers (the program you use to access the Web, such as Netscape) and their numbers are growing rapidly. It would be tempting to say that the best search engines are those which index the largest number of pages, but you will likely determine personal criteria, such as search speed, available help, types of searching supported, etc., which will help you select your own favorites.

- Ross Tyner offers a much more complete discussion of search engines and subject guides (directories) as part of a workshop entitled "Sink or Swim: Internet Search Tools & Techniques" (http://oksw01.okanagan.bc.ca/libr/connect96/search.htm).

- Search.com (http://www.search.com/) is a meta–search engine that will permit you to search via several search engines at the same time.
- Ted Slater's Search Engine Collection (http://www.regent.edu/~tedslat/tools.html) permits one-stop searching, including many major search engines on one page, as well as a dictionary, a Bible, Shakespeare, CNN news, and street-level map making.

Searching for Schools and Universities

- A key place to look for K–12 schools on the Web is Web 66 (http://Web66.coled.umn.edu/schools.html), where you'll find a terrific clickable map. Another easily searchable database is the ClassroomWeb (http://ftp.wentworth.com/classroom/classWeb/) of Classroom Connect.
- Christina DeMello has created a directory to over three thousand colleges and universities in more than eighty countries (http://www.mit.edu:8001/people/cdemello/univ.html).

IX. Technical Help for Web Projects

If there is one way in which the Web is self-reflexive, it is in offering an enormous number of resources on technical help for working within it. Below is an initial sampling; you will find that technical help is ever present within the medium as you begin project development and authoring. The need for expensive workshops, training sessions, and even books for general technical help seems slim indeed given the abundance of Web-based resources.

Understanding the World Wide Web Historically and Conceptually

- An entire workshop on the Internet developed by Patrick Crispen called Internet Roadmap 96 (http://rs.internic.net/nicsupport/roadmap96) is good for someone wanting more background on the Internet and the WWW (lessons 23 and 24). There is also a whole range of accessible lessons on other aspects of the Internet, including e-mail, FTP, listservs, and Gopher.
- Learn the Net (http://www.learnthenet.com/english/index.html) is an excellent introduction to the history and structure of the Internet and the World Wide Web, with plenty of links for those desiring further study. Note also the useful overview of Understanding Web Addresses, which helps to demystify who it is you're communicating with on the Web.

Introductions to Creating Web Pages

These resources include information on hypertext markup language (HTML), the standard language used to produce Web pages. There is little that is mysterious about basic HTML codes, and through new software such authoring is getting easier all the time. Some of these sources also situate the creation of Web pages within the entire process of project design and within broader educational purposes.

- For a no-nonsense Beginner's Guide to HTML, go to the site produced by the National Center for Supercomputing Applications (NCSA) at the University of Illinois at Urbana-Champaign (http://www.ncsa. uiuc.edu/General/Internet/WWW/HTMLPrimer.html).

- Another useful guide for authoring and troubleshooting is the Help Desk (http://Web.canlink.com/helpdesk/), which also discusses more sophisticated Web-weaving with Java, CGI scripts, etc., and offers a large collection of editors.

- Building a Website That Works (http://www.tenet.edu/education/online.html), from the Texas Education Network (TE-NET), offers tips on the development process, links to style guides and exemplary sites, and a template. A good home base for beginning development.

- Harnessing the Power of the Web (http://www.gsn.org/Web/index.html), from the Global SchoolNet Foundation, is intended to help support work on the Web from "an old-fashioned, student-centered, project-based learning point of view." This site situates the entire process of pedagogy on the Web in a particular educational vision and offers background on the Web, examples of student projects, and a step-by-step tutorial on planning, implementing, and reviewing Web work.

- The Interactive HTML Crash Course (http://edWeb.gsn.org/resource.cntnts.html) by Andy Carvin at EdWeb is a great little introduction to Web authoring, complete with self-quizzes. The entire EdWeb site is unique and well worth exploring in that it includes discussions of the history of the Web, its role in education, its relation to educational reform, and competing visions of its future.

- For Web page design, consult Nan Goggin's short guide (http://gertrude.art.uiuc.edu/Webdesign/design.html) from the School of Art at UIUC, or the Web Style Manual by Patrick Lynch at Yale (http://info.med.yale.edu/caim/manual/index.html).

X. Final Reflections

While it is impossible to "conclude" a reference essay on the Web in the sense of reaching closure, I would like to end with a few thoughts, reflections that are directed toward interrupting two dichotomies. First, it is tempting to imagine the Web as either an entirely old space or an entirely new space, and critiques of the Web in education often play at the extremes of this dichotomy—arguing that in the relationship between the Web and education either nothing or everything has changed. An important, related dichotomy is often constructed between the technophobic, Web-shunning naysayer (old teacher) and the technophilic Web-developing wonder educator (new teacher). As we become more familiar with the Web and both absorb and develop it into the everyday work of teaching and learning, we need also to imagine the variable and broad relations that it, and other technologies, can have to our work.

Old Space/New Space

It is important to reflect upon the ways in which the Web is historically related to teaching and learning practices that have developed over long periods of time. In many ways, the Web is an old space, a familiar space. We can and should critique constructions of education on the Web that look like more of the same—more lectures, more course notes and syllabi, more talking teachers and few talking students. At the same time, within our critiques we should recognize and reflect upon our expectations for change as well. The expectation that everything will change with the development of new media is closely related to the expectation that nothing will change: both extremes of the dichotomy express something of the non-relation of technology to other parts of the educational world. In the "old space" view, technology is seen as operating beyond educational life, with no impact upon it, while in the "new space" view, it is tempting to celebrate technology as determining the direction of educational change, rather than being deeply related to other players, including durable and evolving teaching practices, student orientations to learning, and institutional and commercial movements.

Which is to say, in the end, that the Web always confronts us with the old and the new complexly related, and that for understanding, appreciating, and participating in the Web environment it seems important to enter into the dialogue between history and innovation. As the Web moves toward becoming a new(er) space for teaching and learning, this reference essay highlights some developing potentials that are particularly encouraging. Many of the sources indexed and reviewed represent how multimedia can help motivate and enhance student learning, and how such media can also permit students to produce and represent their learning in diverse ways. Related to student construction are the potentials of interaction with diverse communities of practice, which can loosen the boundaries of "schooling," including those of "student" and "teacher" identities. Further, the Web offers avenues of engagement with museums, libraries, and other learning spaces that were formerly much more distant to the student's desk. While all of these issues have been discussed within educational practice and theory for some time, the development of the World Wide Web offers a stimulating space in which to further develop these values as practices, building productive theory-practice relations.

Old Teacher/New Teacher

In many ways the old teacher/new teacher dichotomy is a personalization of old space/new space. It is tempting to group ourselves and others as either technophobes or technophiles, and tempting as well to map these groupings onto "regressive" versus "progressive" teacher identities and pedagogies. Once again, those who are primarily critical of the Web as a learning environment will find plenty of evidence for nonprogressive education with it, and those dubbed "true believers" will find plenty of support for their position as well. In this essay, in exploring a range of Web-based resources as well as a range of pedagogies, I have tried to suggest that the spectrum of engagements with the Web is very broad. This is simply to say in closing that as educators all of us develop complex and unique identities with developing technologies, relations that change over time and that are likely not located on one end of a false dichotomy.

While for some educators complete courses as well as student projects are Web-dependent, for others the Web is merely a reference for students to consult among many. For still other educators, the Web is a personal and not a classroom learning space—a space for professional development courses and reading online journals. As the Web becomes more integrated as a learning space and tool into the daily practice of education, it is likely that individually and collectively we will make fewer distinctions between non-Web-based and Web-based learning and identities, that these worlds will intersect in complex ways. And, at this crossroads, hopefully we will develop a productively broad range of teaching and learning practices that move beyond education as we experience it today.

Note

A version of this chapter also appears online at http://www.ed.uiuc.edu/ students/k-leand/craft/crafthome.html.

Index

Editor

Sibylle Gruber is assistant professor of rhetoric at Northern Arizona University, where she teaches graduate and undergraduate courses in literacy studies, rhetoric and cultures, computers and composition, and the history of composition studies. She is co-editing a book with Laura Gray-Rosendale entitled *Alternative Rhetorics: Challenges to the Rhetorical Tradition*. Gruber's work on cybertheories, feminist rhetorics, composition, and cultural studies can be found in journals such as *Computers and Composition*, *Computer Supported Cooperative Work*, and *The Journal of the Assembly on Computers in English*, and in books such as *Feminist Cyberspaces: Essays on Gender in Electronic Spaces* and *Global Literacy Practices and the WWW: Cultural Perspectives on Information Distribution, Interpretation, and Use*.

Contributors

J. D. Applen received a B.S. in biology from San Diego State University, and an M.F.A. in creative writing and Ph.D. in English from the University of Arizona. He teaches technical writing at the University of Central Florida. Currently, his research interests include composition and poststructuralism, hypertext theory, and environmental rhetoric.

Larry Beason is Director of English Composition at the University of South Alabama, where he teaches composition, technical writing, grammar, and teacher-preparation courses. His research interests include assessment, writing across the curriculum, and the use of e-mail and Web pages in writing courses. His publications include articles in *Research in the Teaching of English*, *Journal of Business Communication*, and *Writing Instructor*.

Jean Boreen is assistant professor in English education at Northern Arizona University. She currently teaches courses in English teaching methods and adolescent literature as well as supervising student teachers. Issues around the use of computer technology in the classroom have long been important to Jean, which is why she created a course called "Surfing the 'Net with Words" for her teacher education students.

Elizabeth Burow-Flak is assistant professor of English at Valparaiso University. She began teaching computer-assisted courses in the Computer Writing and Research Labs at the University of Texas at Austin while completing her Ph.D. in Renaissance literature. At Valparaiso, she teaches courses in composition, the humanities, and English literature of the sixteenth and seventeenth centuries, including a course on the impact of print technology in early modern culture and of Internet technology today.

Enikö Csomay has been working as a teacher educator since 1992 at Eötvös University in Budapest, at the Centre for English Teacher Training. She studied at the University of Reading, UK, and was a Fulbright visiting lecturer in the English department at Northern Arizona University. She taught linguistics and teacher-training courses to both undergraduate and graduate students there, and became devoted to the use of technology in education. Her main professional interests relate to issues in second language acquisition and learning: composition, task, syllabus and curriculum design, and learner autonomy. The title of her latest course offered at Eötvös University is "The CALL of the Information Age." She delivers the course for pre- and inservice teachers about the role and application of technology in the design of the second language curriculum. Further, she is a keen photographer; some of her pictures may be seen at http://jan.ucc.nau.edu/~ec23.

Mick Doherty (mdoherty@dallascvb.com) is Internet Editor for the Dallas Convention & Visitors Bureau in Dallas, Texas. He is completing work toward a Ph.D. in rhetoric and electronic publishing at Rensselaer Polytechnic Institute, but is in no huge hurry to finish. Doherty is founding editor of *Kairos: A Journal for Teachers of Writing in Webbed Environments.* He designed and taught both RPI's initial "Writing to the WWW" class and its first Internet-driven "Technical & Professional Communication" course.

Joy L. Egbert is assistant professor in the School of Education at Indiana University. She received her Ph.D. in higher education from the University of Arizona in 1993. She is an award-winning teacher, researcher, and materials developer whose research interests include computer-assisted learning, computer-mediated communication, and learning environments.

Douglas Eyman is an Instructional Technology Specialist and Webspinner for Cape Fear Community College in Wilmington, North Carolina. He is currently serving on the board of directors of the Alliance for Computers in Writing (ACW) and is the CoverWeb editor for the online journal *Kairos: A Journal for Teachers of Writing in Webbed Environments* (http://english.ttu.edu/kairos/). Eyman received his M.A. from the University of North Carolina at Wilmington in 1995; his thesis, "Hypertextual Collaboration in the Computer-Facilitated Composition Classroom," is available on the World Wide Web (http://localsonly.wilmington.net/~eymand/thesis.htm).

Katherine M. Fischer, M.F.A. (kfischer@keller.clarke.edu), teaches English and directs the Writing Lab at Clarke College in Dubuque, Iowa. Her poetry, essays, and academic writings appear frequently in journals, magazines, and books. Most recently, "Pig Tales: Literature Inside the Pen of Electronic Writing" appeared in *Electronic Communication Across the Curriculum* (Donna Reiss, Art Young, and Richard Selfe, eds. NCTE, 1998). Her main areas of academic interest include teaching with technology, writing centers, and creative writing and composition studies.

David Gillette is assistant professor at the University of Central Florida (Orlando) where he teaches in the technical writing and creative writing programs. He has taught hypertext theory courses for both graduate and undergraduate students, and has also made hypertext creation and analysis a vital part of his other writing courses. For the last six years, Gillette has used computer-aided, hypertext-centered instruction in nontechnical writing and literature courses that range from basic composition to screenwriting to graduate-level courses in modern rhetoric. Gillette's graduate work at the University of New Mexico (Ph.D., 1995) focused on the hypertext interactions between graphical and textual rhetorics on the computer screen. He is currently at work on a number of articles and a small book examining the connections between twentieth-century art (Postimpressionism, Cubism, artist books) and the development and use of the World Wide Web.

Emily Golson is associate professor in the English department at the University of Northern Colorado, where she directs the Writing Center, trains graduate students, and teaches writing. Her research interests are in the application of technology in the writing classroom and in theoretical and applied studies of hypertext. She has presented papers on computers and writing at numerous state, regional, and national conferences. She has published in *Computers and Composition* and has two studies on hypertext forthcoming in book-length collections of essays.

Gail Hawisher (hawisher@uiuc.edu) is professor of English and Director of the Center for Writing Studies at the University of Illinois at Urbana-Champaign. With Paul LeBlanc, Charles Moran, and Cynthia Selfe, she is author of *Computers and the Teaching of Writing in Higher Education, 1979–1994: A History.* She is also co-editor of several books focusing on theoretical, pedagogical, and research questions related to literacy and technology. With Cynthia Selfe, she edits *Computers and Composition: An International Journal for Teachers of Writing.* Other projects include a college reader entitled *Literacy, Technology, and Society: Confronting the Issues* and a collection of essays entitled *Passions, Pedagogies, and 21st Century Technologies.* Her articles have appeared in *College English, College Composition and Communication,* and *Written Communication,* among others. Her most recent work (with Cynthia Selfe) is *Global Literacies and the World Wide Web.*

Leonard M. Jessup is associate professor of information systems and the director of technology for the School of Business at Indiana University, Bloomington. He received his Ph.D. in organizational behavior and management information systems from the University of Arizona in 1989. He is a member of the Association for Information Systems and he holds editorial and reviewer responsibilities for a number of book publishers, research journals, and conferences. He teaches in various areas of management and management information systems and his research interests include electronic commerce, using computer-based tools to support collaborative work, computer-assisted learning, and related topics.

Kevin M. Leander, formerly a high school English and French teacher, is currently assistant professor in the Department of Teaching and Learning, Peabody College, Vanderbilt University. His research involves sociocultural analyses of schooling, including the relationships between discourse, other forms of activity, tools, and artifacts.

Jean W. LeLoup (Ph.D., The Ohio State University) is associate professor of Spanish at State University of New York College at Cortland. **Robert Ponterio** (Ph.D., University of Illinois at Urbana-Champaign) is associate professor of French at State University of New York College at Cortland. They are the co-founders and co-moderators of FLTEACH, the Foreign Language Teaching Forum, a listserv for FL professionals, and the editors of a regular column "On the Net" in the electronic journal *Language Learning & Technology.* Together they have presented at local, regional, and national foreign language conferences and have co-authored several articles on the use of technology and the Internet in FL teaching and learning.

Aijun Anna Li (ali@serve.org) is the project evaluator for the SouthEast and Islands Regional Technology in Education Consortium (SEIR*TEC), funded by the U.S. Department of Education. She is a Ph.D. candidate in the Department of Curriculum and Instruction, University of Illinois at Urbana-Champaign. Her research interests include the integration of technology into teaching and learning, application of technology for children with special needs, teacher education, and evaluation of technology programs.

Ted Nellen has been teaching high school English since 1974, with computers since 1983, and with the Internet since 1985. He is currently teaching Cyber English at a New York City public high school and finishing his doctoral work at Teachers College. He is on the editorial board of *Kairos*. His work can be viewed online at http://www.tnellen.com/ted/.

Margery D. Osborne is assistant professor of science education in the Department of Curriculum and Instruction, University of Illinois at Urbana-Champaign. She is the author of *Constructing and Framing Knowledge in the Elementary School Classroom: Teachers, Students and Science* (forthcoming).

Dean Rehberger is associate professor at Michigan State University and is the associate director of Matrix (http://matrix.msu.edu). He teaches Humanities Computing and Composition Theory and is currently working on a book about computers and composition theory entitled *Computer Compositions.*

Sarah Rilling (srilling@lamar.colstate.edu) is assistant professor of English at Colorado State University and holds a Ph.D. in applied linguistics from Northern Arizona University. Her research interests include classroom-based research, intercultural communications via computer, and literacy in a technological age. She has taught computerized composition, graduate and undergraduate courses in teaching English as a second language, German language, and English as a second/foreign language in the United States and Japan. Her work with textiles and her interest in things coded draw her into Web weaving.

Eric Sagel is a graduate student in the English department at the University of Northern Colorado. As a teaching assistant and Writing Center tutor, Eric is interested in the application of technology in the English classroom. Also, he is interested in studying the use of the Internet and commercial networks outside of traditional institutions. He has given presentations on computers and writing at several local and state conferences. He lives in Greeley, Colorado, with his cat Bo.

Cynthia L. Selfe (cyselfe@mtu.edu) is professor of humanities at Michigan Technological University. A past chair of the Conference on College Composition and Communication and NCTE's College Section, Selfe has served as co-editor of the *CCCC Bibliography on Composition and Rhetoric* (with Gail Hawisher) and has authored a number of journal articles and books on computer use in composition classrooms. Her most recent book, *Technology and Literacy: The Importance of Paying Attention,* describes not only the increasingly close ties between technology and literacy in our culture, but also the increasingly dangerous linkage between technological literacy and intergenerational cycles of illiteracy, racism, and poverty.

In 1983, Selfe founded the journal *Computers and Composition* with Kate Kiefer; she continues to edit that journal with Gail Hawisher. In 1989, Selfe and Hawisher founded the Computers and Composition Press to support the publication of books on computers and their uses in English composition classrooms. Selfe is the winner of the 1996 EDUCOM Medal Award for innovation in educational technology use, the first woman and the first English teacher to be accorded that honor.

Catherine F. Smith is associate professor of writing and English/textual studies at Syracuse University, where she teaches undergraduate writing courses using the World Wide Web and graduate seminars focused on Internet discourse practices. She is currently working on a scholarly web concerned with the history and rhetoric of Congressional hearings. It can be viewed at http://web.syr.edu/~cfsmith.

Elizabeth Sommers is associate professor of English at San Francisco State University. She teaches both undergraduate writing classes and graduate classes in the M.A. Program in English with a concentration in composition. Her research interests include collaborative learning, gender issues in the writing classroom, and critical and feminist pedagogies in addition to computer-mediated language instruction. Recently she has co-authored an article for *Teaching English in the Two-Year College* with Sandra Lawrence of Mount Holyoke College entitled "From the Park Bench to the (Writing) Workshop Table: Encouraging Collaboration among Inexperienced Writers" (1996). With a former tutee and two former staff members of the English Tutoring Center at San Francisco State University, for which Sommers is faculty coordinator, she has recently completed a chapter entitled "Do You Know Who(m) You're Talking To? Critical Pedagogy and ESL Tutoring," to be published by the National Association of Writing Centers in a volume co-edited by Thia Wolf, Carol Haviland et al. As the current College of Humanities Computer Education Coordinator for San Francisco State University, Sommers has also constructed a humanities Web site for teachers and students that can be accessed at http://www.sfsu.edu/~humanity/helpsite/.

Sandye Thompson (sandyet@eaze.net) is a doctoral candidate in the Department of English, Speech, and Foreign Languages at Texas Woman's University in Denton, Texas, where she has taught composition and literature. She is currently the Chief CopyEditor of *Kairos: A Journal for Teachers of Writing in Webbed Environments*. She was also a consultant for a chapter in the 5th edition of the *Scott, Foresman Handbook*, including "Online Style."

Patricia R. Webb is assistant professor at Arizona State University. Her publications include articles in *Computers and Composition*. Her dissertation analyzes technoliteracies in the academy, the workplace, and the community.

Anne Frances Wysocki teaches multimedia, graphic design, and digital photography at Michigan Technological University.

This book was typeset in Palatino and Helvetica.
The typeface used on the cover was Chainlink.
The book was printed by Versa Press.